PHENOMENOLOGY

AND THE

CRISIS OF PHILOSOPHY

Edmund Husserl

PHENOMENOLOGY
AND THE
CRISIS OF PHILOSOPHY

Philosophy as Rigorous Science
and
Philosophy and the Crisis of European Man

TRANSLATED WITH NOTES AND AN INTRODUCTION BY
QUENTIN LAUER

HARPER TORCHBOOKS
Harper & Row, Publishers
New York, Cambridge, Hagerstown, Philadelphia, San Francisco
London, Mexico City, São Paulo, Sydney

PHENOMENOLOGY AND THE CRISIS OF PHILOSOPHY

English translation copyright © 1965 by Quentin Lauer

Printed in the United States of America.

First HARPER TORCHBOOK edition published 1965 by
Harper & Row, Publishers, Inc.
New York, Evanston, and London.

Library of Congress Catalog Card Number: 64–8794

89 90   30 29 28 27 26 25 24 23 22 21

Contents

||||||||||||||||||||||||||||||||||||||||||||||||||||||||||||||||||||||||||||||||||||||||||||||||||||||||||||||||||||||||||||||||||||||||||||||||

v

Introduction   BY QUENTIN LAUER

Despite a strong upsurge of interest among English-speaking readers in the work of phenomenologists, we are still faced with a lamentable dearth of material in English devoted to their efforts. Particularly conspicuous is the lack of translations, above all of the work done by the "father of phenomenology," Edmund Husserl. Chief, perhaps,. among the reasons for this absence of translations is the extremely involuted and, therefore, forbidding style of the author. His thought is not extraordinarily difficult to comprehend (for those who are familiar with modern philosophy from Descartes to Kant), but the words in which this thought is expressed resist translation. There is an early translation by Boyce-Gibson of the first volume of Husserl's *Ideas*,[1] whose accuracy leaves something to be desired, and there is a recent translation by Dorion Cairns of the *Cartesian Meditations*,[2] which reveals as well as anything can the difficulty of presenting a readable English version of Husserl's German. In addition, the present editor has translated for *Cross Currents*[3] the first of the essays

[1] *Ideas,* tr. W. R. Boyce-Gibson (New York: Macmillan, 1941). The preface to this translation was an original essay by Husserl, published in German under the title *Nachwort zu meinen Ideen zu einer reinen Phänomenologie* (Halle: Niemeyer, 1930).

[2] *Cartesian Meditations,* tr. Dorion Cairns (The Hague: Nijhoff, 1960). Throughout the present volume references will be to this translation, according to the original pagination, which is given in the margins.

[3] *Cross Currents,* VI (1956), 228–46, 324–44. The translation is reprinted here with slight emendations.

contained in this volume. Nothing else is available of a thought which has proved so influential, particularly on the European continent, during the twentieth century.

The situation with regard to books in English about Husserl is scarcely better. The interest in phenomenology (most prominent, perhaps, among psychiatrists) seems somehow to have bypassed the "founder" of the movement. We have, of course, the excellent original phenomenological studies of Dietrich von Hildebrand, but aside from a few books and a handful of articles[4] we have little to familiarize us with the roots of the phenomenological method or to help us trace the development of this thought from its beginnings.

It is hoped that the two essays chosen for translation in this volume will contribute toward filling a gap which those who are interested in contemporary phenomenology cannot but feel. The first essay can be said to represent Husserl early in his career, when he was seeking to gain a hearing for his "radically new" scientific manner of philosophizing. The second dates from the years immediately preceding the cessation of Husserl's philosophical activity. Together they constitute a striking testimony to the continuity of Husserl's "scientific" ideal in philosophy. The intervening years saw considerable development of the detailed method for attaining the goal of universal rationality, but it is significant that the position achieved as a result of this development in no way involved relinquishing any major position adopted at the beginning or along the way. Thus we have in these two essays not only an early and a late stage in the genetic growth of Husserl's thought but also an introduction to what can be called his definitive attitude toward the very nature of philosophical thinking.

---

[4] The recent comprehensive study by Herbert Spiegelberg, *The Phenomenological Movement,* 2 vols. (The Hague: Nijhoff, 1960), goes a long way toward filling the gap for the English-speaking world. I have published a small introduction to Husserl's phenomenology, *The Triumph of Subjectivity* (New York: Fordham University Press, 1958).

Chronologically "Philosophy as Rigorous Science"[5] occupies a place of unique interest in the development of Husserl's thought. It was published in 1911, at a time when that thought was in transition from the first practical efforts of *Logische Untersuchungen* (1900) to work out a phenomenological method to *Ideen I* (1913), his first published attempt to justify theoretically a method which had already proved successful in practice.[6] Thus it serves as a link between the pre-transcendental and the transcendental thinking of Husserl.[7]

Though the developed terminology and some of the most important themes of Husserl's later phenomenology are absent from this essay, which was intended as an introduction to the phenomenological ideal rather than to its methods or conclusions, one can find in it strong indications of the direction in which its author's thought is moving. His preoccupation with refuting "naturalism" and "psychologism," the dominant theme in the first volume of *Logische Untersuchungen*,[8] is very much in evidence here as it is also in the later essay. On the other hand, his concern with historicism and *Weltanschauung* philosophy, dating as it does from a period in which he was engaged in controversy and correspondence with Wilhelm Dilthey,[9] is almost unique in his writings. Most revealing for an understanding of Husserl's whole

---

[5] "Philosophie als strenge Wissenschaft," *Logos,* I (1910–11), 289–341.

[6] Many of Husserl's most ardent disciples preferred to base their own investigations on the earlier "practical" method than on the later "idealistic" theory. It is the opinion of this writer, an opinion disputed by many, that the transition from "descriptive phenomenology" to "transcendental idealism" in no way constitutes a break in Husserl's thought; it is but the logical explicitation of what was implicit in the earlier period.

[7] It is true that *Die Idee der Phänomenologie,* ed. Walter Biemel (The Hague: Nijhoff, 1950), which antedates the present essay by several years, had already adopted the transcendental perspective. However, it was not published during Husserl's lifetime.

[8] Under the subtitle *Prolegomena zur reinen Logik* (Halle: Niemeyer, 1900). In later editions this first volume remained unchanged.

[9] Cf. Georg Misch, *Lebensphilosophie und Phänomenologie* (Leipzig: Teubner, 1931).

development and of the character which his philosophizing ultimately assumes is the indication found here of the deliberate
choice involved in his project of laying the groundwork of a
strictly scientific philosophy. In a sense it is an arbitrary choice,
of a value not necessarily the highest,[10] a choice which demanded
of him great asceticism and which precluded his acquiring the
large historical background whose absence is so conspicuous in
his writings.

Perhaps the greatest importance of this early essay is the testimony it gives of Husserl's ambition to establish philosophy on a
basis of unimpeachable rationality. In his mind this ambition can
be realized only by complete dedication to truth, and this in the
combined efforts of generations, all carrying on their researches
according to the phenomenological method. Thus he sees each
individual philosophical problem as, so to speak, autonomous,
demanding for its solution a new beginning, not a prefabricated
system. Each problem is to be taken by itself and investigated in
a rigid application of the phenomenological method, the only
philosophical method worthy of the name because it is the only
method which will guarantee scientific rigor in philosophic thinking.

From the beginning, then, we can see what, according to
Husserl, distinguishes phenomenology from any other philosophy,
i.e., what makes it alone truly a philosophy.[11] Only a phenomenology can be truly scientific, and only a scientific philosophy can
be truly philosophy. Phenomenology, then, will be satisfied only
with a cognition that is absolutely certain, and it will be con-

---

[10] Cf. p. 134 and n. 69, infra.

[11] It is interesting to note that Hegel, whose phenomenology is in its way
as thoroughgoing as Husserl's and who accorded it an extraordinary importance, nevertheless did not look upon it as the whole of philosophy. In
fact, Hegel looks upon his *Phenomenology* as primarily a propaedeutic to
philosophy—an introduction to his *Logic*, which is properly a metaphysics,
the system of philosophy. This may well be one of the reasons why Husserl had no sympathy whatever for Hegel, despite the similarity of both their
aims.

cerned only with an object that is absolutely necessary, in no way contingent or "factitious," which is but another way of saying that it is the object of an absolutely certain (ultimately "rational") cognition. This sort of philosophy will refuse to accept any conclusion that has not been verified as absolutely valid for all men and for all times; thus it wants to be a science in direct contact with absolute being. For Husserl, however, absolute being can only be essential being, and the whole orientation of his phenomenology will be to a knowledge of the essential. He will not deny the existence of a world, not even an extramental existence; he will simply deny that such an existence can have any significance for philosophy, since existence can only be contingent.[12]

Now, for Husserl a strict science of philosophy is one that, though systematic in its procedures, is not a "system." Phenomenologically speaking, he has grasped the "essence" of science in meditating on the positive sciences, where results are verified one after another and thus accumulate to form a store of established truths. The science of philosophy, then, must make a new beginning as it attacks each problem and must accept only those conclusions that have been thoroughly verified according to the only method capable of verifying philosophical truth at all. It is in this sense—and only in this sense—that the philosophical endeavor must be a cooperative endeavor. The establishment of truth after truth in this manner requires time, and it requires the combined efforts of many investigators, all imbued with the same ideal but not belonging to the same "school."

It is not remarkable, then, that with this ideal of philosophical science before him the greater part of Husserl's writings (both

[12] "Philosophy as Rigorous Science" reveals how strong was Hume's influence on Husserl. For the former, whatever could be thought of as not being, could not-be, since its not-being involved no contradiction. Husserl, therefore, will accept as an object of philosophical thought only what cannot not-be, and this is essence. Cf. Gaston Berger, "Husserl et Hume," *Revue internationale de Philosophie,* I (1938–39), 342–53.

published and unpublished) should manifest a distinctly programmatic character. Over and over again he reworks the same
problems; and for the most part they are problems of method.[13]
Only with the method established could the pursuit of any problem result in the kind of absolute knowledge which he regarded
as essential to philosophy. Again and again he pleads for a
restoration of philosophy to its proper dignity—as we shall find
him doing in his latest writings—always with the assumption that
only the phenomenological method can achieve this restoration.
No matter what changes and developments one may seem to
find in Husserl's thought in the course of his long career, the ideal
remains always the same, and the method for attaining to this
ideal, though more and more refined, is still basically the same
phenomenological method.

It is for this reason that the second essay translated in this
present volume becomes important as part of an introduction to
the transcendental phenomenology of Husserl.[14] It shows as
clearly as anything can how, toward the end of his life, he still
viewed the ideal of scientific philosophy.

Husserl's last major philosophical work, treating a problem
that between the years 1934 and 1937 (when he ceased writing
entirely) had occupied him almost exclusively, was *Die Krisis
der europäischen Wissenschaften und die transzendentale Phänomenologie*.[15] Parts I and II of this work were published in the
Belgrade review *Philosophia* in 1936. It was Husserl's intention
to publish Part III in the same review, but the manuscript was
never sent to the publisher. The entire work, in which for the

[13] Only rarely after *Logische Untersuchungen* (1900–1901), and then only
with indifferent success, does Husserl himself engage in actual phenomenological analyses.
[14] It is my opinion (cf. p. 3, n. 6, supra) that Husserl would have been
untrue to his own insights had his phenomenology not become consciously
"transcendental."
[15] Published 1954 by Martinus Nijhoff, The Hague, as Vol. IV of the
Husserliana, being edited by the Husserl Archives of Louvain.

first time the author dealt explicitly with the relation between history and philosophy, grew out of a lecture he had delivered on May 7, 1935, at the University of Prague. Thus if, as Husserl himself wrote in his introduction to the text published in *Philosophia*, the *Krisis* is "an independent introduction to transcendental phenomenology," the lecture out of which it grew can be called an "introduction to an introduction." The "crisis of the European sciences" is for Husserl the "crisis of European Man" and can be resolved only in transcendental phenomenology, wherein "human reason comes to itself." It is almost inevitable, then, that the lecture should be included in one volume with the much earlier introduction, "Philosophy as Rigorous Science." The task which Husserl set himself as a lifework was, after all, that of "saving human reason," which is but another way of saying that his task was one of giving a meaning to "rigorous science," when this is said of philosophy.

With regard to both translations, a slight apologia seems to be in order. Even German readers recognize Husserl's style as not only difficult but quite un-German. In an effort, then, to secure accuracy rather than elegance, the translator has regretfully retained for the most part the unwieldliness of Husserl's style, language, and grammar. This difficulty is compounded in the second selection, a lecture delivered practically extempore,[16] making it simply impossible to achieve a smooth-flowing English style in translation and at the same time to remain faithful to the original. It has seemed preferable, then, to be consistently faithful to the text in both selections rather than to risk falsification by rendering the translation more readable.

The close relationship of the two texts, whereby together they form a unified introduction to transcendental phenomenology, will stand out in a rapid summary of each.

---

[16] Cf. *Krisis,* p. xiii.

THE IDEAL OF PHILOSOPHICAL SCIENCE

"Philosophy as Rigorous Science" begins with a brief backward glance at the history of Western philosophy.[17] This survey reveals to Husserl that philosophy has always felt a need of being scientific, a need that up to the present has remained unfulfilled. A rapid leap carries him over twenty centuries of thought to modern times, where he finds the ideal realized in a certain number of particular natural sciences, but in philosophy not at all. Philosophy is as yet not merely an incomplete or imperfect science, it simply is not science at all; there is no objectively valid philosophical "system"; there are only philosophical "tendencies," which do not add up to "philosophy."

Philosophy's constant failure to develop into a rigorous science might lead one to conclude that it is philosophy's essence to be nonscientific and that it should abandon its misguided efforts to become scientific. This is a conclusion, however, which Husserl refuses to accept, though only later will appear the reasons for his refusal, i.e., that the possibility of rigorous science in any domain whatever entails the possibility of a rigorous science of philosophy, since only the latter can ultimately guarantee the genuinely scientific character of any particular science.[18]

With this conclusion as a point of departure Husserl institutes a brief historical critique of past philosophies. He finds that up to the Romantic period they were all motivated by the desire of finding a genuinely scientific basis. Though Hegel's goal was unquestionably absolute knowledge, it is in his wake that the scientific exigency in philosophy tends to weaken or to be given a false

---

[17] Not until the later date will he say explicitly that only Western thought can be called truly philosophical at all. Cf. p. 171 and n. 35, infra.

[18] One is reminded of Descartes's insistence on the same point, *Discourse on Method*, ed. Adam & Tannery, p. 22. Husserl will constantly claim that his ideal is the same as that of Descartes. Both share the conviction that only reason is a reliable instrument of truth.

orientation. As a reaction to Hegel there arose a dissatisfaction with every known philosophy, which turned into a distrust of philosophy as such and terminated in historical relativism. Today we are still without a scientific philosophy, but the quest for such a philosophy is certainly not foreign to the contemporary spirit, nor do we lack good reason to hope that the quest will succeed— provided that the critique of the pretenders to such a dignity be an attack on their principles and methods, not merely on their conclusions. There follows a criticism of "naturalism," the strongest contemporary pretender to the title of scientific philosophy. Naturalism, it is true, recognizes the need of a scientific philosophy, but it is the greatest obstacle to the realization of such a philosophy, based as it is on principles that make philosophy impossible.

Naturalism, as Husserl here characterizes it, is the doctrine that recognizes as real (*wirklich*) only the physical. As a science of the factual it either refuses any reality to the ideal or else "naturalizes" it by making it a physical reality. It is precisely by naturalizing consciousness and ideas, however, that it defeats itself. The objectivity which it presupposes, without which it could itself lay no claim to being scientific, is essentially ideal and therefore a contradiction of naturalism's own principles. Thus in its theoretical procedure it is idealistic, even though it refuses all idealism and makes of ideas physical realities. What is more, any attempt to see in the ideal a nonphysical reality is simply branded by naturalism as "Scholasticism."

The sort of criticism which attacks only the consequences of naturalism, however, results only in the conclusion that a scientific philosophy is impossible, since mere "science" cannot make it so. Husserl institutes, therefore, a positive critique of naturalism, i.e., of psychophysical psychology's pretention to be *the* scientific philosophy. On the supposition that philosophy's rôle is to provide a foundation for normative disciplines (ethics, axiology, etc.)—ideal disciplines that transcend facts—he shows that no science of facts can provide them with a foundation. Because modern psychology is essentially bound to the physical, it shares the naïveté of all natural sciences; it is caught up in the contingency of empirical existence and cannot itself be absolute or necessary. Experience alone cannot answer the most important questions about experience but must seek the answers in a theory of cognition from which every positing of existence has been rigorously eliminated. A theory of cognition that is to study the relation between being and consciousness must concern itself with that being which corresponds to consciousness (ideal being)[19] rather than with a consciousness that would correspond to (existential) being.

Now, the demands that psychology cannot satisfy, phenomenology does satisfy. What phenomenology does is to analyze consciousness, where alone objectivity is absolute. Phenomenology, then, is a study of consciousness, but it is not a psychology, a notion impossible to grasp until one sees consciousness as not a physical something.

Moreover, not only is empirical psychology not philosophy, it is not even psychology in the most significant sense. Because it is afraid of introspection, it refuses any direct grasp of the data of consciousness, thus blocking any access to the essence of the very concepts with which it must work. Nor is it aware of the deficiencies in its own procedures but seeks to overcome the essential weaknesses of its methods by employing these same methods. In doing this it rejects the only method that would make it truly a psychology, the phenomenological method. It wants to get to "things themselves" without even knowing what "things" are. In this its basic error is a confusion between the comprehension of experience precisely as experience and the analysis of the experience of nature merely as a psychological process. In other words, in describing experience we are forced to employ a set of

[19] Ideas (or essential concepts) precede their existential (and therefore contingent) realizations.

concepts that are derived not from experience but from an essential analysis of the acts of consciousness. It is true, of course, that we must have experiences in order to have concepts, but the concepts are not justified by experience; their validity transcends experience. The question, then, of a scientific knowledge of what experience presents cannot be answered by experience; it is a question of "sense," which is a trans-empirical element in all knowledge. By "naturalizing" consciousness psychology is bound to miss this its essential character.

The confusion here comes from the supposition that there must be absolute uniformity of method in sciences and that the method is that of the empirical sciences. True science, on the other hand, conforms itself to its objects, regardless of methodological prejudices based on the success of one method in other scientific endeavors. Now, the concept of nature applies, properly speaking, only to the spatio-temporal world and not to the psychical. Therefore it is only corporeal being that can be submitted to empirical investigation, wherein it is experienced as identical in a number of diverse appearances, since only corporeal being is distinct from its appearances, only it is subject to laws of causality in the physical sense. The world of the psychical, on the other hand, is composed of monadic beings whose relation to each other is not causal. It is a world where there is no distinction between being and appearance; the being of the psychical is its appearing, a phenomenal being constantly in flux, graspable only in an essential intuition.

The problem, of course, is to explain how a sphere of constant change such as that of the psychical can yield up objectively valid and therefore stable cognitions. It is a problem, says Husserl, only if we persist in naturalizing both consciousness and ideas. In the ideal order phenomena have no nature, but they do have an essence, whereby they manifest an objective validity. A perception, a memory, a judgment can be grasped as what they are essentially, nor can any judgment regarding them, based as it is on an essential intuition, be either verified or contradicted by experience.[20] As a matter of fact, the physical identity of an object is intelligible only through the acts in which the object is present to consciousness, since it is precisely the relation to consciousness (in these acts) that makes it an object. Essences, then, that belong to the ideal sphere can be grasped as immediately in intuition as physical reality is in perception—and only thus can they be grasped at all. Thus phenomenology is a study of essences only, whereby it escapes the objections against introspection, which is an observation of factual psychological processes and not of ideal objectivities.

In addition to this strictly naturalizing psychological attitude there is another that does not deny the psychical but will study it only in its connection with the corporeal. Husserl does not deny this relation nor the legitimacy of studying it. In fact, it is only in this area that the psychical is related to objective time, the time that is characteristic of nature and not of consciousness.[21] Still, there are other psychological concepts that do not represent natural unities and that demand a strictly phenomenological study. For this reason an experimental psychology must presuppose a phenomenology; in no other way can the essence of the psychical be known, and without such a knowledge any psychology would be without adequate foundations.

For Husserl two conclusions are to be drawn from the preceding analysis: (1) though psychology is not philosophy, its dependence on phenomenology relates it very closely to philosophy; and (2) to recognize the deficiencies of psychologism does not involve abandoning the ideal of a rigorous science of philosophy.

[20] One sees readily that the terminology here antedates the development of *Erfahrung und Urteil* (Prague: Akademia-Verlag, 1939; rev. edn., Hamburg: Claasen & Govert, 1948) and the *Cartesian Meditations.*

[21] Cf. *Vorlesungen zur Phänomenologie des inneren Zeitbewusstseins* (Halle: Niemeyer, 1928), where Husserl promises someday to conduct a phenomenological investigation of "objective" time, which, however, he never did. — Husserl will never deny that measurement can be significant in psychological studies or that measurement can only be in terms of space and time.

After this the author turns his attention to historicism and *Weltanschauung* philosophy, tendencies diametrically opposed to the one just studied. Whereas Husserl rejects the philosophic claims of naturalism and psychologism because they are inadequately scientific, the tendency represented by historicism and *Weltanschauung* philosophy finds naturalistic science too scientific for philosophy. In so far as this tendency remains immersed in a certain relativism based on the empirical facts of psychic life, however, it resembles naturalism and is no less to be rejected by those who seek the ideal of a rigorous science of philosophy.

One can look at the life of the spirit from a historical point of view and legitimately recognize in it a "structure of becoming," but he must not be led by this to conclude that in it nothing is stable, not even objective truth.[22] Thus, while recognizing that history provides important bases for research in various areas, one must resist the temptation of falling into a relativistic attitude toward objective truth.

The "historicism" that Husserl now criticizes is not history; rather it is an attempt to interpret all reality and all truth as relative to historical development. Taking Dilthey as the most significant representative of this attitude, Husserl agrees that history manifests a vast diversity of philosophical positions in the ongoing life of the spirit.[23] He will deny, however, that such a factual diversity can deprive any particular position of objective validity or, worse still, eliminate the possibility of any objectively valid position whatever. History testifies to a similar variety of positions in the "exact" sciences, yet they have attained to objective validity. One must distinguish clearly between an objectively valid science (or art, religion, or axiology), whose validity is independent of its concrete realization, and the historical fact that this or that scientific position has existed. Nor is it history

---

[22] Precisely because the objective is ideal and not empirical can it be stable amid factual diversity.

[23] Like Descartes, Husserl finds the very existence of opposed philosophies disturbing.

that decides which of these positions is objectively valid; in fact, mere history cannot even establish the *fact* that up to the present there has existed no absolutely valid metaphysics. To do this requires a value judgment, which simply is not a historical judgment. Even less can history say that such an absolute metaphysics is impossible. In fact, the very attempt to prove the *fact* shows at least the *possibility* of a basis of criticism, and in this, historicism refutes itself. Thus, though history is a legitimate discipline, inherent in it is the temptation to treat all historical positions as equally invalid.

Weltanschauung philosophy, unlike historicism, does not consider the variety of successive philosophical positions. Rather it looks upon a certain loose unity of all scientific thought at any time as expressing the spirit of that time; and this it calls "philosophy." Precisely because it is not a unifying "science," however, but only a unifying *Anschauung,* this sort of thing is suspect. Its attitude is humanistic; looking at the same historical facts as does historicism, it finds that they are not all equally invalid, but rather all equally valid, since each performs in its age an important function in the development of the human spirit. Thus philosophy serves to develop the person (or the community); its concern is not objective truth. Ultimately it is practically synonymous with "culture," whose goal is to give within the limits of a particular time and place as good an answer as possible to the problems of life. It is, then, a sort of "wisdom" or "science of living," and it calls itself a "philosophy" of the loftiest human values.

Without denying to this conception a certain attractiveness and even a certain value, Husserl finds it completely illegitimate as a substitute for strict science. A rigorously scientific philosophy is a human value which must be attained; nothing can be a substitute for it. Past philosophies may have been *Weltanschauungen,* but modern consciousness has clearly distinguished culture from strict science and will accept no substitutes for the latter. *Weltanschauung* is neither the path to strict science, nor is it an imperfect temporal realization of the genuinely scientific ideal; up to the present the ideal simply has not been realized, not even imperfectly. Nor will it ever be realized by an isolated individual; it would not be science in the modern sense if it could be so realized.

Weltanschauung and rigorously scientific philosophy, then, are distinct human values. Whether one chooses one or the other depends on the fundamental inclination by which one is guided, be it theoretical or practical.

If, as in the sciences of nature, a strictly philosophical discipline had already been constituted, the man whose inclination is to the theoretical would have no choice at all—*Weltanschauung* would have no attraction for him. Since, however, the necessities of life can dictate a decision, even the scientific spirit cannot always wait to make practical decisions. Where a decision must be made, even an *Anschauung* is better than nothing. Still, our responsibility to future generations forbids undue haste; philosophy is an eternal value which is not to be sacrificed for a temporal one, no matter how attractive the latter—only a scientific philosophy can satisfy modern scientific man. The only solution, then, is that such a philosophy be constituted, no matter how great the labor involved. The triumphant advance of science will not stop short before philosophy, and no compromise with a *Weltanschauung* can be tolerated. Still, scientific fanaticism need not go to the other extreme and destroy *Weltanschauung*. There are still personal and cultural values to be assured, and thus *Weltanschauung* will retain its significance for humanity.

To some, science implies obscurity, but this is false; true science is essentially clear. Even the exact sciences, it is true, have had their long periods of obscurity, and just as they have passed this stage in their development, never to return to it, so may we expect philosophy to attain maturity. If, however, it is to satisfy the exigencies of science, such as the modern world understands them, philosophy must rid itself of all presuppositions, it must begin anew. The new philosophy will not come from old philosophies; it will be dictated by the very sense of the problems to be solved.

If our age understands what is to be accomplished and has the will to do so, it will accomplish it. Great names will mean nothing to it; a valid position is to be adopted, no matter who held it; truth is truth. We must begin at the beginning. We must see with our own eyes and forget prejudice. The fact that the positive sciences have succeeded by the use of indirect methods does not mean that these methods are essential to science as such. The true scientific method in philosophy is that of the direct, intuitive grasp of essences. It is such a science, phenomenological science, which opens up infinite perspectives for philosophical investigation.

"Philosophy and the Crisis of European Man" can be summarized more briefly. Many of its basic notions have already been outlined above. Its theme, after all, is really the same; only the manner of exposition is somewhat different.

Like "Philosophy as Rigorous Science" the selection here under consideration is well ordered and easy to follow, despite its somewhat obvious extempore character. The purpose of the lecture, stated in the very first paragraph, is to delineate philosophy's role in making Western man the spiritual being that he is. Conversely, it is Western man's failure to live up to his philosophical destiny that has brought him to the crisis before which he now stands. He is sick, and there seems to be no available cure for his illness. There is a science of medicine to cure his sick body, but there is no science of the spirit to cure his sick soul. If there is to be such a science—and there must be—it cannot simply satisfy itself with empirical observation; only a strict science will do. Nor can such a science of the spiritual subject who is man be a merely psychophysical science—though it cannot spurn the help of this latter. It is important to realize that it cannot be a science of nature at all; it cannot be "objective" the way a science of nature must be. The world it is to study is not the objective world of nature but the "environing world" (*Umwelt*) of the spiritual subject.

To make his point more tellingly, Husserl points out that science itself is a product of "spirit" and cannot, therefore, be investigated by the kind of science whose object is "nature." Thus the problem of Western man is not one that "objective" science can solve; its solution lies in a science of the spirit—and its task is to grasp the spirit that characterizes and animates Western civilization. It is in this framework that we can see the significance of history—its unity of space and unified succession of time constituting the supranational unity called "Europe"— as a teleological process. The spiritual birthplace of this "en-telechy" is in Greece, where philosophy is discovered as a universal science that ramifies into the particular sciences, forming a special type of cultural structure characteristic of Europe (as a spiritual unit) alone. Not until philosophy and science had spread before men's minds an infinite possibility of development and an infinite task of investigation could spiritual Europe be said truly to have been born. Only because the character of scientific achievement is enduring, not limited to either the time or the place in which it occurs, is this birth significant.

Just as it is in Greece that we discover the birth of Western man's philosophical ideal (and, properly speaking, philosophy is indigenous only to the West), so too it is in Greece that we can trace its early growth. This growth, paradigmatic for all philosophical growth, is manifested in the gradual subsumption of finite aims in the infinite. That this should come about, however, a transformation of "attitude" was essential. Man had always lived in a world and been conditioned by it. Not until he made this world the theme of theoretical investigation, however, could this attitude be said to be philosophically significant—and not until his attitude is genuinely theoretical does the history of Western man in the proper sense begin. Here a caution is in order: there can be no complete change of attitude, such that man's environing world becomes entirely and permanently other than it was; the transformation of attitude (*Umstellung*) results in an "habitual" thematizing of the world, which is taken up

over and over again during those periods when the practical attitude toward the workaday world in which men must live can be
suspended. What really characterized the transformation is the
dominance of the philosophical (for Husserl, always "theoretical") attitude, at least in those who are called "philosophers."
"Wonder" in the face of the world replaces the desire to explain
it mythically, and that for practical reasons. When man can no
longer be satisfied with mere opinion, he thirsts for knowledge,
and this can be found only in *theoria*. Man's thirst drives him to
an infinite world that transcends his particular *Umwelt*. This
drive, beginning in ancient Greece, necessarily spreads from a few
individuals to the interested group (scientific community), and
from this group to the nation, until finally an international community is formed, in which the guiding light is the philosophical
ideal. (An unfortunate side result is that it brings about a sharp
cleavage between the learned and unlearned.) Under the guidance of this ideal there comes into being and grows a more and
more generalized concern for "truth in itself"—which is necessarily critical of all mere traditions and presuppositions.

As in the earlier essay, Husserl now leaps over centuries to
contrast the "true rationalism" of the Greek spirit with the "objectivistic" rationalism of Europe from the seventeenth to the
nineteenth centuries. It is in this mistaken rationalism, this "objectivism," that he finds the roots of Europe's cultural crisis. It is
reason that distinguishes man from the beast; and it is philosophical reason ("universal rationality") that raises him to a new
level and characterizes all his culture—the philosophical ideal, in
fact, is the nerve center of European culture, without which
Europe is not Europe.

In speaking of philosophy in this way Husserl is, of course,
speaking of the "idea" of philosophy, not of this or that particular realization of it. Still, he recognized that the path to the universal scientific ideal leads through a certain one-sidedness and
naïveté—culminating in a realization that the goal can only be
infinity, never particularity. In this connection mathematics is

worthy of high praise, since it is a pioneer in making the infinite a goal toward which man knows he can strive. It is unfortunate, however, that the spirit of man, where infinite goals and infinite possibilities reside, should have mistakenly been studied according to the methods of natural science—spirit simply is not nature, nor is it "real" in the way that nature is. Thus we are not faced with two equal "realities" that can be studied according to the same "objective" methods. If spirit is to be studied scientifically (and it must), psychology itself must be reformed and become a science of the human subject; "objectivistic" prejudices must be abandoned.

The conclusion reached here is that not only *must* spirit be studied scientifically, but only spirit *can* be studied scientifically, in the full sense of that term. The kind of rationality required by an ultimate science can be gained only in genuine insight, and only in "intentional" investigations do we have the required intellectual insight. To investigate intentionality, however, is to investigate the spiritual subject, the ultimate source of all intentionality.

In summary, then, it is necessary to say that the only goal worthy of Western man is the infinite goal set by strictly scientific reason. This we can understand in the light of an historical teleology of reason; and if Western man is to meet the "crisis" which faces him, he must be reborn in the spirit of scientific philosophy.

REALIZING THE IDEAL

Having said this much of the scientific ideal that Husserl sets himself as the only goal for a philosophy worthy of the name, it might be well to spell out in some detail the lines along which he sought to realize this ideal. For the most part the two selections presented here are intelligible by themselves, but since no work of Husserl can really be understood unless the whole of his work is understood, at least in its broad outlines, an overall picture seems necessary simply in order to understand this "introduction." First, however, a word about the three philosophers whose writings were most influential on the development of Husserl's thought in the direction of a "transcendantal" phenomenology. In chronological order they are Descartes, Hume, and Kant, though this is not the order in which Husserl became acquainted with them.

It was Descartes who, in his *Meditations,* revealed to Husserl the possibility (or, perhaps, the inevitability) of seeking a universally rational science of being by turning from a consideration of the objective world to a reflective consideration of the thinking subject. Unlike Descartes, however, Husserl will not look upon this knowledge of the subject as a first indubitable principle from which all other knowledge can be derived.[24] Instead, taking the *cogitatum* as the objective correlate of the *cogito,* he will see in subjectivity the one and only (transcendental) source of all absolute, objectively valid knowledge, because in the subjectivity of consciousness and only here is the being of objectivity absolute.

The influence of Hume is peculiar; it is at once positive and negative. As for Kant, so for Husserl nothing was more important in life than to safeguard the rights of science by refuting the scepticism of Hume. Still, Husserl had great respect for Hume and was convinced that he had effectively put an end to the possibility of any causal metaphysics or theory of knowledge. Hume had refused to see in appearances anything more than appearances—they reveal only themselves and not something which appears. In this Husserl agrees, but the conclusion he draws is diametrically opposed to that of Hume. The latter had never advanced beyond a "phenomenism," according to which appearances yield no necessary knowledge at all. Husserl, on the con-

---

[24] Husserl seems never to have fully grasped the significance of the *cogito* as the paradigm for Descartes of all certain knowledge. Descartes does not actually derive all knowledge from knowledge of the ego; rather he uses knowledge of the ego as a criterion for the qualities that any genuine knowledge must have.

trary, will find in phenomena all the knowledge he wants, and it will be an absolute knowledge. Granted that phenomena tell us nothing about the existence of anything, they do afford us a knowledge of essences, and this is necessary knowledge in the fullest sense. It will be the task of "phenomenology" to make phenomena give up the secrets they contain—the essences of things. The path to this knowledge will be an examination of the experiences in which "things" are given.

The first of the great philosophers to influence Husserl was Kant (though much of the influence was indirect, being filtered through the neo-Kantians). It was Kant who convinced Husserl that objectivity could never be the measure of subjectivity. Kant had effected the "Copernican revolution" in philosophy, and henceforth the subject's thinking activity was to afford the only criterion of its own validity. True thought, then, would no longer be that which corresponded with objective reality; rather the objectively real would be that which corresponded with true thought, i.e., a thougth that fulfilled all the conditions necessary for it to be valid.[25] As Husserl saw it, however, Kant refused to advance beyond a necessary knowledge that was purely formal. Knowledge was guaranteed if its form was unimpeachable, but this said nothing about its content. This, Husserl was convinced, revealed the "dualist" presupposition of Kant's thinking. Though Kant's *Critique of Pure Reason* could do nothing with it, the thing-in-itself was still "out there," making a completely rational science of all reality an impossibility. Husserl would find the entire essential content of reality in the phenomena themselves, thus rendering the contents of consciousness as known as are the a priori forms according to which they are known. There could be no need even to speak of things-in-themselves, since *what* things are is adequately revealed in consciousness.

[25] The very notion of a "transcendental logic," that was to be so important for Husserl, is derived from Kant (cf. *Critique of Pure Reason,* B, 74–82). The difference is that Husserl makes this into a "logic of experience," which Kant refused to do.

Two other influences should be mentioned if we are to understand the direction taken by Husserl's quest for a rigorous science of philosophy during a long life of analysing his own thought.[26] The first of these was Franz Brentano, who has the distinction of having turned Husserl's attention from mathematics to philosophy. It was Brentano's insight into the essentially intentional character of every act of consciousness that provided the key enabling Husserl to overcome the Kantian dichotomy of noumenon and phenomenon. On the other hand it was the mathematician Bernard Bolzano, to whom Brentano had directed Husserl's attention, who enabled the latter to complete a consistent theory of intentionality in terms of an objectivity at once thoroughly immanent to the thinking subject and thoroughly valid for all thinking subjects.[27] An immanent objectivity must, of course, be ideal and only ideal, prescinding from all factual existence of "objects" in the world. By the same token, the "ideality" both of objects and of the conscious acts in which objects are "intended" makes available to the thinking subject the very "essence" of the objects which it intends. Such a grasp of ideal essences is, in Husserl's view, infallible and constitutes the philosophic "science" he has been seeking. Since, however, essences cannot be inferred from the data present to consciousness —inference would demand the sort of causal metaphysics and epistemology that Husserl, under the influence of Hume, has rejected—the only pathway to essences open to such a theory is that of intuition. Essences cannot be *derived from* appearances, they can only be *seen in* the appearances. To follow the development of Husserl's phenomenology, then, is to see how for him

[26] For a fuller account of a large number of influences on Husserl and on the whole phenomenological movement, see Spiegelberg, I, Part I. We might note, in particular, the influence of Carl Stumpf (ibid., pp. 53–65).

[27] According to Husserl, the objective correlate of intentional consciousness was, in Brentano's theory, not really immanent to consciousness. In the last analysis, then, Brentano continued to be a "dualist," utterly incapable of absolutizing the object of knowledge.

the essence of whatever is is ultimately contained ideally and objectively in the very subjective acts whereby what is is present to consciousness. It is a "phenomenology" because it refuses to go beyond the only data available to consciousness, i.e., appearances. It is a "transcendental" phenomenology because all that is required can be discovered by reflection on subjective acts with their inevitable objective correlates. It is a "science" because it affords a knowledge that has effectively disposed of all the elements that could render its grasp "contingent." Only an apodictic grasp of essences at all merits the title "knowledge," and only a grasp that has effectively disposed of all contingent elements in our affirmations can be apodictic. Phenomenology, then, is the "science of science," since it alone investigates that which all other sciences simply take for granted (or ignore)—the very essence of their own objects.

There is a sort of dialectic discernible in the development of Husserl's scientific philosophy, but it is a dialectic wholly immanent in consciousness. A philosophy so conceived gradually reveals the essence of its own object, and in so doing, it progressively modifies itself in accord with this object, since it is the object, not the subject, that determines what the science must be.[28] An examination of Husserl's works (published and unpublished) from *Die Philosophie der Arithmetik* (1889) to *Die Krisis der europäischen Wissenschaften* (1936) will reveal the course of this development. Perhaps the most important step in this process, however, comes with *Ideen I* (1913), in which the reduction of all objectivity to ideal immanence is spelled out theoretically for the first time. "Philosophy as Rigorous Science" (1911) is, then, an important transitional document as an introduction to the "transcendental" phase of phenomenology. On the other hand, what happens between *Ideen I* and *Krisis* constitutes a working out of the implications contained in an ideal

[28] It is the character of what is to be known, not the character of the knower, that makes phenomenology the only viable philosophical method.

science so conceived. From this point of view, "Philosophy and the Crisis of European Man" is representative of the last stage in the developmental process, looking back over a process anticipated only vaguely in the earlier selection.

STRUCTURE OF THE IDEAL

Coming as they did at the end of the nineteenth and the beginning of the twentieth centuries, Husserl's contentions that both consciousness and ideas have a being of their own, that they have nothing in common with the "factual" being of physical reality, that there can be a "pure" psychology concerned not with the processes of conscious activity but only with the ideal being of consciousness and its objects, struck the philosophical world either as revolutionary or as a throwback to an outmoded "scholastic" way of thinking. Even among his own early disciples, though there was considerable enthusiasm for the descriptive method which revealed "objective essences," many refused to follow him in his thoroughgoing idealization of these essences. They were content to follow the Husserl of the *Logische Untersuchungen,* where he so masterfully employed a phenomenological description of experience, but they balked at following the Husserl of *Ideen I*, as he turned the searchlight of his investigations more and more inward to the subject of this experience. Nor were they reconciled when, in *Formale und transzendentale Logik* and the *Cartesian Meditations,* he made his idealism so thoroughly transcendental that not only the form but also the content of experience was constituted in subjectivity (even Kant was preferable to that).

Whether or not the thoroughgoing rationalization of experience through an ideally constitutive intuition, such as is presented in the *Cartesian Meditations,* represents a break with the descriptive phenomenology *practised* in the *Logische Untersuchungen,* is a question that need not be answered here. To anyone who reads the later works, however, it is clear that Husserl himself saw no break in the entire development but only the inevitable working out of implications that were there from the beginning. It is impossible, of course, in a brief introduction to spell out the details of this development and thus to show its continuity. By showing how three major themes present from the beginning guide the whole development, however, we can give a unified picture of the whole phenomenological endeavor as Husserl saw it. These three themes are: the ideal of universal science, the goal of absolute truth, and the mediation of apodictic evidence.

Philosophy as Universal Science

Though one can say—and it has been said more than once—that Husserl is singularly unenlightened regarding the actual historical origins of philosophical thinking in ancient Greece, there can be no doubt that he has grasped in a sort of intuition the unique significance of the Greek philosophical attitude for all subsequent thinking in the West. It is true, too, that greater historical erudition on his part would have made his account of constant dominance by the scientific ideal more convincing. Still there is a grandeur of vision and an accuracy of insight not to be gainsaid in Husserl's account of the ever-present philosophical "wonder," which has refused to let Western man rest in his desire to know. The sciences as we know them have grown out of this "wonder," and philosophy itself has advanced in proportion as it has been dissatisfied with non-rational presuppositions, mere traditions of authority, and mythological explanations of the way things are. That reason, too, has had its "myths" is recognized by Husserl in his criticism of the naïve rationalism of seventeenth- and eighteenth-century enlightenment. Nor can one dispute his contention that the shift from a merely objectivistic to a subjectivistic thematic was necessary if the scientific ideal was to be approached. That rationalism itself, however, has a non-rational foundation, in the sense that it must begin with an act of faith in reason (for which there is no *reason*)—this Husserl does not seem to have realized explicitly.[29]

Husserl would not insist—in his early works, at least—that knowing rationally is the *only* way to know. He will insist, however, that this kind of knowing is a value that the human race and Western man in particular cannot forego and that the acquisition of it demands the sacrifice of other values. He will, then, devote his entire life to the promotion of the rational ideal—precisely in philosophical thinking. The first task to be accomplished, if this ideal was to be realized even partially, was the elimination of the contingent, the merely "factual," from the philosophical horizon. He saw clearly that Kant's rational endeavor to achieve universality had failed precisely because it had stopped short of rationalizing experience itself. But having refused the Hegelian dialectic "system," he had no recourse but to a Fichtean "transcendental idealism," wherein he could identify reason and experience by an appeal to the transcendental source of both reason and experience, the absolute subject. He differs from Fichte, however, in not invoking this absolute subject at the beginning but only at the end of a methodological procedure. The goal is absolute knowledge, science in the fullest sense; but before the goal could be reached, there was work to be done, a work of purification. Only after the non-subjective had been systematically—and painfully—eliminated could the subjective source of all objective validity stand revealed and yield up its scientific secrets.

The work began where Hume had left off, in the determination to accept only the phenomenal, because only the phenomenal was indubitably "given." In the phenomenally given, however, Husserl will find (unlike Hume) a whole world of scientific knowledge, precisely because in the purely phenomenal, where

---

[29] The refusal to be satisfied with other than a genuinely rational explanation may well be justified. But the refusal itself is scarcely rational.

contingency and factuality play no part, what remains is only what is given "absolutely."[30] Methodologically, however, the procedure is the reverse. With a view toward achieving pure phenomenality, the contingent is deliberately eliminated in the phenomenological *epoché* (a Greek word to which Husserl gives his own peculiar meaning rather than coin a word in his own language), which simply leaves out of consideration, as philosophically (scientifically) irrelevant, any form of existential positing of that which appears, retaining only the appearance. This negative procedure is then followed by the more positive technique of "reduction,"[31] whereby the phenomenal residue is rendered more and more emphatically present to consciousness. The further technique of "ideation," which in the genetic development of Husserl's thought is chronologically prior to the two just mentioned, proceeds by a method of variation in point of view to extract the ideal essence common to the various manners of viewing the phenomenal object. Despite a superficial similarity, this last technique is not intended to be a process of induction, since it in no way depends on a multiplication of actual experimental observations—it is ideal through and through.

It is significant that the techniques here so sketchily described are employed with good results in the *Logische Untersuchungen* long before they have been theoretically elaborated in *Ideen I*. It is equally significant that after *Ideen I* Husserl himself rarely employs them, rarely institutes a phenomenological analysis of objectivity. The reason, it would seem, was that, having constantly before him the need of perfecting the procedure in all its details and implications, Husserl for the most part left to others the task of conducting actual phenomenological investigations. The character of his own work remains almost exclusively pro-

[30] Cf. *Krisis,* pp. 186–88, 271.

[31] In another work, *The Triumph of Subjectivity* (pp. 50–52), I have distinguished six reductions (or perhaps better, six stages in the process of reduction) designed to afford a progressive exploitation of what is phenomenally given. Cf. supra, n. 4.

grammatic; his main concern is to make the transcendental sub-ject, the source of all objectivity, available for investigation.[32]

It is obvious that the implications of the scientific ideal here described are not found in either of the selections contained in this volume. It is equally clear, however, that the ideal is the same at the beginning as at the end and that the intervening development has only spelled out what the ideal implied for Husserl's whole manner of thinking. According to this no judg-ment is scientifically philosophical until it has been completely justified, and such a complete justification (or validation) is pos-sible only in the immanence of consciousness, since only there is the contact between consciousness and objectivity such that ob-jective being can be said to be "given itself," which is but another way of saying that the true being of objectivity is being in con-sciousness (*Bewusst-Sein*). Only a careful reading of Husserl's principal works will reveal how this completely justified cognition is to be achieved, but there are three factors at least indicated in the present selections that point the direction in which Husserl's thought on the scientific ideal moves. They are: the notion of a cognition whose objective validity can be determined by an ex-amination of the act of knowing itself, the constant necessity of beginning over again in the acquisition of scientific knowledge, and science as an accumulation of established truths achievable only by the cooperative efforts of a community of investigators.

Objectively valid cognition

Though the ideal of rational knowledge which Husserl kept be-fore himself demanded that he go beyond Kant and rationalize prescientific experience itself, there can be no doubt that his

---

[32] Significant exceptions are found in Husserl's analysis of time in *Vorle-sungen zur Phänomenologie des inneren Zeitbewusstseins;* two brief essays on Space, (posthumous); the psychological investigations of *Ideen III;* and the attempts to elucidate intersubjectivity in the Fifth Cartesian Meditation and in *Ideen II*.

attitude toward knowledge and toward a theory of knowledge is conditioned by the Kantian approach to the problematic. Like Kant, then, he is directly concerned not with the truth or falsity of what is judged but rather with the validity or invalidity of the act of judging. Nor will he recognize any criterion for the validity of the act other than that contained in the act itself. An objectively valid judgment, it is true, will "say of what is that it is and of what is not that it is not," but from the Husserlian point of view one determines "what is or is not" from an examination of the judgment, not vice versa; if a judgment is valid, then the state of affairs which corresponds to it *is truly so.* So, too, with experience. The question to be asked is not "what do I experience" but rather "what is my experience?"[33] If the experience is fully grasped, its object (the "noematic" aspect of the act) is fully grasped, which is to say, it is "known." No element outside the act enters into this validation; the act itself reveals its own validity or invalidity—based on the necessary a priori conditions or rules for valid thinking: an act completely in accord with the rules for this type of act is valid.[34]

When Husserl says of an act that it is not only valid but "objectively valid," he sees great significance in the added qualification. Not only does such an act intend its object as that object truly is, but when nothing is lacking to the perfection of the act, then its very perfection will demand that any act of the same kind which intends the same object will necessarily agree with it. Thus the notion of objectivity, as Husserl sees it, involves both permanence and universality: an objectively valid act is so for all time and for all possible subjects. Such permanence and universality can be secured phenomenologically precisely because no existential position of objectivity can intervene; only the act and its

[33] Cf. *Krisis,* pp. 236–37.

[34] This, of course, presupposes that the essence of the act in question has been revealed in a phenomenological investigation of its type. Obviously Husserl cannot completely escape circularity in the process.

immanent object is of significance in the phenomenological analysis.

Thus, though it is true that Husserl's direct concern in the employment of his method is to establish a theory of cognition, a "transcendental critique of reason," there can be no mistaking the metaphysical overtones which his theory carries. The act of philosophical cognition or, ultimately, the systematic connection of cognitions that constitute a body of philosophical knowledge,[35] is rigorously scientific if its objective validity has been established according to the rules of the "critique." If it has established this objective validity, transcendental phenomenology has done its job. If, however, absolute being is by definition the object of such an objectively valid act, then a theory concerned with validating the act of cognition will by the same token be concerned with absolute being, which is to say that such a theory will be a metaphysics. It will, of course, be an essential and not an existential metaphysics, but it will be, nonetheless, a theory of being.

In the mature thought of Husserl, most eloquently expressed in *Formale und transzendentale Logik* and *Cartesian Meditations,* the identification of theory of knowledge and metaphysics is completed in the theory of "intentional constitution." According to this theory being can be absolute (and thus an object of "science") only if it has been constituted in the mode of necessity proper to reason. The true "critique of cognition," then, is this very constitution of being, since it is this constitution which validates both cognition and the being which is its object. The ideal of a strictly scientific philosophy demands that its object be apodictically given, and the ideal of "objective validity" demands that the apodictic givenness of the object be completely established within the structure of the cognitive act iself. Two such demands can be satisfied only where "to be given" and "to be constituted" are identified. A philosophy will be strictly scientific,

---

[35] In this sense phenomenology can be called a philosophy and not merely a method.

in the sense in which Husserl understands that designation, when all its objectivity, which by definition is "absolute being," has been drawn from the only possible source of "apodictic givenness," transcendental subjectivity.[36]

Philosophizing as a constant return to beginnings

Like so many philosophers before him, notably Descartes and Kant, Husserl was convinced that there was a radical cleavage between philosophical thinking and the mind's natural tendencies. For Descartes this conviction meant a constant insistence on "method" in order to overcome the mind's proneness to accept unquestioningly its naïve certainties. For Kant the same conviction meant a systematic refusal to allow the mind to indulge its "metaphysical" urges—which urges, incidentally, he considered inseparable from human thinking. Husserl, for his part, was convinced that his philosophizing was more radically new than any philosophy had ever been, precisely because it was more thoroughgoingly subjective than any other philosophy had ever dared to be.[37]

[36] The foregoing interpretation is not intended as a definitive solution of the dispute between those who see in Husserl's "transcendental idealism" a departure from his earlier descriptive analyses of experience and those who see in the later stage a perfectly consistent development of the earlier. The only contention here is that, in Husserl's own terms, the only way to achieve the rigorous science of philosophy is in a transcendental subjectivity.

[37] Without reading too much between the lines, one can enumerate on the basis of the two selections presented here and *Die Krisis der europäischen Wissenschaften* what Husserl would consider the four most important philosophical revolutions in the history of thought: the Socratic-Platonic revolution, which represented the definitive turn to the "logos" of being, thus preparing the way for all future "scientific" developments; the Cartesian revolution, with its emphasis on the subjective thematic in both experience and reason; the "transcendental" revolution of Kant, in which subjectivity becomes the "source" of all necessity and, therefore, of all knowledge in the strict sense; and, finally, the "phenomenological" revolution, that so radically reforms all knowing that not only the form but also the content of every act of knowing has its source in subjectivity. Incidentally, one might wonder

According to Husserl, Descartes was by virtue of his *cogito* on the threshold of discovering the truly transcendental subjectivity but failed to see what was within his grasp, because of his dualistic and causalistic presuppositions.[38] This situation, Husserl feels, could have been remedied by Hume, who was nearer to a solution than anyone else. Had he, we read in "Philosophy as Rigorous Science," recognized the implications of his own reduction of all givenness to the phenomenal, he would have become the great transcendental phenomenologist instead of the great sceptic. Hume, however, was unable fully to overcome the naïve naturalism that he had inherited from Locke, with the result that his rejection of any causal solution to the problematic relation between object and subject in cognition led him to reject any solution whatever. With regard to Kant, though it is impossible in a short space to enter into the subtleties of Husserl's criticism, we can say that Husserl takes him to task for not being sufficiently radical; he was correct as far as he went, but he did not go far enough, his "Copernican revolution" was not thoroughly revolutionary. Kant had recognized the necessity of a transcendental subjectivity if ever philosophy was to escape the Humean dilemma, but he destroyed the purity of this subjectivity by his concession to transcendence under the guise of the "thing-in-itself." As a result Kant achieves, not a universal science of philosophy, not a rationalization of all objectivity, but only a formal critique of knowledge that sets the limits of reason and in no way extends its domain. It is for this last reason that Husserl feels himself closer in spirit to Descartes than to Kant, even though superficially he may resemble the latter more than the former.

Husserl's philosophy, then, is in his own eyes the only subjective philosophy that is truly radical, the only philosophy that has succeeded in closing the gap between subjectivity and ob-

whether this last position is any more revolutionary than those of either Berkeley or Fichte. The answer, presumably, is that Husserl provides what neither Berkeley nor Fichte did, a method for "reducing" all objectivity to subjectivity and thus guaranteeing it.

[38] Cf. *Cartesian Meditations,* First Meditation, No. 10.

jectivity. In the entire history of thought it is the only philosophy that has been genuinely (and thoroughly) transcendental, and by the same token it is the only philosophy that has ever been thoroughly objective—which is but another way of saying that it is the only philosophy ever to be thoroughly philosophical. Now, precisely because this philosophy is radically new, and because its newness consists in the degree of its subjectivity, Husserl feels the constant need of returning at every moment to its subjective foundation. The reduction to subjectivity cannot be accomplished once and for all: unless constantly forced to make this reduction, the human mind will follow its natural bent and once more become lost in "objectivism." Husserl's philosophy is radically revolutionary because the revolution is constantly going on: it is not merely a revolt against the way things have been; it is a constant war against the mind's natural tendency to go in a counter direction.[39]

Since, then, man's attitude in the world that environs him is not naturally a scientific one, and since the phenomenological attitude adopted for scientific investigation is not a complete transformation of the natural attitude (in the sense that it replaces it in all the affairs of life), a distinct effort of will must enter in during those times when the philosopher is philosophizing. Thus the transcendence that, so to speak, imposes itself on us in normal, everyday affairs must be deliberately put aside each time we turn to philosophical thinking. The repeated act of the will required for adopting the necessary scientific attitude betokens a repeated return to the beginning in the kind of thinking involved. This can, of course, become habitual, in the same way that the attitude required for any task can be called habitual, if it is called into play only at such times as the task is being accomplished. For the phenomenologist this will mean that he can at will eliminate transcendence in favor of that immanence which is the source

[39] One is reminded of Bergson's "laborious, and even painful, effort to remount the natural slope of the work of thought" (*Introduction to Metaphysics*, tr. T. E. Hulme; The Liberal Arts Press, 1950, p. 44).

and center of all objectivity, all absolute being. It will also mean, however, that there is no once-and-for-all adoption of an attitude that will then automatically carry through in all one's thinking.

In respect to philosophy as such, however, this return to the source of absolute being which strict science requires has an even more radical aspect. Philosophy has never before been phenomenological, and it must, therefore, be totally reconstituted on the foundations that phenomenology affords. Husserl does not deny that philosophies in the past have come up with valuable, even true, conclusions. He does deny, however, that these conclusions have ever been adequately established, nor will they be established until they are re-examined phenomenologically—they must justify themselves, so to speak, before a new board of examiners, and the new examination will be at once a critique and a constitution of that which is genuinely true. To paraphrase Spinoza, the validity constituted will be at once the criterion of its own truth and of the false. From this point of view, then, there is, properly speaking, no history of philosophy, since as a strict science of being it has never existed in order to have a history. Of course, there may be a history of the tendency towards a strictly scientific philosophy—and in this sense "teleology" has a meaning for Husserl—but philosophy itself has no history, since up to his time not even the foundations for genuine philosophy had been laid. Nor, it would seem, need the aspiring philosopher study the history of thought, unless it be to familiarize himself with the kind of problems that have been called "philosophical" or perhaps to derive from the thought of others the impetus to his own investigations. Strictly speaking, however, what other "philosophers" have thought is of no importance; the whole of philosophy could begin today and be constituted phenomenologically, even if we did not know what any former thinker had said. There may, too, have been a subjective history of consciousness—Husserl will not claim that phenomenology as such could have come into being sooner than it did—but this would

not be a history of thought, only a history of the long prepara-
tions for the definitive manner of thinking. Aspiration toward
a truly scientific manner of philosophical thinking was present
in Socrates and Plato; the thinking itself, however, begins only
with Husserl.[40]

That this should be so is not difficult to see, from Husserl's
point of view. Philosophy can be truly philosophy only if it is
strictly scientific, both in its procedures and in its grasp of its object. It can be strictly scientific only when the being which is its
object is grasped absolutely; and this being can be grasped absolutely only when it is given apodictically. Now, an object can be
given apodictically only when it is intentionally constituted in
the immanence of consciousness acting as reason, the "faculty of
necessity." Only when the object of consciousness has been thus
intentionally constituted does the philosophical object, absolute
being, begin to be—and philosophy begins to be when its object
begins to be. In these terms, returning to the beginning means
returning to the beginning of philosophy; each aspiring philosopher must do this, and each philosopher must do this over and
over again if he is not to sink back into the unphilosophical attitude of his forebears.

Small wonder, then, that the major portion of Husserl's work
is purely programmatic in character. With phenomenology, philosophy is only beginning, and Husserl feels within himself a sort
of messianic responsibility to assure this beginning. If it had
taken more than twenty-five centuries for philosophy to begin,
then the complete dedication of a single lifetime would not be
too much in getting it safely on its way. In both his published
works and his unpublished manuscripts Husserl tortures himself
constantly in an effort to lay firmly the foundation upon which
the philosophical edifice would be constructed. If one reads con-
tinuously from *Ideen I* to *Die Krisis der europäischen Wissenschaften*, one is aware of covering the same ground over and over

[40] Cf. *Krisis*, pp. 4, 72.

again. Apart from the inherently unsatisfactory analyses, such as those of time, intersubjectivity, death, etc., that fill so many tortured pages of the manuscripts he left behind, Husserl is never quite satisfied that he has expressed himself adequately even in describing the method. If the method is to provide the groundwork for a truly rigorous science of philosophy, the rough spots must be smoothed out, and Husserl must achieve by constant repetition what he could not achieve by a style of writing that is so tantalizingly involved. Nor do all Husserl's efforts to lay the foundations of phenomenology preclude the necessity incumbent on every subsequent philosopher to cover the same ground—to begin from the beginning and to realize a radical reflection on his own subjectivity, a reflection in which is again accomplished the fundamental constitution of absolute being. All this does not mean, however, that philosophy is not susceptible to progress. The radical reconstitution that each philosopher must accomplish need not be so long and so painful, once Husserl himself has laid the groundwork. There is in all Husserl's work a note of the noble self-sacrifice that he is willing to undergo so that others may be spared the torture—and so that philosophy may live!

Thus, though no one can absolve himself of the obligation to accomplish in himself the phenomenological reflection, we should not conclude that this sort of philosophy cannot be taught. Like Hegel, Husserl disagrees vigorously with Kant on this point in particular. There is even a sense in which history is significant for this teaching. The efforts of individuals and groups can assuredly shorten or lighten the task that subsequent thinkers must accomplish, if only by showing them the dead-end streets down which they should not wander. Philosophy can be taught, just as the particular sciences can be taught; and just as in the latter there is no need for each investigator to go through all the experiments or all the thought-processes whereby the science was established, so in philosophy the beginner can profit by the gigantic efforts made before him. What alone is indispensable is that philosophy should begin for each with the radical effort of will to adopt the proper attitude, the only attitude that will make scientific philosophy possible. This attitude once assured, each will approach the philosophical problems with which he is faced and will constitute from the ground up as scientific certitude what was previously mere opinion. One cannot, it is true, teach philosophy by simply handing over a body of conclusions, but one can help to abbreviate the process through which the student must go in constituting intentionally the truths that the master himself has labored long to establish.[41]

Philosophic growth by accumulation of findings

Like Descartes, whose spirit he sought in so many ways to reincarnate, Husserl had little confidence in the possibility of philosophical development achieved through the confrontation of conflicting opinions. He saw no possibility of progress without the phenomenological method, a method inseparable from the philosophy involved in it. Theoretically both Descartes and Husserl welcomed intelligent criticism as an instrument for correcting weaknesses in their procedures or inadequacies in their conclusions. Practically speaking, however, neither was impressed by the quality of the criticism to which their efforts were submitted. Such criticism provoked little more than a more vigorous reaffirmation of their already firm convictions. Each was essentially (perhaps temperamentally) a monologist, more impressed by his own capacity for self-criticism than by the significance of what either friend or enemy might express by way of correction.[42] In both men this attitude resulted in a practical rejection

[41] The problem is not really very different from that which any "intuitional" philosopher meets in seeking to communicate his intuitions. He cannot hand over the intuition ready made, but he can prepare the ground for a personal intuition on the part of the student. Bergson's efforts are an obvious case in point. One wonders whether there is any other way of teaching philosophy, no matter what one's theory may be.

[42] Husserl could not, of course, entirely escape the influence of his con-

of dialogue as genuinely significant in philosophical development. Growth, of course, there could and must be if philosophy
was to be vital. The model of growth, however, was to be sought
in the perfectly established science, where the possibilities of
expansion are limitless but where the expansion is accomplished
by an accumulation of discoveries, not by an organic growth of
scientific thinking as such. Despite disavowals dictated by a certain conventional modesty, there was no question in the mind
of either Descartes or Husserl that he had discovered (and established) *the* philosophical method. If there was to be growth,
then, it could come about only by the more and more widespread
adoption of the method and the application of it to the solution
of more and more problems. The very nature of those problems
precluded solution by any other method.

Husserl, it is true, enjoyed one advantage over Descartes;
coming at the end of the nineteenth and the beginning of the
twentieth centuries, he did not share the scientific optimism of
the seventeenth century. As a child of his time, Descartes might
be forgiven for envisaging science's task as finite (its accomplishment hampered only by "brevity of life or even paucity of
experiments").[43] Husserl, on the other hand, saw clearly enough
that science's task was infinite. Still, the asymptotic approach of
the "scientific community" toward the accomplishment of this
task was to be in the hands of "like-minded scientists," all devoted
to the same method and each contributing his own solutions, the
sum total of which would constitute the science of philosophy
at any given time. From a practical point of view Husserl sought
to promote this attitude and these results by assigning to his
students a series of "phenomenological investigations," much as
a professor of science might assign to his students a number of
laboratory experiments.[44]

---

temporaries. The prominence in his later writings on such themes as intersubjectivity, temporality, and the *Lebenswelt* is evidence of such influence.

[43] *Discourse on Method*, p. 63.

[44] Many of the studies thus undertaken were published in the *Jahrbuch*

Since, prior to Husserl's own efforts, there simply had been no scientific philosophy (and hence no philosophy worthy of the name), growth can at any time be measured by the number of problems (in various areas: logical, metaphysical, moral, aesthetic, sociological) that have been solved in phenomenological investigations. There can be no end to the problems that can arise and hence no end to the solutions to be sought. The newness of this need not mean that all the solutions will be different from those advanced in former ages, but it must mean that the solutions have been validated to an extent that they never had been previously. What Husserl seeks in philosophy is scientific knowledge, not true opinions. The content of what one man knows and what another believes may very well be the same; the difference will be in the justification for their affirmations. Science, according to Husserl, is an accumulation of completely verified affirmations, and this the "science" of philosophy must be.

It is significant in this characterization of philosophical science that Husserl has arrived, by means of a phenomenological analysis, at an intuition revealing the very "essence" of science. Thus, he has "seen" that philosophy cannot consist in a scholastic analysis of traditional concepts; it cannot be deduced from a first apodictic principle, as Descartes would have it; it cannot be forced within the confines of a unified system à la Spinoza. It boasts a unity of method, in which sense it is "systematic," but it consists in a multiplicity of cognitions, each of which is, so to speak, autonomous, having been established in an independent application of the method, starting from the beginning. This is not to say that the truths which phenomenology discovers (or "constitutes") are unrelated among themselves, only that

---

für Philosophie und phänomenologische Forschung, edited by Husserl himself. They are remarkably penetrating studies, whose philosophical value is unquestionable. It is significant, however, that his best students quickly traveled out in directions to which Husserl himself was somewhat less than sympathetic. One need but mention the directions taken by Edith Stein, Hedwig Conrad-Martius, Martin Heidegger, and Alexander Pfänder.

they are not inferred from each other.[45] It is precisely for this reason that the immense number of truths with which philosophy (or any science) will be occupied simply exceeds the physical capacities of any one man—or even of one generation—to accomplish. Like any positive science, then, philosophy will demand the contributions of a large number of scholars, all animated by the same purpose and all employing the same phenomenological method. The unified method will make of philosophy a unified body of knowledge because all its truths will be linked together in their source, which is the universal a priori of transcendental subjectivity—whose normative rules are invariant from concrete subject to concrete subject.

A science, however, as a body of knowledge can be genuinely significant only if it is the common property of a concrete multiplicity of subjects. And knowledge can be common property only if it is somehow communicable from one to another. It was this rather obvious fact that brought Husserl face to face with a most tantalizing problem, which the phenomenological method can scarcely be said to have solved adequately and to which in later years Husserl devoted some of his most tortured pages. It is the problem of "intersubjectivity." Among the works published during the author's lifetime, it is *Cartesian Meditations* (Fifth Meditation) which devotes the most space to this problem. One can also find an extensive treatment of the problem in *Ideen II,* recently published from the manuscript collection he left.[46] In a phenomenological context the problem of communication is really a double one. Though it is true that any cognition recognized by the subject as "objectively valid" will be recognized as being necessarily such for any possible other subjects, communication can be significant only if there are actual other subjects. The first problem, then, is that of knowing

[45] Unlike Kant, Husserl saw no inevitable "antinomies of pure reason" marring the smoothness of philosophical progress. The phenomenological method correctly employed eliminates the possibility of lasting antinomies.

[46] *Ideen zu einer reinen Phänomenologie und phänomenologischen Philosophie,* II, ed. Walter Biemel (The Hague: Nijhoff, 1952).

other actual subjects, in a framework where nothing is known unless it is constituted subjectively as an object of cognition. Thus the other subject must be an object constituted as a subject (i.e., as constituting its own objects, including subjects other than itself).

The problem, of course, is not peculiar to phenomenology; it plagues any philosophy that will accept only those solutions provided by "pure reason." Still, the difficulties are multiplied for a philosophy so radically essentialist as "transcendental" phenomenology must necessarily be. Add to this that Husserl himself chose to confine the philosophical problematic to the solipsistic level until forced beyond it by the need of a concrete universality of scientific knowledge, and the problem becomes practically insoluble on his terms.

If the problem is not sufficiently complicated already, one need but stress the necessity that a communicated knowledge be reconstituted in each individual subject and that the common body of knowledge called "science," which no single subject can command, must be commonly constituted by a community of subjects. A brief introduction is not the place to go into the details of Husserl's attempts to answer the questions that have been raised. It is important, however, to know that he was not unaware of the complex problem involved and that he gives no indication of being quite satisfied with the only solutions his phenomenological analyses could provide. Had Husserl chosen to devote his efforts less to the programmatic aspects of phenomenology and had continued along the line of the promising descriptive analyses presented in *Logische Untersuchungen,* the solution which eluded him on the theoretical level might have presented itself in a more practical manner. On the other hand, it does seem to be true that Husserl would not have been faithful to his own insights had he not followed out the implications of the scientific ideal already mapped out in "Philosophy as Rigorous Science." But since might-have-beens are scarcely in place in a discussion of this kind, it seems imperative to move on to the second theme announced in the 1911 essay and reiterated in the lecture of 1935.

THE GOAL OF ABSOLUTE KNOWLEDGE

As already mentioned, it was Husserl's great respect for Hume's profound analysis of the knowledge problem which led him to take Hume so seriously and to see in his theories the most significant objections to a rigorous science of philosophy. Following Leibniz, Hume had distinguished radically between "truths of reason" and "matters of fact," according only to the former the possibility of being strictly known. Since, however, only a proposition whose predicate could be seen to belong with absolute necessity to its subject could be said to embody a truth of reason, Hume was forced to deny that there is knowledge in the strict sense of anything but tautologies. With regard to matters of fact, there can be no knowledge of them, since what is said of them could always be otherwise. From one point of view, then, Hume has come to be characterized as a "phenomenalist" who would limit man's grasp of reality to the consciousness of appearances and subjectivity itself to a "bundle of sensations."

With this theory Hume might be said to have delivered the death blow to traditional rationalism, particularly the rationalism of the seventeenth and eighteenth centuries. If, then, the claims of rationalism are to be heard again, a new approach must be sought, an approach that does not make the mistake of ignoring Hume. In his *Critique of Pure Reason* Kant pays tribute to Hume by distinguishing sharply between a world of noumena and a world of phenomena, the first of which can be thought about but only the second of which can be known. It is also a token of Kant's respect for Hume that he will recognize as known only that which is the object of a priori cognition. Unlike Hume, however, Kant will not limit knowing to cognition by analysis; he will in fact refuse any great significance to analytic cognition, since it involves no progress in knowledge. For this reason he introduces one of the notions for which he is most famous, that of synthetic a priori cognition. The *Critique of Pure Reason,* however, limits itself to setting down the conditions for such cognition, thus stopping short before even seeking to outline a scientific philosophy.

Like Kant, Husserl takes Hume's destruction of traditional rationalism as his point of departure. More than that, he agrees with Kant that the only solution to the Humean dilemma lies in a subjective a priori, whose content is phenomenal, and not in any problematic relation of consciousness to noumenal reality. Unlike Kant, however, he is not content that the subjective a priori extend only to the form of cognition, leaving the content of cognition where it was. With all due respect to Kant for having supplied a "how" for a strictly scientific philosophy, Husserl will seek to render a grasp of the "what" equally scientific, equally apodictic. Given the framework in which Husserl had chosen to work out a solution, only one alternative was open to him: he must guarantee the same apriority for the content of cognition as Kant had for its forms. But since a content can be given only in intuition, an a priori grasp of content necessarily implies an a priori intuition that goes far beyond the a priori forms of sensibility that Kant had recognized as pure intuition. Characteristically, Husserl did not shrink before the alternative. Like Kant's immediate successor Fichte, he would posit an intellectual intuition and thereby totally rationalize his grasp of reality. Ultimately this would demand that the a priori source of all objective cognition be found in the subject's self-intuition. Still, unlike Fichte, he would not begin the process of rationalization with self-intuition; instead, his whole phenomenological method would lead up to it. The ultimate guarantee of rationality would not be his point of departure but rather his point of arrival. The phenomenological themes that have come to be so closely associated with Husserl's name—intentionality, *epoché,* transcendental reduction, objective constitution—all are step-ping stones to the transcendental subjectivity in which knowl-edge is guaranteed, in which it is rendered apodictic, absolute.

Although it would be a mistake to look upon Husserl's phe-nomenology as primarily a theory of knowledge rather than as a total philosophical science (at least in intent), it should be clear by this time that there can be no radical separation between the Husserlian critique of cognition and the Husserlian "universal" philosophy. For Husserl the critique is not a propaedeutic to philosophy, it is philosophy. The aim of the critique is to render knowledge absolute, but an absolute knowledge can only be that which has absolute being as its object—and it is in the very act of knowing that the absoluteness of its object is revealed, or bet-ter still, in the act of knowing being is constituted as absolute. Now, it is precisely this character of absoluteness that character-izes the science of philosophy as Husserl envisages the ideal. The positive sciences, it is true, are the examples he has before his mind when he seeks by phenomenological analysis to determine the very essence of science, but the absoluteness of the knowledge to be yielded by philosophy and the correlative absoluteness of its object outstrip anything that positive science can achieve. Ultimately, in fact, only the absoluteness of the knowledge at-tainable in philosophy will guarantee any genuinely scientific character in the positive sciences themselves, since only in phi-losophy can the norms of scientific thinking be themselves val-idated.

Philosophy, then, is to be a science, but it is to be so in a way that no other science is. This is not to say that the positive sciences are not rigorously scientific in their procedures and their results. They are, however, scientific in the manner which their subject matter demands—and their subject matter does not de-mand what philosophy's does. So long, therefore, as the notion of rigorous science is applied only to the positive sciences, the goal which science has in view can justifiably be a practical one. These sciences cannot, of course, be entirely lacking in theoretical character, since they seek a knowledge objectively valid, but this objective validity of cognition is not their primary aim. What they seek is the establishment of "laws" that will enable the scientist to predict what "things" will do in given circumstances. Positive science simply is not interested in what "things" are. However, when the science in question is philosophy, when the object under investigation is being—whether the being of a "thing," a "state of affairs," a process, an event, a social reality, or a culture—the investigator cannot be satisfied with a knowledge only practically valid. It is the philosopher's task to penetrate to the deeper validity rooted in the very essence of the object under investigation, which essence, of course, is also the ultimate explanation for the way things act—because they are what they are. More importantly, from Husserl's point of view, the essences of things will be the truth of knowledge about them. Absolute being and absolute truth become identified, then, and they are identified in the absolute knowledge to which only philosophy can lay claim—absolute being is philosophically known being.

Here, then, is the root of the phenomenological method as opposed to any other method in philosophy. Only in consciousness is being not infected with the "facticity" that is an impediment to absoluteness. For the philosopher only being in consciousness (*Bewusst-Sein*) can be absolute, since only in consciousness is being free from the sort of existential positing that Hume's attacks on causality had rendered forever suspect, and this being in consciousness must be characterized by the necessity and universality only reason can confer upon it. If, then, to know things absolutely is to know their essences, phenomenology must be able to reveal the essential whatness of whatever is proposed to its investigations, and this whatness must be discoverable in appearances. For Husserl the dichotomy of "thing-in-itself" and "thing-as-it-appears" (noumenon-phenomenon) is an illegitimate concession to dualistic, causalistic metaphysics. Only "truths of reason" can be objects of knowledge in the strict sense, but only what is essentially, necessarily true can be a truth of reason. Finally, only where there are no non-rational elements in the act of knowing—no elements of conjecture, of facticity, of contingency—can there be a knowing which has the absolutely true as its object.

In all this there is a strange paradox never resolved by Husserl and that he seems never to have tried to resolve. One is tempted, in fact, to ask whether he was even aware of the paradox. It is indubitable that Husserl saw how important for his philosophy—perhaps more than for any other philosophy—was the question of truth, the "essence" of truth. Yet—and here is the paradox—he never really asked himself the question. He does, of course, constantly speak of "truth" (*Wahrheit*), particularly in *Logische Untersuchungen* and *Formale und transzendentale Logik,* but since his philosophy is primarily concerned with the essence of what is (*das Seiende*) rather than with the essence of being (*das Sein*), the form of expression he uses is somewhat deceiving. He speaks of the essence of truth (*Wahrheit*), but he seeks the essence of the true (*das Wahre*). His problem, then, is not to discover the essence of either being or truth, but rather to guarantee that knowledge is of "what is" and that it is true.

This is important. Kant had said that man's ultimate concerns were God, freedom, and immortality, but that "pure speculative reason" was incapable of coming to terms with these concerns. Without even entering into man's ultimate concerns, Husserl confines himself to philosophy's ultimate concerns, and these, he feels, are what philosophy can know with absolute, apodictic certitude. If God, freedom, and immortality cannot be known this way, then they simply are no concern of philosophy. He does, of course, admit (at least, in 1911) that man's theoretical interests need not be his highest interests, but he does insist—and insisted to the end—that Western man is characterized by his theoretical interests, and that it is phenomenology's task to promote these and only these. That these interests will carry over into the practical order he does not deny, but his own task and that of philosophy as a science he conceives as the safeguarding of the theoretical. Philosophically speaking, God is replaced by "absolute being," freedom by "absolute knowing," and immortality by "pure rationality."

Thus, though one can discern in transcendental phenomenology a theory of being and a theory of truth, these are in reality indistinguishable from its theory of the validity of cognition, which in its turn is ultimately a theory of evidence. Absolute being is the object of a cognition that is absolutely true, and a cognition is absolutely true when its object is presented in it with absolute evidence. The process of knowing is the process of making evident, rendering the object present-in-itself to consciousness. All of which comes down to saying that transcendental phenomenology, the only possible strict science of philosophy, is a quest for a being which is given to consciousness in such a way that the impossibility of its being given otherwise is *seen*. Only if the wall of separation between being and consciousness is completely removed can being be so completely given to consciousness, and only when philosophy confines itself to an investigation of phenomenal being is the wall of separation down to stay. The task of phenomenology, then, is not so much to describe phenomena (as Husserl himself first conceived the task and as the majority of "phenomenologists" still conceive it). Rather its task is to "reduce" all being to phenomenality, since only thus is being given in such a way that a description of it can be significant.

Though one can detect as early as "Philosophy as Rigorous Science" the main outlines of this progressive search for an "absolutely given," it is only gradually that the full implications of his own program were brought home to Husserl. Still, it is remarkable that as early as the *Logische Untersuchungen* he saw the problem of evidence as the fundamental problem of his whole philosophical endeavor. This endeavor, however, has a history that only begins here. It will develop as phenomenology (or the phenomenologist) becomes progressively aware that the quest for absolute being is a quest for an absolutely true cognition and that cognition is true to the extent that its object is absolutely given, or apodictically evident. Such a growth in awareness would of course remain absolutely sterile if it were not accompanied by a concrete means of realizing the ideal of apodictic givenness. This means was at hand, long before "descriptive" phenomenology became "transcendental" phenomenology, in the notion of "intentionality" that Husserl had inherited from the teachings of Franz Brentano. It was Brentano who set Husserl to reading Bolzano, Leibniz, and Descartes, and it was in a synthesis of these three that Husserl found the "ideal objectivity" that was to transform Brentano's somewhat limited concept of intentionality into the instrument for a thoroughgoing investigation of "essences."[47]

Like so many mathematicians turned philosophers, Husserl was keenly aware of the constitutive function exercised by mind in regard to the mathematical "essences" with which it operates. These essences are not found in or abstracted from the world of things, and yet they are infallibly "given." If their givenness is not that of some sort of sensible presence, they must be given intellectually. This, however, is but another way of saying that they are ideally objective, seen by the mind as necessarily exactly what they are. The being proper to essences such as these is the being proper to the objective term of an act of knowing. The rules for their being, for their relationships, for the operations in which they function, are a priori rules, in no way dependent on experience (in the narrow sense), since they are rules inherent in the subjectivity from which all intentionality flows. Because the world of mathematical "intentions" is a self-contained world, not only need no appeal be made outside the

[47] For a brief acknowledgement on Husserl's part of his debt to Brentano together with an account of the significant differences that separate him from his erstwhile teacher, see *Ideen III* (The Hague: Nijhoff, 1952), p. 59.

intentional order, but the accuracy of operations within this order demands that the mathematician eliminate from his consideration the contingencies involved in whatever is outside this order.

Despite the highly psychological character of the analyses contained in Husserl's earliest published work, *Die Philosophie der Arithmetik* (a "psychologism" he will later repudiate), there emerges from its investigations regarding number an awareness of the intentionality of mathematical entities. Along with this went an awareness that the scientific rigor achievable in mathematics is due to the purely intentional character of the objectivities with which it deals. From this awareness the step is short to the conviction that scientific rigor (not necessarily mathematical exactitude) will be achievable only where a similar limitation of investigation to the intentional order can be assured.

At what point in Husserl's career this sort of scientific rigor became a philosophical ideal cannot be determined, but the important witness contained in "Philosophy as Rigorous Science" can be invoked in this connection. Here we find not only an affirmation of the scientific ideal that will dominate Husserl's thought thereafter but also a consciousness that the path toward a universal philosophy marked throughout by scientific rigor lies in a thoroughgoing exploitation of intentionality. The whole of Husserl's philosophical career was devoted to just this exploitation, and the major works he published between 1900, the date of the first edition of *Logische Untersuchungen,* and 1936, when Part I of *Die Krisis der europäischen Wissenschaften* appeared, will be milestones in the genesis of transcendental phenomenology, wherein the implications of intentionality are gradually explicited.[48]

Perhaps the most significant period in this development is

---

[48] In an earlier work, *La phénoménologie de Husserl* (Paris: Presses Universitaires de France, 1955), I have sought to trace this genesis through a careful analysis of Husserl's published works.

from 1900 to 1913, culminating in the almost simultaneous publication of *Ideen I* and the second edition of *Logische Untersuchungen*. To appreciate fully the development taking place in
this period, one would have to examine carefully everything that
came from Husserl's pen during these years: the articles on logic,
which appear as rapid surveys of the books that were appearing
on the subject in Germany (it is in one of these, in 1904, that
Husserl first repudiated his own characterization of phenomenology as "descriptive psychology") ;[49] the unpublished manuscripts testifying to the intellectual struggles through which Husserl was going, admirably summed up in the manuscript of this
period recently published by the Husserl Archives of Louvain,
Die Idee der Phänomenologie; his correspondence, particularly
with Brentano, Dilthey, and Meinong. Without going into these
details, however, we can trace the major steps in the development by giving some attention here to the major works that
mark it.

It was *Logische Untersuchungen* that established Husserl as
a figure to be reckoned with in the European philosophical world
at the beginning of the twentieth century. Reactions to it were
varied, but on all sides they were strong. Opponents decried the
Logical Investigations as the revival of an outmoded metaphysics,
a relapse into "Scholasticism." Adherents found in it a magna
carta of objective philosophical thinking. The first volume, *Prolegomena zur reinen Logik,* was an all out attack on psychologism, mechanism, and relativism in thinking (the attacks are
repeated more briefly in "Philosophy as Rigorous Science"). It is
significant that this volume was reprinted without alteration[50] in
subsequent editions. The second volume contained the actual

---

[49] Cf. pp. 115–16, n. e, infra.

[50] In a careful comparison of both editions I was able to find only one
word added in the second edition. The addition, incidentally, is very interesting. On p. 256 he adds the name of Descartes to that of Leibniz as a
witness in favor of an ideal norm for sciences of fact. Apparently the influence
of Descartes had much to do with Husserl's development during the years
between the two editions.

"investigations" and was devoted to a rationalization of discourse as the form of scientific expression. Herein the phenomenological method is employed to great advantage, though its methodology and above all its philosophical bases have not yet been established. The investigations are "intentional" (more consciously so in the second edition), concerned as they are with meaning. Thus, to give meaning to an expression is an intentional act on the part of the one who uses the expression, while to grasp the expression's meaning is an intentional act on the part of him who understands it. In short, it is the "intention" of meaning which gives sense to expression, and it is an investigation of intentional acts which reveals the essence of meaning. However, since meaning is not justified by the mere fact that it is meaning (as intentional), it must be justified (or "fulfilled") by an immanent vision that Husserl calls "intuition." The thoroughly intentional character of this justifying intuition is hinted at but not developed in the *Investigations;* the techniques for assuring the immanence and apriority of intuition must await the revolutionary analyses of *Ideen I.*

If the reactions to the *Logische Untersuchungen* were mixed, those occasioned by the publication of *Ideen I* were confused. Both opponents and adherents were disturbed. The former could not find here the traditional metaphysics, the "Scholasticism," that they could facilely reject. Here was a subjectivism that went beyond anything psychologism or relativism had ever proposed, but it was an a priori subjectivism that claimed to reveal "objective essences," rooted as they were in the essential character of the acts that intended them. Enthusiastic supporters of the *Logische Untersuchungen* suddenly found Husserl propounding a transcendental idealism exceeding anything proposed by Kant; its closest analogue was the absolute ego of Fichte. Many of Husserl's disciples felt not so much that they had to part company with him as that he had become unfaithful to his original vision and had therefore parted company with them.

The ideal of an absolute science of philosophy still dominated

Husserl's thought, but in *Ideen I* he was moving toward that goal by simply immanentizing all objectivity. In order that philosophy as the "science of being" might be rigorously scientific, he would make reason the very source of being itself. This meant the elimination of all that is contingent or merely factual in the positing of being and the retention of only what reason saw as absolutely necessary. It is here that phenomenology consciously seeks to reduce all being to phenomenality, since only phenomenally can being be absolute. The key to a knowledge of being in its essentiality is an analysis of the intentional structures of consciousness, wherein being appears. The groundwork is laid for a philosophy that will find the essence of whatever can be said to be in an analysis of intentional conscious acts, with their noetic-noematic structures (i.e., their subjective structure as acts and their objective structure as acts *intending* objects). Not until the second edition of *Ideen I* in 1922, it is true, does Husserl see in all this the implication that such an analysis must be an intentional "constitution" of all that is known, but even in 1913 he is well on his way to that conclusion. By this time the intentional act had already revealed itself as a structure objectively analysable, permitting an essential knowledge of objectivity within the immanence of consciousness itself. At this time, too, he began to see the validating (or fulfilling) function of intuition in a new light. Intuition, too, is intentional, but it has a necessity that mere meanings do not have, because its source is reason. Already the purely formal a priori of Kant is being transformed by the Husserlian analysis into a formal *and* material a priori—both form and content of knowledge would be purely a priori, both equally immanent, both equally subjective. The hopeless "dualism" of the Kantian noumenon–phenomenon structure would be overcome. At this point, however, Husserl has only an inkling of what is to come, as he sees meaning and intuition unified in the operation (*Leistung*) of intentional consciousness. Describing just what this operation is must await a later period.

With the exception of *Die Phänomenologie des inneren Zeit-*

bewusstseins, edited by Martin Heidegger and published in the 1927 issue of Husserl's own *Jahrbuch für Philosophie und phänomenologische Forschung,* Husserl published no important new work between 1913 and 1929, the year he published *Formale und transzendentale Logik.*[51]

Although Husserl's investigations of "time consciousness" are unquestionably both interesting and important, containing as they do the first significant application of the method of intentional analysis since the *Logische Untersuchungen,* they must be passed over here in favor of *Formale und transzendentale Logik,* which marks a most important step in phenomenological theory and methodology. Like the earlier work on logic, this book is concerned with the validation of those structures that function in logical—and scientific—thinking. In the later work, however, the rationalization of the synthetic structures of objective thinking is much more consciously subjective in its orientation. Husserl had found fault with Kant for not subjecting logic itself to a critique. Like mathematics, formal logic had always been eminently successful in its procedures and was unimpeachable on the merely formal level. But just as mathematics was in need of a philosophy that would establish the very essence of its fundamental concepts, so formal logic required a validation of the structures and categories with which it operated. Such a validation, Husserl was convinced, could only be "transcendental," accomplished in a profound penetration into the subjective source whence flowed all objective validity. It is here that he sees all intentional operations as forms of subjective constitution in consciousness. The objective relationship present in conscious acts, which formerly could be described, must now be constituted. This did not mean the substitution of new structures and categories for old ones, but it did mean the "reconstitution" of the old ones, whose validity could be established only in being con-

[51] Two recently published volumes of the *Husserliana, Die erste Philosophie* and *Ideen II* and *III,* published earlier, belong to this period, but Husserl himself never saw to their publication.

sciously constituted. Transcendental logic, then, is a "critique" of cognition, because it validates the fundamental forms in which cognition occurs; it does not merely "discover" the a priori norms of thought, it establishes them in constituting them. In doing this it links all cognition, even the most formal, to experience; there is, we might say, a "transcendental experiencing" of logical structures. Unlike Kant, however, Husserl will not be satisfied to exclude the content of experience from rationalization—his phenomenology will be a complete rationalization of objectivity, because it will thoroughly eliminate the opaqueness of the noumenal. He will admit that "conceptions without intuitions are empty," but intuition itself will be a fundamentally rational operation because it, too, will be intentional through and through. Husserl will not be brought up short before an unknowable thing-in-itself; he will simply reject any "thing" which is only "in-itself"; what is not phenomenally given, is not. The instrument of this thoroughgoing rationalization is intentional constitution: what is given in intuition is evident, because to be given is to be constituted, and to be given apodictically is to be constituted rationally; there simply is no objectivity that is not subjective through and through. The task is not to reconcile experience and reason but to make experience a rational function.[52]

Like most of Husserl's published works, the *Cartesian Meditations* contain much that is simply repetitious of the program already outlined. They do, however (particularly the Fourth and Fifth Meditations), break new ground in seeking to rationalize subjectivity as the ultimate source of constituted objectivity. The transcendental subject, without which, according to Husserl, phenomcnology would lack its ultimate justification, has a genesis of its own; it, too, must be constituted. It does not come into the world fully equipped, like Minerva springing from the head of

---

[52] *Erfahrung und Urteil,* publ. Louis Landgrebe, contains a number of papers written by Husserl at various times and covers a major part of his productive career. It evidences the extent to which the problem of rationalizing experience occupied him through the years.

Jove. All experience is constitutive of objectivity, but there is an order in experience; the subject grows with experience, and experience grows as the subject grows. In the Fourth Meditation, Husserl calls this growth of the subject "subjective constitution." This is something radically different from though allied to the intentional constitution of objects in consciousness. Wherever there is objectively valid cognition, it is true, the object known is constituted in consciousness, and the ultimate validation of this cognition is contained in a reflection on the subjective source of the objective constitution. The subject that knows, however, is different from the subject that does not know. Thus as knowledge grows, the subject grows, and the progressive constitution of objectivity is at the same time the progressive constitution of subjectivity. Progress in knowledge, then, involves more than the accumulation of objectively valid cognitions; it means the growth of a subject progressively better equipped to know and to be the validating source of the knowledge it has or acquires.

In the Fifth Meditation, Husserl comes to grips with a problem that had forced itself upon him as far back as the early twenties, as is revealed in the now-published *Ideen II*. A transcendental subject standing in isolation may well be the source of genuinely essential knowledge, which it recognizes as necessarily universalizable. If it remains isolated, however, it cannot but fear a certain arbitrariness in its own grasp of objectivity. An objectively valid cognition is one that is recognized as compelling not only for the subject who has the cognition but also for any possible subject who thinks properly (anything less would be meaningless in a rationalistic framework). Even to speak of other "possible" subjects, however, is to speak of "transcendental" subjects, whose intentional operations would be constitutive of objectivity. If, then, objectively valid cognition is to be infallibly true, there must be agreement among subjects whose cognition is objectively valid; theirs must be a commonly constituted world, where the validity of constitution, and not the pre-given world, is responsible for the community. Since, however, a knowing subject must be subjectively constituted, and a known subject must be objectively constituted, and a known world must be commonly constituted, there arises an extremely complex problem of intersubjectivity and intersubjective constitution. It can scarcely be said that Husserl solves the problem, either in the *Cartesian Meditations* or in *Ideen II*. The best that can be said is that he describes the elements of the problem—and indicates the necessity of coming to grips with it if one is to rise above the level of solipsistic phenomenology.

Unconsciously, perhaps, but nonetheless effectively Husserl points the direction that such a solution must take with the historical and "teleological" investigations instituted in *Die Krisis der europäischen Wissenschaften und die transzendentale Phänomenologie,* the theme also of the second selection in this volume and of a number of manuscripts dating from the period 1934 to 1936. The progress of consciousness toward science is the progress of being (and truth) toward absoluteness. Since, however, such teleological progress is meaningless in terms of this or that isolated subject, it is "humanity" which progresses, it is subjects in communication with each other, either socially or historically; and the march of science somehow transcends both the individual subject and the sum total of individual subjects. Transcendental subjectivity becomes a concrete totality of subjects in historical dimensions—though it is never quite clear what this can mean in a world where the social and the historical is subsequent to the individual, where the intersubjective is an extension of the subjective. The fact remains that Husserl saw, however vaguely, that transcendental phenomenology would ultimately be viable only in a historical framework; philosophy could be a "strict science" only if it became a strict science in a historical process of development.

Although Husserl's philosophical productivity did not begin with *Logische Untersuchungen* nor end with *Formale und transzendentale Logik,* these two avowedly logical texts can serve as two poles between which to trace the development of Husserl's thought. Both works are concerned with the problem of truth, but the differences in the approach each takes to the problem are a measure of the development that had taken place in transcendental phenomenology between 1900 and 1929. In a large measure *Logische Untersuchungen* is a work of controversy, concerned with refuting psychologism and empiricism as theories of truth (a point of view still dominant in "Philosophy as Rigorous Science"). As a result much stress is laid on the ideal objectivity of truth (and correlatively on the being of the ideal), on the fact that logical truth is independent both of contingent, factual reality and of the psychological activity of any existing subject or subjects. Much is said of "fulfilling" ideal meanings in intuition, but little is said of the ontological status of either meaning or intuition. *Formale und transzendentale Logik,* on the other hand, is more "metaphysical" in its approach. Still convinced that objective truth can only be ideal, Husserl is here concerned with elaborating a theory and a method that will specify the subjective conditions for ideal objectivity and assure its acquisition in philosophical thinking. The later work presents more clearly a "logic of experience," wherein the ultimate contact with being is to be logically justified—which ultimately means a transcendental justification of logic itself.

In neither work, however (and for that matter nowhere in his writings), does Husserl institute an essential analysis of truth. Rather, as we have already indicated, he is concerned throughout with the true, with the conditions requisite for a cognition to be true. One could say, of course, that truth is the ideal characteristic whereby the true is true, but a phenomenological investigation that does not seek to uncover the very essence of this ideal characteristic has really said nothing about truth itself.[53] The fact is that although Husserl insists on a clear distinction between

---

[53] Heidegger, *Vom Wesen der Wahrheit* (Frankfurt/M.: Klostermann, 1949), contends that the traditional stress on logical truth as opposed to ontological truth has obscured the whole issue. The essence of truth is the essence of being, or better still, truth is the essence of being.

truth and evidence, the distinction has very little bearing on his own investigations, since he constantly identifies the true with that which is evident, thus turning the phenomenological quest for truth into a quest for evidence.

It is true that in both *Logische Untersuchungen* and *Formale und transzendentale Logik* Husserl does try to define the ideal of truth, but it is characteristic that in the two works he defines the ideal in terms of evidence. The ideal, then, remains the same from one work to the other, but the means of attaining the ideal undergoes considerable development; we might say that it has been progressively "transcendentalized." The reduction to transcendental subjectivity elaborated during the intervening years put the accent on the constitution of true being in the intentionality of consciousness. True being has become the being which is "given-in-itself," which is but another way of saying "evident" being. There results an ideal truth just as independent of transcendent reality and of psychological subjectivity as it was in the earlier work, but now it is an ideal truth more consciously rooted in pure consciousness, or to use the later terminology, in the universal a priori of transcendental subjectivity. With *Formale und transzendentale Logik* phenomenology has become more radically subjective, but in doing so, thinks Husserl, it has become more radically objective. Being, truth, and evidence are now thoroughly rooted in phenomenological consciousness—and at the same time they are thoroughly independent of both subjective and objective factuality.

EVIDENCE

After what has just been said, it might well seem superfluous to add a section on the Husserlian conception of evidence. But since it is possible to characterize Husserl's entire philosophical endeavor, particularly in its epistemological overtones, as a quest for the kind of evidence that will make knowledge "scientific," there is no better point of view from which to assess the advances made over the years in Husserl's thought about the nature of phenomenology itself. No philosophy, it is true, can be indifferent to the evidences available to it in the employment of its method, but it is not common to find the very concept of evidence assuming such importance as it does in transcendental phenomenology. If, however, a philosophy is to be conceived as a strict science never to be satisfied with a cognition whose objective validity is less than unimpeachable, it must devote considerable attention to just what meaning evidence is going to have for it. This is particularly true of transcendental phenomenology, where the motivating force behind the identification of absolute being and phenomenal being is the desire to attain to a being given in such a way that the impossibility of it being otherwise imposes itself on consciousness.

One need not, after all, be a phenomenologist in order to recognize (as did Hume, for instance) that an act of consciousness—be it perception, imagination, memory, or desire—is given in itself and as itself in such a manner that the subject of the act cannot doubt the being of the act. This is precisely the significance that Husserl sees in the Cartesian *cogito*, which to him revealed not the existence of a substantial subject—an invalid inference from the *cogito*—but revealed only itself and whatever is contained in it. What neither Descartes nor Hume saw, says Husserl, is that in the *cogito* the *cogitatum* is given with the same immediacy and certainty as is the *cogito* itself. Had either seen this, he would have discovered the essential intentionality of consciousness, and the step to transcendental phenomenology would have been inevitable. According to this theory, the being of an object as *cogitatum* is its veritable being, which is but another way of saying that in the intentionality of consciousness an object is "absolutely" given, provided that the act in which it is given is rational.

When one sees things thus, one *is* a phenomenologist, having deliberately chosen to center one's attention on phenomenal being because of its givenness. It is for this reason, according to Husserl, that being and consequently truth are functions of evidence. To be is to be given to consciousness; to be absolutely is to be given absolutely to consciousness, to be present to consciousness in such a way as to manifest the impossibility of being given otherwise. Though one must avoid the temptation to oversimplify—the phenomenological process is an extremely elaborate one—one can say that absolute givenness and hence absolute being are available to a careful reflection on the acts of consciousness. In the act itself is revealed the manner in which the intentional object of the act is given, which is to say that the act contains its own evidence, its own guarantee of givenness. The reasoning process is supremely logical: if the only being that can be absolute is the being that can be absolutely given, and if the only being that can be absolutely given is phenomenal being, then only phenomenal being can be absolute being. Of course, the first supposition, that absolute being is what is absolutely given, could be disputed, but since in this situation it is but a definition of what is meant by "absolute being," the dispute cannot get very far. Transcendental phenomenology wants a being absolute in this sense, and it chooses phenomenal being as the only being that can fulfill the requirements.

It is readily apparent that a philosophy that remains at this level is little more than a phenomenism, à la Hume. In it an absolute certainty has been secured, but it is found to be an empty certainty, for being in any significant sense still eludes one. It is in order to escape this trap of phenomenism that Husserl gradually elaborated his theory of evidence. He saw as clearly as anyone that no new theory was required in order to show that cognition gains in certainty in proportion as it is more immanent. He saw equally clearly, however, that a new theory was necessary in order to show that the certainty thus obtained is not empty, a theory that would effectively unite immanence and genuine objectivity. If Husserl could show that his own theory united absolute certainty with a genuinely objective knowledge of a real world, his task would be accomplished. This, then, is the double movement of Husserl's philosophy, which reveals itself in the gradual unfolding of a theory of evidence, a movement in the direction of ever greater certainty and a movement toward more assured objectivity. He seeks to assure objectivity in cognition by insisting on the essential necessity that manifests itself in imma- nent analysis of conscious acts. The essential is the ideal, and the locus of the ideal is in the acts of consciousness wherein it is consti- tuted. Thus the essential necessity of objectivity is contained in the necessity according to which objectivity is constituted in the various acts of consciousness. A subjective necessity that is logical rather than psychological is by that very fact a guarantee of ob- jectivity.

Returning to *Logische Untersuchungen,* we find there the foundations for a theory of evidence in the notion of intuitive "fulfillment" of the intention of meaning, an intention by itself "empty." Language functions in communication because the meaning given to it by the one who uses it is the meaning grasped by the one who understands it. The intention of meaning is the effective link between a conscious subject and the "state of affairs" expressed in language. For both parties in a communica- tion, however, the conscious relationship can be an illusion if it is no more than an intention of meaning. What rescues it from illusion is the verification furnished by an intuition, wherein an object or "state of affairs" is not simply "intended" but rendered, so to speak, "bodily present" or "present-in-itself" to the con- sciousness that intends it. When the object intended and the object given in an intuition are identical, and the conscious sub- ject is aware of the identification, the object, or better still, the proposition, is evident, its intention has been fulfilled.[54]

Up to this point the newness of Husserl's theory of verification might justifiably be questioned; it differs but slightly from that of

[54] "The vital experience of the agreement between the intending and the self-present which it intends, between the actual sense of the expression and the self-given content, is evidence, and the idea of this agreement is truth" (*Log. Unt.,* I, 190–91).

Kant, of the empiricists, or of the positivists. Yet there is something definitely new in the theory, which, we must remember, is not clearly formulated as a theory until *Ideen I*. The novelty lies in Husserl's insistence that intuition, in the full sense of the term, is the presence to consciousness of an essence, with all that that implies by way of necessity and universal validity. Phenomenological intuition is essential intuition,[55] which is to say an intellectual intuition, the impossibility of which Kant had so vigorously asserted. It is plain to see, then, that such an intuition must be something more than the simple view contained in perception or imaginative representation, even though these latter acts are the examples from which the notion of intuition is derived. For Husserl intuition means more than empirical contact with an object. On the other hand, it is not some sort of mystical penetration into a world of essences inaccessible to merely rational thought. The whole secret of the phenomenological method, as conceived by Husserl, is that it is a laborious process wherein objects are brought to "self-givenness" in intuition. The phenomenological techniques elaborated over a long period of years and culminating in the intentional constitution whereby experience itself is rationalized, are but the implementation of the original determination to accept as evident only what presents itself to consciousness with the same immediacy as does the *cogito*.[56]

There is no need here to describe once more the techniques devised by Husserl to effect the essential intuition demanded by the ideal of evidence as he sees it. If essences are to present themselves immediately to consciousness, they can do so only as ideal, since immediacy to consciousness and ideality are inseparable.

[55] Spiegelberg, I, 11, goes so far as to define phenomenology (in the sense that it is common to the whole "movement") as an "intuitive method for obtaining insights into essential structures."

[56] The similarity with Descartes here is striking. Descartes sought in the *cogito* the model for all certain knowledge. Thus he determined to accord the same evidence to whatever presented itself with the same clarity and distinctness as did the "I am." Husserl will adopt the same model for evidence, though he will seriously question that the Cartesian "I am" is part of the evidence.

Thus the technique of ideation, which plays such a large part in *Logische Untersuchungen,* must be completed by the techniques of *epochē* and "reduction," if it is to be more than a process of very imperfect induction. An essence that would somehow be in-itself, standing behind the appearances present to consciousness, could only be conjectured, it could never be evident. On the other hand, an essence constructed by the mind on the basis of the appearances present to it would be no more than a subjective projection—an ideal, it is true, but without guarantee of objectivity. Only in appearances stripped of all that is foreign to their appearing can essences legitimately be found. Thus the *epochē* is necessary in order to strip objectivity of all that is not phenomenal. Our everyday way of looking at things may clothe them with attributes our philosophical thinking cannot justify, but we must have the courage to eliminate such attributions from our consideration. This done, we must then "reduce" the phenomenal residue to its positive content and find there the essential richness we seek. With nothing but phenomena to go on, we can find by noetic-noematic analysis all the objectivity available to us in a reflection on the acts of consciousness themselves. The apparent negativity of these techniques may seem to offer only very impoverished results, but we must be willing to sacrifice the dross of conjecture for the pure gold of essential knowledge.

To speak of essential knowledge, however, is to speak of what is necessarily so, and to speak of what is necessarily so is to speak of reason, the faculty of necessity. What reason genuinely sees to be necessary, is necessary—in one way or another this is the presupposition of all rationalism. However, the condition for the sort of necessity seen by reason is that reason suffer no interference from what is not reason. One way to assure noninterference is to eliminate the very possibility of interference—and this Husserl has done in his *epochē* and reductions. More than that, one must hand over everything to reason, and this Husserl does with the development of "intentional constitution." Whatever is an object of consciousness, to the extent that it is an object of consciousness, has its source in consciousness itself and is constituted as an object, according to the "mode" of constitution which is necessity. The object so constituted is an object of reason. This is at one and the same time thoroughly consistent rationalism and thoroughly consistent transcendental phenomenology. Notwithstanding the fact of logic to the contrary, the ultimate rationalist and phenomenologist explanation of knowledge must be, "I see it that way."[57] Logic or phenomenological method may be the means of assuring that I see correctly, but the ultimate court of appeal is still seeing—what I see to be rationally necessary, I see to be absolutely true. This sort of seeing, however, is possible only if in the context it leaves nothing unseen, and this is possible only if what is seen is constituted as seen in reason.

In all this there is a certain inevitability. Given the original purpose of securing apodictic certitude in matters philosophical, without which philosophy would not be "science," whatever makes for uncertainty must be eliminated from philosophical consideration. But where there is not merely question of postulatory definition, as in mathematics, or of propositional functions, as in logic, there is ultimately only one source of apodictic certainty, and that is seeing. Philosophy, then, is either a seeing, or it is no science at all. Furthermore, if all that is not seen is eliminated from consideration, only what is constituted in consciousness is left (unless, of course, reason is to be considered as a finite participation in universal reason, and of this Husserl would have no part). The structure of reality is to be looked for in reason, since only there is it revealed. But Husserl could not be satisfied with a parallelism of reason and reality, that would after all still be a mystery and could not itself be rationalized. Only a reality whose source is reason is a reality with nothing of the irrational about it; its being and its intelligibility are constituted in reason.

[57] The objection has often been raised that different phenomenologists can come up with contradictory "essential intuitions," with no criterion for choosing between them. Husserl answers quite simply that one genuine essential intuition cannot contradict another (cf. *Log. Unt.*, I, 191; II, Part 2, 127).

Yet along with the inevitability of this there goes also a certain opportunism. Phenomenology began as a quest for objectivity, but what it has done is to define objectivity in terms of what it has found. There can be no question, as Kant saw so well, that by suppressing transcendence, the source of all doubt, one can arrive at an absolutely certain cognition. This phenomenology has done. Then, by a detailed analysis of this certain cognition it has arrived at a unique and unifying "sense" in the multiple modes manifested by the objective relation immanent in this certain cognition. Finally, it has defined objectivity as this unified sense it has found, without even questioning whether it has sacrificed reality in the process, whether perhaps uncertainty is the price one must pay for a genuine contact with reality. By eliminating the factual, it is true, one may arrive at the essential, but philosophically speaking, the price may be more than we can afford, if the essential must be identified with the hypothetical.[58]

There is nevertheless a remarkable consistency to this way of thinking. Taking as its point of departure the conviction that a strictly scientific knowledge of being should be accessible to man (a somewhat sentimental conviction, since such a knowledge is conceived as necessary if man's dignity is to be safeguarded), it rejects successively a transcendent objective essence and a subjective psychological necessity of thinking as explanations of objectively valid cognition. Once granted that Husserl's scientific ideal in philosophy is possible, the only alternative left is an objectivity based on an essential necessity revealed in cognition itself, insofar as this latter is an act proceeding from pure phenomenological consciousness. Such an essential necessity (be it ever so hypothetical) is the only objectivity available to such a way of thinking. Consciousness being what it is, only the act of consciousness can be absolutely given. If, then, objectivity is to be given, it must be given in the act of consciousness; but the only

---

[58] A Hegelian might well say that Husserl has made the mistake of stopping at essential intuition instead of seeing it as merely a "moment" in a larger process.

objectivity given in consciousness is the ideal term of its intentional orientation. The only objective analysis that phenomenology can consistently accept is the immanent analysis of intentionality, and the only possible source of this intentionality is consciousness itself—or, in the final analysis, transcendental subjectivity. This latter, however, is meaningless if it is not constitutive of its own cognition, both in its formal and its material aspects. Husserl has succeeded in thoroughly rationalizing cognition, even down to its experiential bases. Whatever escapes this rationalization is conjecture, not knowledge.

If Husserl's phenomenology has done nothing else, it has drawn attention in a very striking way to the unquestionably subjective elements in all "rational" knowledge, especially the rational knowledge of "essences." Who can question that facts have about them a definite impenetrability? It has become almost axiomatic in our positivistically oriented culture to look askance at essences, as being simply unknowable. The conclusion we can draw from Husserl would seem to be exactly the reverse: only essences are knowable at all. We know to the extent that we grasp essences. Beyond this we opine.

One last word: despite Husserl's insistence on being in consciousness (*Bewusst-Sein*) as the being with which philosophy is concerned, it would be a mistake to interpret his philosophy as in any sense a metaphysical idealism. More than once he insisted that phenomenology is metaphysically neutral—it declares neither for nor against extra-mental reality; it simply is not interested. As he declared in *Ideen I,* phenomenology is a "doctrine of essences,"[59] and such a doctrine simply ignores the question of the extra-mental realization of essences—it is concerned with what things are, not with whether they are. He does not, it is true, ask whether there are other non-rational grounds for attributing

[59] *Ideen I* (The Hague: Nijhoff, 1950), p. 154; and cf. p. 171. All references will be to this critical edition.

reality to the extra-mental, as does Scheler, for instance, and even Kant, because the "science" of philosophy that he sought permitted him simply to leave the question unasked (and, of course, unanswered).

In all this Husserl was recognizing something that had always been true of philosophy and since Kant had been explicitly recognized by philosophers, i.e., that philosophy is a methodical reflection on consciousness as revelatory of being.[60] Because Husserl was at the same time convinced that consciousness could reveal only being in consciousness, he made a deliberate choice to confine himself to such being in his investigations. Any other being could only be conjectured, and that would place it outside the scope of a "science" of philosophy. But since to affirm that its only being was in consciousness would be equally unwarranted, he avoided that, too. Enough for him that in consciousness was the "absolute" being with which philosophy is concerned—his is not a theory of being, as the metaphysician understands it, but only a theory of philosophical (scientific) being.

For that reason Husserl in his later years could without contradiction make so much of the "environing world" (*Umwelt*) and the "everyday world" (*Lebenswelt*). These concepts do not represent the reintroduction of a "real" world of experience into a philosophy from which it had been excluded. Rather they are a manifestation of the growing importance for Husserl of prereflexive, pre-scientific, pre-philosophic consciousness for the philosophic endeavor. The "world" of which he speaks is still a world in consciousness, but it is a world that somehow guides and colors philosophic reflection. For Husserl reflection had always meant a "turning inward," not to the psychological activity of consciousness but to the ideal act of consciousness, to which belonged inescapably an objective structure. The *Umwelt* or *Lebenswelt*, then, is the objective counterpart of pre-philosophical consciousness: it is a world in consciousness that has not been rendered "thematic," which is simply taken for granted—it is

[60] Cf. Hegel, *Wissenschaft der Logik*, ed. Lasson, II, 3–4.

the familiar world in which men perforce live. Philosophic reflection upon such a world revealed to Husserl two facts: that
even though pre-reflexive, it, as objective to consciousness, is still
constituted in its being, i.e., that the being it has in consciousness
is a being whose source is consciousness itself; and when this
world is rendered thematic in a rational investigation, it is "reconstituted" according to the necessary laws of reason and thus
becomes a world of essences, or an essential world. It is still indifferent to the phenomenologist as phenomenologist whether this
world "exists." What is important to him is that he knows it and
that his knowledge of it is scientific because his knowledge has
its essence as its object. Phenomenology is what it is because it
neither seeks nor accepts evidence other than that offered by
consciousness itself.

PHENOMENOLOGY
AND THE
CRISIS OF PHILOSOPHY

Philosophy as Rigorous Science

Notes indicated by superior italic letters in the text are Husserl's original notes. Those indicated by figures are by the translator.

From its earliest beginnings philosophy has claimed to be rigorous science. What is more, it has claimed to be the science that satisfies the loftiest theoretical needs and renders possible from an ethico-religious point of view a life regulated by pure rational norms. This claim has been pressed with sometimes more, sometimes less energy, but it has never been completely abandoned, not even during those times when interest in and capacity for pure theory were in danger of atrophying, or when religious forces restricted freedom of theoretical investigation.

During no period of its development has philosophy been capable of living up to this claim of being rigorous science; not even in its most recent period, when—despite the multiplicity and contradictory character of its philosophical orientations—it has followed from the Renaissance up to the present an essentially unitary line of development. It is, in fact, the dominant characteristic of modern philosophy that, rather than surrender itself naïvely to the philosophical impulse, it will by means of critical reflection and by ever more profound methodological investigation constitute itself as rigorous science. But the only mature fruit of these efforts has been to secure first the foundation and then the independence of rigorous natural and humanistic

71

sciences[1] along with new purely mathematical disciplines. Philosophy itself, in the particular sense that only now has become distinguished, lacked as much as ever the character of rigorous science. The very meaning of the distinction remained without scientifically secure determination. The question of philosophy's relation to the natural and humanistic sciences—whether the specifically philosophical element of its work, essentially related as it is to nature and the human spirit, demands fundamentally new attitudes,[2] that in turn involve fundamentally peculiar goals and methods; whether as a result the philosophical takes us, as it were, into a new dimension, or whether it performs its function on the same level as the empirical sciences of nature and of the human spirit—all this is to this day disputed. It shows that even the proper sense of philosophical problems has not been made scientifically clear.

Thus philosophy, according to its historical purpose the loftiest and most rigorous of all sciences, representing as it does humanity's imperishable demand for pure and absolute knowledge[3] (and what is inseparably one with that, its demand for pure and absolute valuing and willing), is incapable of assuming the form of rigorous science. Philosophy, whose vocation is to teach us how

[1] We have rendered "Geisteswissenschaften" as "humanistic sciences." They study the products of human genius, particularly in so far as those products are an expression of a common spirit in men.

[2] Husserl never tires of insisting that philosophy cannot return to a pre-Cartesian point of view, i.e., to a merely objective mode of looking at reality—particularly nature. Essential to all philosophical discussion is the subjective element, the element of "spirit." Reality is susceptible of philosophical investigation only to the extent that it is in consciousness.

[3] At this point it is not easy to give an exact meaning to the terms "pure" and "absolute." In general, Husserl employs the word "pure" to signify that which is unmixed, i.e., a cognition that involves no elements of conjecture or construction. "Absolute," on the other hand, concerns primarily the manner in which a subject knows. In the later writings (e.g., *Formale und transzendentale Logik, Die Krisis der europäischen Wissenschaften*) the term concerns the degree of evidence involved in the "intentional constitution" of the known. Ultimately philosophy will be scientific to the extent that it assures the most perfect (apodictic) evidence.

to carry on the eternal work of humanity, is utterly incapable of teaching in an objectively valid manner.[4] Kant was fond of saying that one could not learn philosophy, but only to philosophize. What is that but an admission of philosophy's unscientific character? As far as science, real science, extends, so far can one teach and learn, and this everywhere in the same sense. Certainly scientific learning is nowhere a passive acceptance of matter alien to the mind. In all cases it is based on self-activity, on an inner reproduction, in their relationships as grounds and consequences, of the rational insights gained by creative spirits.[5] One cannot learn philosophy, because here there are no such insights objectively grasped and grounded, or to put it in another way, because here the problems, methods, and theories have not been clearly defined conceptually, their sense has not been fully clarified.

I do not say that philosophy is an imperfect science; I say simply that it is not yet a science at all, that as science it has not yet begun. As a criterion for this, take any portion—however small—of theoretical content[6] that has been objectively grounded.

[4] Like Kant, Husserl will seek the criterion of knowledge in the act of cognition itself. By examining the subjective act phenomenologically, he will determine what its "essence" is. An act found in this way to be essentially one of knowledge, not opinion, is by this very fact verified; its object is true. The same can be said for "science," whose essence is not fully realized in any of the positive sciences precisely because their "evidences" have not been subjectively constituted as absolute, or "apodictic."

[5] As a philosopher Husserl can be called an "idealist," but only if we realize that as a man he is a "realist." What he asserts is that to be genuinely philosophical, knowledge's source must be subjective, and that a prescientific grasp of reality can be rendered philosophical only when it has been "interiorized"; cf. *Krisis*, pp. 255, 271; *Cart. Med.*, pp. 115–18. In this sense any philosophy that rebels against a Lockean sort of empiricism will be "idealist"—a fortiori, a philosophy of essences will be.

[6] It is this notion of the ideal "content" of the sciences that caused Brentano and Dilthey to label Husserl a "Platonist." Though the theory of intentional constitution does much to tone down the ideal independence of this content, it continues to have a sort of being of its own, even in Husserl's later works. Cf. *Nachwort zu meinen Ideen*, No. 1; *Formale und*

All sciences are imperfect, even the much-admired exact sciences. On the one hand they are incomplete, because the limitless horizon of open problems, which will never let the drive toward knowledge rest, lies before them; and on the other hand they have a variety of defects in their already developed doctrinal content, there remain evidences here and there of a lack of clarity or perfection in the systematic ordering of proofs and theories. Nevertheless they do have a doctrinal content that is constantly growing and branching out in new directions. No reasonable person will doubt the objective truth or the objectively grounded probability of the wonderful theories of mathematics and the natural sciences. Here there is, by and large, no room for private "opinions," "notions," or "points of view." To the extent that there are such in particular instances, the science in question is not established as such but is in the process of becoming a science and is in general so judged.*

The imperfection of philosophy is of an entirely different sort from that of the other sciences as just described. It does not have at its disposal a merely incomplete and, in particular instances, imperfect doctrinal system; it simply has none whatever. Each and every question is herein controverted, every position is a

---

transzendentale Logik (Halle: Niemeyer, 1929), No. 62, p. 148; *Ideen III*, p. 37 and No. 36. In his earliest works Husserl is concerned to show that what is truly objective must be ideal (the struggle against psychologism); in his later works he is concerned to show how the ideal can be objective (the struggle for constitutive intentional analysis).

a Obviously I am not thinking here of the philosophico-mathematical and scientific-philosophical controversies that, when closely examined, do involve not merely isolated points in the subject matter but the very "sense" of the entire scientific accomplishment of the disciplines in question. These controversies can and must remain distinct from the disciplines themselves, and in this way they are, in fact, a matter of indifference to the majority of those who pursue these disciplines. Perhaps the word philosophy, in connection with the titles of all sciences, signifies a genus of investigation that in a certain sense gives to them all a new dimension and thereby a final perfection. At the same time, however, the word dimension indicates something else: rigorous science is still rigorous science, doctrinal content remains doctrinal content, even when the transition to this new dimension has not been achieved.

matter of individual conviction, of the interpretation given by a school, of a "point of view."

It may well be that the proposals presented in the world-renowned scientific works of philosophy in ancient and modern times are based on serious, even colossal intellectual activity. More than that, it may in large measure be work done in advance for the future establishment of scientifically strict doctrinal systems; but for the moment, nothing in them is recognizable as a basis for philosophical science, nor is there any prospect of cutting out, as it were, with the critical scissors here and there a fragment of philosophical doctrine.[7]

This conviction must once more be expressed boldly and honestly, and precisely in this place, in the first issue of *Logos,* whose aim is to testify to a significant revolution in philosophy and to prepare the ground for the future philosophical "system." For with this blunt emphasis on the unscientific character of all previous philosophy, the question immediately arises whether philosophy is to continue envisioning the goal of being a rigorous science, whether it can or must want to be so. What is this new revolution supposed to mean to us? Some sort of departure from the idea of a rigorous science? And what meaning should be given to the "system" for which we yearn, which is supposed to gleam as an ideal before us in the lowlands where we are doing our investigative work? Is it to be a philosophical "system" in the traditional sense, like a Minerva springing forth complete and full-panoplied from the head of some creative genius, only in later times to be kept along with other such Minervas in the silent museum of history?[8] Or is it to be a philosophical system of doc-

---

[7] Husserl is not so much concerned with criticizing already existing philosophical thought as with constituting philosophy anew. In his eyes, only a thought rendered "scientific" by the phenomenological method can from now on be called philosophical at all.

[8] Husserl will constantly insist that he has constructed no "system." It is characteristic of a "system," he thinks, to go beyond the data in its explanations. It is interesting to note that, though his aims and those of Hegel are in many respects similar, particularly in their opposition to Kantian

trine that, after the gigantic preparatory work of generations, really begins from the ground up with a foundation free of doubt and rises up like any skillful construction, wherein stone is set upon stone, each as solid as the other, in accord with directive insights? On this question minds must part company and paths must diverge.

The revolutions decisive for the progress of philosophy are those in which the claim of former philosophies to be scientific are discredited by a critique of their pretended scientific procedure. Then at the helm is the fully conscious will to establish philosophy in a radically new fashion in the sense of rigorous science, determining the order in which tasks are undertaken. First of all, thought concentrates all its energy on decisively clarifying, by means of systematic examination, the conditions of strict science that in former philosophies were naïvely overlooked or misunderstood, in order thereafter to attempt to construct anew a structure of philosophical docrine. Such a fully conscious will for rigorous science[9] dominated the Socratic-Platonic revolution of philosophy and also, at the beginning of the modern era, the scientific reactions against Scholasticism, especially the Cartesian revolution. Its impulse carries over to the great philosophies of the seventeenth and eighteenth centuries; it renews itself with most radical vigor in Kant's critique of reason and still dominates Fichte's philosophizing. Again and again research is directed toward true beginnings, decisive formulation of problems, and correct methods.

Only with romantic philosophy does a change occur. However much Hegel insists on the absolute validity of his method and his

---

formalism, Husserl had no sympathy for the great "system builder." He finds the latter's system "unscientific," relativistic, lacking a critique of reason, and ultimately giving rise to a "naturalistic" reaction.

[9] Scepticism in all its forms, especially that of Hume, was particularly distasteful to Husserl precisely because he considered philosophical certitude a value necessary to humanity. Only if we recognize the value judgment basic to Husserl's quest for a scientific philosophy can we follow the argumentation here.

doctrine, still his system lacks a critique of reason, which is the foremost prerequisite for being scientific in philosophy. In this connection it is clear that this philosophy, like romantic philosophy in general, acted in the years that followed either to weaken or to adulterate the impulse toward the constitution of rigorous philosophical science.

Concerning the latter tendency to adulterate, it is well known that with the progress of the exact sciences Hegelianism gave rise to reactions, as a result of which the naturalism of the eighteenth century gained an overwhelming impetus; and with its scepticism, which invalidated all absolute ideality and objectivity, it has largely determined the *Weltanschauung*[10] and philosophy of the last decades.

On the other hand, as a tendency to weaken the impulse toward philosophic science Hegelian philosophy produced after-effects by its doctrine on the relative justification of every philosophy for its own time—a doctrine, it is true, that in Hegel's system, pretending to absolute validity, had an entirely different sense from the historistic one attributed to it by those generations that had lost along with their belief in Hegelian philosophy any belief whatever in an absolute philosophy. As a result of the transformation of Hegel's metaphysical philosophy of history into a sceptical historicism, the establishment of the new *Weltanschauung* philosophy has now been essentially determined. This latter seems in our day to be spreading rapidly, and what is more, warring as it does for the most part against naturalism and, when the occasion offers, even against historicism, it has not the least desire to be sceptical. To the extent, however, that it does not show itself, at least in its whole intention and procedure, any longer dominated by that radical will to scientific doctrine that constituted the great progress of modern philosophy up to Kant's

[10] We have chosen not to translate the term "Weltanschauung" because it has been taken over into practically every modern tongue. It expresses at one and the same time the shades of meaning contained in "ideology," "world view," "global attitude," "interpretation of reality," "concrete view of things," etc.

time, what I said regarding a weakening of philosophy's scientific impulse referred particularly to it.[11]

The following arguments are based on the conviction that the highest interests of human culture demand the development of a rigorously scientific philosophy; consequently, if a philosophical revolution in our times is to be justified, it must without fail be animated by the purpose of laying a new foundation for philosophy in the sense of strict science. This purpose is by no means foreign to the present age. It is fully alive precisely in the naturalism that dominates the age. From the start, naturalism sets out with a firm determination to realize the ideal of a rigorously scientific reform of philosophy. It even believes at all times, both in its earlier and in its modern forms, that it has already realized this idea. But all this takes place, when we look at it from the standpoint of principle, in a form that from the ground up is replete with erroneous theory; and from a practical point of view this means a growing danger for our culture. It is important today to engage in a radical criticism of naturalistic philosophy. In particular, there is need of a positive criticism of principles and methods as opposed to a purely negative criticism based on consequences. Only such a criticism is calculated to preserve intact confidence in the possibility of a scientific philosophy, a confidence threatened by the absurd[12] consequences of a naturalism built on strict empirical science. The arguments contained in the first part of this study are calculated to afford just such a criticism.

However, with regard to the remarkable revolution in our times, it is in fact—and in that it is justified—anti-naturalistic in its orientation. Still under the influence of historicism, it seems

[11] If absolute certainty is to be characteristic of philosophy, a thought (such as Dilthey's; cf. pp. 123–24 infra) that denies that any philosophy can be absolute is itself unworthy of being called a philosophy.

[12] For the meaning of "absurd" as Husserl uses it, cf. *Ideen I,* p. 123, n. 1: "In this work absurdity is a logical term, connoting no extra-logical emotional evaluation. Even the greatest savants have at one time or another been guilty of absurdity, and if it is our scientific duty to bring this out, our respect for them is thereby in no way diminished."

to desire a departure from the lines of scientific philosophy and a turn toward mere *Weltanschauung* philosophy. The second part of this study is devoted to an exposé, based on principles, of the differences between these two philosophies and to an evaluation of their respective justifications.

NATURALISTIC PHILOSOPHY

Naturalism is a phenomenon consequent upon the discovery of nature, which is to say, nature considered as a unity of spatio-temporal being subject to exact laws of nature. With the gradual realization of this idea in constantly new natural sciences that guarantee strict knowledge regarding many matters, naturalism proceeds to expand more and more. In a very similar fashion historicism developed later, consequent upon the "discovery of history," constantly guaranteeing new humanistic sciences. In accord with each one's dominant habit of interpretation, the natural scientist has the tendency to look upon everything as nature, and the humanistic scientist sees everything as "spirit," as a historical creation; by the same token, both are inclined to falsify the sense of what cannot be seen in their way. Thus the naturalist, to consider him in particular, sees only nature, and primarily physical nature. Whatever is is either itself physical, belonging to the unified totality of physical nature, or it is in fact psychical, but then merely as a variable dependent on the physical, at best a secondary "parallel accompaniment." Whatever is belongs to psychophysical nature, which is to say that it is univocally determined by rigid laws.[13] From our point of view, there

13 For a definition of the kind of naturalism Husserl was combating, we can turn to an avowed "naturalist": "a philosophical position, empirical in method, that regards everything that exists or occurs to be conditioned in its existence or occurrence by causal factors within one all-encompassing system of nature, however spiritual or purposeful or rational some of these things and events may in their functions and value prove to be" (S. P. Lamprecht, in *Naturalism and the Human Spirit,* ed. Y. H. Krikorian [New York: Columbia Univer. Press, 1944], p. 18). According to Husserl, there

is no essential alteration in this interpretation, when in the positivistic sense (whether it be a positivism that bases itself on a naturalistically interpreted Kant or one that renews and consistently develops Hume) physical nature is sensualistically broken up into complexes of sensations, into colors, sounds, pressures, etc., and in the same way the so-called "psychical" is broken up into complementary complexes of the same or of still other "sensations."

Characteristic of all forms of extreme and consistent naturalism, from popular naturalism to the most recent forms of sensation-monism and energism, is on one hand the naturalizing of consciousness, including all intentionally immanent data of consciousness, and on the other the naturalizing of ideas and consequently of all absolute ideals and norms.

From the latter point of view, without realizing it, naturalism refutes itself. If we take an exemplary index of all ideality, formal logic, then the formal-logical principles, the so-called "laws of thought," are interpreted by naturalism as natural laws of thinking. That this brings with it the sort of absurdity that characterizes every theory of scepticism in the fullest sense has elsewhere been demonstrated in detail.[b] One can submit naturalistic axiology and practical philosophy (including ethics) as well as naturalistic practice to a radical criticism of the same sort. For theoretical absurdities are inevitably followed by absurdities (evident inconsistencies) in actual theoretical, axiological, and ethical ways of acting. The naturalist is, one can safely say, idealist and objectivist in the way he acts. He is dominated by the purpose of making scientifically known (i.e., in a way that compels any rational individual) whatever is genuine truth, the genuinely beautiful and good; he wants to know how to determine what is its universal essence and the method by which it [namely, that

---

is in every act of consciousness an element which is simply irreducible to nature. This we might call the basic intuition that set Husserl on the path to transcendental phenomenology. Cf. *Ideen I,* Nos. 33, 34, 39, 42, 50.

[b] Cf. my *Logische Untersuchungen,* Vol. I (1900). [Nos. 25–29. — Tr.]

which is genuinely true, or genuinely beautiful, or genuinely good] is to be obtained in the particular case. He believes that through natural science and through a philosophy based on the same science the goal has for the most part been attained, and with all the enthusiasm that such a consciousness gives, he has installed himself as teacher and practical reformer in regard to the true, the good, and the beautiful, from the standpoint of natural science. He is, however, an idealist who sets up and (so he thinks) justifies theories, which deny precisely what he presupposes in his idealistic way of acting, whether it be in constructing theories or in justifying and recommending values or practical norms as the most beautiful and the best. He is, after all, going on presuppositions, to the extent that he theorizes at all, to the extent that he objectively sets up values to which value judgments are to correspond, and likewise in setting up any practical rules according to which each one is to be guided in his willing and in his conduct. The naturalist teaches, preaches, moralizes, reforms. (Häckel and Ostwald are good examples.) But he denies what every sermon, every demand, if it is to have a meaning, presupposes. The only thing is, he does not preach in express terms that the only rational thing to do is to deny reason, as well theoretical as axiological and practical reason. He would, in fact, banish that sort of thing far from him. The absurdity is not in his case evident, but remains hidden from him because he naturalizes reason.

From this point of view the controversy has been factually decided, even if the flood of positivism and pragmatism, which latter exceeds the former in its relativism,[14] mounts still higher. It is manifest, of course, by this very circumstance how slight is the practically effective force of arguments based on consequences. Prejudices blind, and one who sees only empirical facts and grants intrinsic validity only to empirical science will not be particularly disturbed by absurd consequences that cannot be

[14] As a phenomenologist, Husserl looks on any "science of facts" as relativistic, precisely because only ideas, and not facts, can be "absolute." Cf. *Log. Unt.* I, No. 38; *Die Idee der Phänomenologie*, p. 33.

proved empirically to contradict facts of nature. This sort of argument he will put aside as "Scholasticism." What is more, arguments drawn from consequences lead easily to an undesired result in the other direction, that is, for those who are inclined to credit them with demonstrative force.

Since naturalism, which wanted to establish philosophy both on a basis of strict science and as a strict science, appears completely discredited, now the aim of its method seems to be discredited too, and all the more so because among non-naturalists, too, there is a widespread tendency to look upon positive science as the only strict science and to recognize as scientific philosophy only one that is based on this sort of science.[15] That, however, is also only prejudice, and it would be a fundamental error to want for that reason to deviate from the line of strict science. Precisely in the energy with which naturalism seeks to realize the principle of scientific rigor in all the spheres of nature and spirit, in theory and practice, and in the energy with which it strives to solve the philosophical problems of being and value—thinking it is proceeding in the manner of "exact natural science"—lies its merit and the major part of its strength in our era. There is, perhaps, in all modern life no more powerfully, more irresistibly progressing idea than that of science. Nothing will hinder its victorious advance. In fact, with regard to its legitimate aims, it is all-embracing. Looked upon in its ideal perfection, it would be reason itself, which could have no other authority equal or superior to itself. There belong in the domain of strict science

[15] There is an important double misapprehension to be recognized here— one on the part of phenomenology's critics, the other on the part of its advocates, both based on the presupposition that the scientific must be positivistic. The former find that phenomenology is not positivistic, and they conclude that it is not scientific. The latter are convinced that it is scientific, and they conclude that it is positivistic. For Husserl, a non-idealist philosophy would simply not be phenomenological—and, by the same token, not genuinely philosophical (cf. supra., p. 73, n. 4). "The term [phenomenology] has become popular. It seems that today every author who undertakes to give the world a philosophical reform wants to introduce his ideas under the title of phenomenology" (*Ideen III,* p. 57, n. 1).

all the theoretical, axiological, and practical ideals that naturalism, by giving them a new empirical meaning, at the same time falsifies.

Still, general convictions carry little weight when one cannot give them a foundation; hopes for a science signify little if one is incapable of envisioning a path to its goals. If, then, the idea of a philosophy as a rigorous science of the aforesaid problems and of all problems essentially related to them is not to remain without force, we must have before our eyes clear possibilities of realizing it. Through a clarification of the problems and through penetration into their pure sense, the methods adequate to these problems, because demanded by their very essence, must impose themselves on us. That is what has to be accomplished, so that at one and the same time we may acquire a vital and active confidence in science and an actual beginning of it. For this purpose the otherwise useful and indispensable refutation of naturalism based on its consequences accomplishes very little for us.

It is altogether different when we engage in the necessary positive and hence principiant criticism of its foundation, methods and accomplishments.[16] Because criticism distinguishes and clarifies, because it compels us to pursue the proper sense of the philosophical motivations that are usually so vaguely and equivocally formulated as problems, it is calculated to call up representations of better ends and means and to promote our plan in a positive manner. With this end in view we comment more in detail on that characteristic of the controverted philosophy that was particularly highlighted above, i.e., the naturalizing

---

[16] Only much later (*Formale und transzendentale Logik* and *Cartesian Meditations*) that "critique" becomes intentional constitution of scientific objectivity by reason. The same meaning is to be found in the "clarification" of which Husserl speaks in *Ideen III*. The principle of this "critique" is expressed in *Cartesian Meditations* (p. 54): "It is plain that I . . . must neither make nor go on accepting any judgment as scientific that I have not derived from evidence, from experiences in which the affairs and affair-complexes in question are present to me as 'they themselves' " (cf. *Ideen I,* Nos. 143–49; *Form. u. trans. Log.,* pp. 27–71).

of consciousness. The more profound connections with the above-mentioned sceptical consequences will of their own accord come forward in what follows, and by the same token the extent to which our second objection regarding the naturalizing of ideas is intended and is to be given a foundation will be made clear.

Obviously we are not directing our critical analysis toward the more popular reflections of philosophizing natural scientists. Rather we are concerned with the learned philosophy that presents itself in a really scientific dress. Above all, however, we are concerned with a method and a discipline whereby this philosophy believes that it has definitely attained the rank of an exact science. So sure is it of this that it looks down disdainfully on all other modes of philosophizing. They stand in relation to its exactly scientific philosophizing as the muddy natural philosophy of the Renaissance to the youthful exact mechanics of a Galileo, or like alchemy in relation to the exact chemistry of a Lavoisier. If we ask about exact though as yet scarcely developed philosophy, the analogue of exact mechanics, we are shown psychophysical and, above all, experimental psychology, to which, of course, no one can deny the rank of strict science. This, they tell us, is the long-sought scientific psychology, that has at last become a fact. Logic and epistemology, aesthetics, ethics, and pedagogy have finally obtained their scientific foundation through it; they are in fact already on the way toward being transformed into experimental disciplines. In addition, strict psychology is obviously the foundation for all humanistic sciences and not less even for metaphysics.[17] With regard to this last, of course, it is not the preferential foundation, since to the same extent physical natural science also has a share in supplying a foundation for this general theory of reality.

[17] For a sketch of the philosophical situation at the beginning of the twentieth century, especially in Germany and Austria, see Marvin Farber, *The Foundation of Phenomenology* (Cambridge: Harvard Univ. Press, 1943), pp. 4–13.

In answer to this, these are our objections. First of all, it should be seen clearly, and a brief consideration would show, that psychology in general, as a factual science, is not calculated to lay the foundations of those philosophical disciplines that have to do with the pure principles for the establishing of norms, of pure logic, pure axiology, and practical discipline. We can spare ourselves a more detailed exposition: it would evidently bring us back to the already discussed sceptical absurdities. With regard to the theory of knowledge, however, which we do distinguish from pure logic, in the sense of pure *mathesis universalis* (having as such nothing to do with knowing), much can be said against epistemological psychologism and physicism, whereof something should be indicated here.

All natural science is naïve[18] in regard to its point of departure. The nature that it will investigate is for it simply there. Of course, things there are, as things at rest, in motion, changing in unlimited space, and temporal things in unlimited time. We perceive them, we describe them by means of simple empirical judgments. It is the aim of natural science to know these unquestioned data in an objectively valid, strictly scientific manner. The same is true in regard to nature in the broader, psychophysical sense, or in regard to the sciences that investigate it— in particular, therefore, in regard to psychology. The psychical does not constitute a world for itself; it is given as an ego or as the experience of an ego (by the way, in a very different sense), and this sort of thing reveals itself empirically as bound to certain physical things called bodies. This, too, is a self-evident pre-datum.[19]

[18] As Husserl uses it, the term "naïve" need not have a pejorative connotation. According to him, a science of nature is following its own essence in being naïve, and in doing so it achieves important results. His only criticism is that a naïve science is inadequate if not grounded ultimately in a strictly scientific philosophy (cf. *Nachwort,* pp. 1–3; *Form. u. trans. Log.,* p. 240; *Die Idee der Phän.,* pp. 17–18).

[19] Pre-datum, because prior to scientific reflection. Much of phenomenology's significance consists in the attempt to get behind reflection to an

It is the task of psychology to explore this psychic element scientifically within the psychophysical nexus of nature (the nexus in which, without question, it occurs), to determine it in an objectively valid way, to discover the laws according to which it develops and changes, comes into being and disappears. Every psychological determination is by that very fact psychophysical, which is to say in the broadest sense (which we retain from now on), that it has a never-failing physical connotation.[20] Even where psychology—the empirical science—concerns itself with determination of bare events of consciousness and not with dependences that are psychophysical in the usual and narrower sense, those events are thought of, nevertheless, as belonging to nature, that is, as belonging to human or brute consciousnesses that for their part have an unquestioned and coapprehended connection with human and brute organisms. To eliminate the relation to nature would deprive the psychical of its character as an objectively and temporally determinable fact of nature, in short, of its character as a psychological fact. Then let us hold fast to this: every psychological judgment involves the existential positing of physical nature, whether expressly or not.

As a result, the following is clear: should there be decisive arguments to prove that physical natural science cannot be philosophy in the specific sense of the word, can never in any way serve as a foundation for philosophy, and can achieve a

---

analysis of the original data of experience. The result may be a confirmation of the naïve view of things, but as a confirmation it is different. Perhaps the greatest difference between Kant and Husserl is that the former will recognize only an intuition that is sensible, whereas the latter, more in tune with Fichte and Schelling, will insist on a genuinely intellectual intuition, that can be such only if it is constitutive of its own data. It is intuition, ultimately, that makes objectivity evident.

[20] In the Husserl Archives of Louvain is Husserl's personal copy of this article, with the following annotation at this point: "All psychology is psychophysical." It is a question of fact that does not conflict with his insistence in the *Encyclopedia Britannica* article "Phenomenology" and in *Krisis* (Nos. 68, 69, 72) that there must be a pure (phenomenological) psychology. This will be a psychology of consciousness as such, independently of its subject (animal or human).

philosophical value for the purposes of metaphysics only on the basis of a prior philosophy, then all such arguments must be equally applicable to psychology.

Now, there is by no means a lack of such arguments. It is sufficient merely to recall the "naïveté" with which, according to what was said above, natural science accepts nature as given, a naïveté that in natural science is, so to speak, immortal and repeats itself afresh, for example, at every place in its procedure where natural science has recourse to pure and simple experience —and ultimately every method of experiential science leads back precisely to experience. It is true, of course, that natural science is, in its own way, very critical. Isolated experience, even when it is accumulated, is still worth little to it. It is in the methodical disposition and connection of experiences, in the interplay of experience and thought, which has its rigid logical laws, that valid experience is distinguished from invalid, that each experience is accorded its level of validity, and that objectively valid knowledge as such, knowledge of nature, is worked out. Still, no matter how satisfactory this kind of critique of experience may be, as long as we remain within natural science and think according to its point of view, a completely different critique of experience is still possible and indispensable, a critique that places in question all experience as such and the sort of thinking proper to empirical science.

How can experience as consciousness give or contact an object? How can experiences be mutually legitimated or corrected by means of each other, and not merely replace each other or confirm each other subjectively?[21] How can the play of a con-

---

[21] Husserl attempts to solve a Humean difficulty by invoking a new notion of objective validity. For Hume there is nothing in the constancy of a multiplicity of experiences that guarantees their objectivity. For Husserl this is precisely what objective validity means: the constant identity of content in experiences—without existential implications. "The identity of the object in the face of multiple experiences referring to the former is the fundamental problem of constitutive phenomenology whose aim is to account for the object or existent in terms of the pertinent experiences" (Aron

sciousness whose logic is empirical[22] make objectively valid statements, valid for things that are in and for themselves? Why
are the playing rules, so to speak, of consciousness not irrelevant
for things? How is natural science to be comprehensible in absolutely every case, to the extent that it pretends at every step
to posit and to know a nature that is in itself—in itself in opposition to the subjective flow of consciousness? All these questions
become riddles as soon as reflection on them becomes serious.
It is well known that theory of knowledge is the discipline that
wants to answer such questions, and also that up to the present,
despite all the thoughtfulness employed by the greatest scholars
in regard to those questions, this discipline has not answered in
a manner scientifically clear, unanimous, and decisive.

It requires only a rigorous consistency in maintaining the level
of this problematic (a consistency missing, it is true, in all theories
of knowledge up to the present) to see clearly the absurdity of a
theory of knowledge based on natural science, and thus, too, of
any psychological theory of knowledge. If certain riddles are,
generally speaking, inherent in principle to natural science, then
it is self-evident that the solution of these riddles according to
premises and conclusions in principle transcends natural science.
To expect from natural science itself the solution of any one of
the problems inherent in it as such—thus inhering through and
through, from beginning to end—or even merely to suppose that
it could contribute to the solution of such a problem any prem-

---

Gurvitsch, "On the Object of Thought," *Philosophy and Phenomenological
Research,* VII [1946–47], 351).

[22] "Das erfahrungslogische Bewusstsein." Philosophy has traditionally
sought to synthesize reason and experience. Husserl, however, is not content
with a synthesis; experience must be included in reason, must be thoroughly
rationalized so that logic, the science of reason, may be a "logic of experience," too. This, of course, presupposes the complete rationality of being,
which causes Husserl no trouble, since being in its fullest sense, absolute
being, is for him precisely rational being; cf. *Erfahrung und Urteil,* No. 7;
Form. u. trans. Log., No. 86. Only in consciousness (*Bewusstsein*) can being
(*Sein*) be absolute—and that only in the highest form of consciousness,
which is reason.

ises whatsoever, is to be involved in a vicious circle.

It also becomes clear that just as every scientific, so every prescientific application of nature must in principle remain excluded in a theory of knowledge that is to retain its univocal sense. So, too, must all expressions that imply thetic existential positings of things in the framework of space, time, causality, etc. This obviously applies also to all existential positings with regard to the empirical being of the investigator, of his psychical faculties, and the like.[23]

Further: if knowledge theory will nevertheless investigate the problems of the relationship between consciousness and being, it can have before its eyes only being as the correlate of consciousness, as something "intended" after the manner of consciousness: as perceived, remembered, expected, represented pictorially, imagined, identified, distinguished, believed, opined, evaluated, etc. It is clear, then, that the investigation must be directed toward a scientific essential knowledge of consciousness, toward that which consciousness itself "is" according to its essence in all its distinguishable forms. At the same time, however, the investigation must be directed toward what consciousness "means," as well as toward the different ways in which—in accord with the essence of the aforementioned forms—it intends the objective, now clearly, now obscurely, now by presenting or by presentifying,[24] now symbolically or pictorially, now simply, now mediated in thought, now in this or that mode of attention, and so in countless other forms, and how ultimately it "demonstrates" the objective as that which is "validly," "really."

[23] Though Husserl does not employ the terms at this date, we can see here an adumbration of his theory of *epochē* and "reduction," without which the phenomenality of being cannot be assured. The actual theory is not proposed until 1913, with the publication of *Ideen I*. From then until his last work (cf. *Krisis*, Nos. 55, 68, 69) it remains absolutely central to the whole phenomenological effort.

[24] *Gegenwärtigend–Vergegenwärtigend:* from the standpoint of the subject, perception is the act in which reality is present; imagination, memory, anticipation, etc., are acts that render present objects that may or may not be real, but whose presence is not that of reality.

Every type of object that is to be the object of a rational proposition, of a prescientific and then of a scientific cognition, must manifest itself in knowledge, thus in consciousness itself, and it must permit being brought to givenness, in accord with the sense of all knowledge. All types of consciousness, in the way they are, so to speak, teleologically[25] ordered under the title of knowledge and, even more, in the way they are grouped according to the various object categories—considered as the groups of cognitive functions that especially correspond to these categories—must permit being studied in their essential connection and in their relation back to the forms of the consciousness of givenness belonging to them. The sense of the question concerning legitimacy, which is to be put to all cognitive acts, must admit of being understood, the essence of grounded legitimation and that of ideal groundableness or validity must admit of being fully clarified, in this manner—and with respect to all levels of cognition, including the highest, that of scientific cognition.

What it means, that objectivity is, and manifests itself cognitively as so being, must precisely become evident purely from consciousness itself, and thereby it must become completely understandable.[26] And for that is required a study of consciousness in its entirety, since according to all its forms it enters into possible cognitive functions. To the extent, however, that every consciousness is "consciousness-of," the essential study of consciousness includes also that of consciousness-meaning and consciousness-objectivity as such. To study any kind of objectivity whatever according to its general essence (a study that can pursue interests far removed from those of knowledge theory

[25] For the notion of "teleology" as Husserl understands it, see the second essay in this volume.

[26] Since objectivity is a function of pure consciousness (cf. supra., pp. 85–86, n. 19), the role of philosophy is to ground objectivity by investigating consciousness. To the very end Husserl will insist on the philosophical task as one of "self-knowledge" (cf. *Krisis,* pp. 263–65).

and the investigation of consciousness) means to concern oneself with objectivity's modes of givenness and to exhaust its essential content in the processes of "clarification" proper to it. Even if the orientation is not that which is directed toward the kinds of consciousness and an essential investigation of them, still the method of clarification is such that even here reflection on the modes of being intended and of being given cannot be avoided. In any case, however, the clarification of all fundamental kinds of objectivities is for its part indispensable for the essential analysis of consciousness, and as a result is included in it, but primarily in an epistemological analysis, that finds its task precisely in the investigation of correlations. Consequently we include all such studies, even though relatively they are to be distinguished, under the title "phenomenological."

With this we meet a science of whose extraordinary extent our contemporaries have as yet no concept; a science, it is true, of consciousness that is still not psychology; a phenomenology of consciousness as opposed to a natural science about consciousness.[27] But since there will be no question here of an accidental equivocation, it is to be expected beforehand that phenomenology and psychology must stand in close relationship to each other, since both are concerned with consciousness, even though in a different way, according to a different "orientation." This we may express by saying that psychology is concerned with "empirical consciousness," with consciousness from the empirical point of view, as an empirical being in the ensemble of nature, whereas phenomenology is concerned with "pure" consciousness, i.e., consciousness from the phenomenological point of view.

If this is correct, the result would then be—without taking away from the truth that psychology is not nor can be any more

---

[27] The task of "pure" psychology as opposed to psychology as a science of nature (psychophysical). This does not say, however, that there cannot be a science of psychology that is legitimately psychophysical, provided it looks to phenomenology for the very "sense" of the nature it investigates (cf. *Krisis,* Nos. 65, 72).

philosophy than the physical science of nature can—that for essential reasons psychology must be more closely related to philosophy (i.e., through the medium of phenomenology) and must in its destiny remain most intimately bound up with philosophy. Finally, it would be possible to foresee that any psychologistic theory of knowledge must owe its existence to the fact that, missing the proper sense of the epistemological problematic, it is a victim of a presumably facile confusion between pure and empirical consciousness. To put the same in another way: it "naturalizes" pure consciousness. This is in fact my interpretation, and it will be illustrated somewhat more clearly in what follows.

It is true that what has just been said by way of general indication, and particularly what was said of the close affinity between psychology and philosophy, applies very little to modern exact psychology, which is as foreign to philosophy as it can possibly be. No matter how much this psychology may consider itself on the strength of the experimental method the sole scientific psychology and look down on "armchair psychology," I am obliged to declare its opinion that it is the psychology, psychological science in the full sense, a serious error heavy with consequences. The ubiquitous fundamental trait of this psychology is to set aside any direct and pure analysis of consciousness (i.e., the systematic realization of "analysis" and "description" of the data that present themselves in the different possible directions of immanent seeing) in favor of indirect fixations of all psychological or psychologically relevant facts, having a sense that is at least superficially understandable without such an analysis of consciousness, at best an outwardly understandable sense. In determining experimentally its psychophysical regularities, it gets along in fact with crude class concepts such as perception, imaginative intuition, enunciation, calculation and miscalculation, measure, recognition, expectation, retention, forgetting, etc. And of course, on the other hand, the treasury of such concepts with which it operates limits the questions it can ask and the answers it can obtain.

One can very well say that experimental psychology is related to originary psychology in the way social statistics is related to originary social science. A statistics of this sort gathers valuable facts and discovers in them valuable regularities, but of a very mediate kind. Only an originary social science can arrive at an explicit understanding and a real clarification of them; that is, a social science that brings social phenomena to direct givenness and investigates them according to their essence.[28] In like manner, experimental psychology is a method of determining psychophysical facts and norms, which may be valuable but which without a systematic science of consciousness that explores the psychic in respect of what is immanent in it lack every possibility of becoming understood more deeply or utilized in an ultimately valid scientific manner.

Exact psychology is not aware that herein lies a serious defect in its procedure, especially as it becomes alarmed at the method of introspection[29] and expends its energy in trying to overcome the defects of the experimental method by the experimental method itself. It seeks to overcome the defects of a method that, as can be shown, has no competence in regard to what is to be accomplished here. The compulsion of facts, however, which are precisely psychical, proves too strong for analyses of consciousness not to be made from time to time. But as a rule these

[28] "Phenomenology, whose only aim is to be a doctrine of essences in the framework of pure intuition" (*Ideen I*, p. 124). "As for phenomenology, it aims only at being a descriptive theory of the essence of pure transcendental experiences in the framework of the phenomenological orientation" (ibid., p. 139). As a methodology, phenomenology has as its aim a grasp of essences—and this grasp is philosophy.

[29] It is important to note the difference between "introspection" and "reflection" (a distinction which Brentano had recognized). The former simply "observes" interior states; the later grasps them vitally. One is reminded of Bergson's "intellectual sympathy." Cf. Scheler, *Formalismus in der Ethik und die materiale Wertethik*, 4th ed. (Bern: Francke Verlag, 1954), pp. 397–98.

are of a phenomenological naïveté that stands in remarkable contrast to the indubitable seriousness with which this psychology strives for—and in some spheres (when its aims are modest) achieves—exactness. This latter is true wherever experimental determinations are concerned with subjective sensible appearances, the description and characterization of which is to be accomplished precisely as it is with "objective" appearances, i.e., without any introduction of concepts and elucidations that go over into the proper sphere of consciousness. Something is also achieved where the determinations are related to roughly circumscribed classes of the properly psychical, to the extent that these determinations from the very beginning present themselves sufficiently without more profound analysis of consciousness, so long as one foregoes the pursuit of the properly psychological sense of the determinations.

The reason for the lack of anything radically psychological in the occasional analysis, however, lies in the fact that only in a pure and systematic phenomenology do the sense and method of the work to be accomplished here come to the fore. The same is true in regard to the extraordinary wealth of consciousness-differences, which for the methodologically inexperienced flow into each other without differentiation. In this way modern exact psychology, by the very fact that it considers itself as already methodically perfect and strictly scientific, is actually unscientific wherever it will pursue the sense of the psychical element that enters into psychophysical regularities, i.e., wherever it will penetrate to a real psychological understanding. On the other hand, it is equally unscientific in all those cases where the deficiencies of unclarified representations of the psychical lead to obscure posing of problems and consequently to mere apparent results. The experimental method is indispensable particularly where there is question of fixing intersubjective connections[30] of facts. Still, it presupposes what no experiment can accomplish, the analysis of consciousness itself.

[30] It is a bit disconcerting to read here of "intersubjective connections,"

Rare psychologists like Stumpf, Lipps, and others of their kind, have recognized this defect of experimental psychology and have been able to appreciate Brentano's truly epoch-making impulse. In accord with it they have made an effort to continue a thorough analytical and descriptive investigation of intentional experiences begun by him, but are either denied full recognition by the experimental fanatics or, if they were experimentally active, are appreciated only from this point of view. Again and again they are attacked as scholastics. It will be quite a source of wonder to future generations that the first modern attempts to investigate the immanent seriously and in the only possible manner, which is that of an immanent analysis, or as we now say with better insight, by means of an essential analysis,[31] could be treated as scholastic and thus brushed aside. The only reason for this is that the natural point of departure for such investigations is the ordinary terminology designating the psychical. Only after we have made their meanings our own do we look into the phenomena to which such designations are first of all vaguely and equivocally related. Of course, even scholastic ontologism is guided by language (by which I am not saying that all scholastic research was ontologistic), but it loses itself by deriving analytical judgments from word meanings, in the belief that it has thereby gained knowledge of facts. Is the phenomenological analyst to be branded scholastic, too, because he derives no judgments at all from word concepts but rather looks into the phenomena that language occasions by means of the words in question, or because he penetrates to the phenomena

upon which any "pure" science of psychology must be based, long before Husserl has even attempted a theory of intersubjectivity (a poser for transcendental phenomenology!). Not until the Fifth Cartesian Meditation, *Ideen II,* and the third part of *Krisis* do we find the theory worked out in any kind of detail.

[31] The expression "immanent analysis" is undesirable because of its ambiguity. It could mean merely an analysis of ·immanent activity. "Essential analysis," Husserl thinks, eliminates the ambiguity, though it is meaningful only as an analysis of what is immanent in consciousness.

constituted by the fully intuitional realization of experimental concepts, etc.?

There is food for thought in the fact that everything psychical (to the extent that it is taken in that full concretion wherein it must be, both for psychology and for phenomenology, the first object of investigation), has the character of a more or less complex "consciousness-of";[32] in the fact that this "consciousness-of" has a confusing fullness of forms; that all expressions that at the beginning of the investigation could help toward making clearly understandable and toward describing objectively are fluid and ambiguous, and that as a result the first beginning can obviously only be to uncover the crudest equivocations that immediately become evident. A definitive fixation of scientific language presupposes the complete analysis of phenomena—a goal that lies in the dim distance—and so long as this has not been accomplished, the progress of the investigation, too, looked at from the outside, moves to a great extent in the form of demonstrating new ambiguities, distinguishable now for the first time, ambiguities in the very concepts that presumably were already fixed in the preceding investigations. That is obviously inevitable, because it is rooted in the nature of things. It is on this basis that one should judge the depth of understanding manifested in the disdainful way the professional guardians of the exactness and scientific character of psychology speak of "merely verbal," merely "grammatical," and "scholastic" analysis.

In the epoch of vigorous reaction against Scholasticism the war cry was: "Away with empty word analyses! We must question things themselves. Back to experience, to seeing, which alone can give to our words sense and rational justification." Very

---

[32] An essential analysis of consciousness has revealed to Husserl that every act of consciousness is necessarily "intentional," which is to say, it contains within itself an objective relation; it is "consciousness-of." Because this is true, an analysis of consciousness will ultimately be an analysis of objectivity (cf. supra., p. 90, n. 26).

much to the point! But what, then, are things? And what sort of experience is it to which we must return in psychology? Are they perhaps the statements we get from subjects in answer to our questions? And is the interpretation of their statements the "experience" of the psychical? The experimentalists themselves will say that that is merely a secondary experience, that the primary lies in the subject himself, and that with the experimenting and interpreting psychologists it must be in their own former self-perceptions, that for good reasons are not and must not be introspections. The experimentalists are not a little proud of the fact that they, as critics par excellence of introspection and of —as they call it—armchair psychology based exclusively on introspection, have so developed the experimental method that it uses direct experience only in the form of "chance, unexpected, not intentionally introduced experience,"[o] and that it has completely eliminated the ill-reputed introspection. Though in one direction, despite strong exaggerations, there is in this something unquestionably good, still, on the other hand, there is a fundamental error of this psychology that should be brought out. It places analysis realized in empathetic[33] understanding of others' experience and, likewise, analysis on the basis of one's own mental processes that were unobserved at the time, on the same level with an analysis of experience (even though indirect) proper to physical science, believing that in this way it is an experimental science of the psychical in fundamentally the same sense as physical science is an experimental science of the physical. It overlooks the specific character of certain analyses of conscious-

---

[o] Cf. in this connection Wundt, *Logic,* II (2nd edn.), 170.

[33] *Einfühlenden:* Husserl has taken over this term but has stripped it of much of its emotional content. It seeks to penetrate to some extent the mystery whereby one subject can somehow enter into the experience of another. It constitutes on Husserl's part a somewhat reluctant concession to the non-rational, but his rationalistic predispositions render his explanations of it hopelessly involved; cf. Fifth Cartesian Meditation; Theodor Lipps, *Aesthetik,* I, 2nd edn. (Leipzig: Voss Verlag, 1914), pp. 96–223; II (1920), pp. 1–32.

ness that must have previously taken place, so that from naïve experiences (whether observational or nonobservational, whether taking place in the framework of actual presence to consciousness or in that of memory or empathy) they can become experiences in a scientific sense.

Let us try to make this clear.

The psychologists think that they owe all their psychological knowledge to experience, thus to those naïve recollections or to empathetic penetration into recollections, which by virtue of the methodical art of the experiment are to become foundations for empirical conclusions. Nevertheless the description of the naïve empirical data, along with the immanent analysis and conceptional grasp that go hand in hand with this description, is affected by virtue of a fund of concepts whose scientific value is decisive for all further methodical steps. These remain—as is evidenced by a bit of reflection—by the very nature of experimental questioning and method, constantly untouched in the further procedure, and they enter into the final result, which means into the empirical judgment, with its claim to be scientific. On the other hand, their scientific value cannot be there from the beginning, nor can it stem from the experiences of the subject or of the psychologist himself, no matter how many of them are heaped up; it can in fact be obtained logically from no empirical determinations whatever.[34] And here is the place for phenomenological analysis of essence, which, however strange and unsympathetic it may sound to the naturalistic psychologist, can in no way be an empirical analysis.

Beginning with Locke and continuing down to our own day there is a confusion between the conviction drawn from the history of the development of empirical consciousness (which

[34] Husserl later added at this point the following comment: "There is wanting a precise distinction between the formation of naturalistically psychological concepts and the formation of immanently psychological concepts that have undergone only exteriorly an apperceptive naturalizing. There is here an important methodical distinction."

therefore already presupposes psychology) that every conceptional representation "stems" from former experiences, and the
entirely different conviction that every concept derives from
experience the justification of its possible use, for example in
descriptive judgments. Now that means here that only in considering what actual perceptions or recollections afford can
legitimizing grounds be found for the concept's validity, its correspondence to an essence (or correspondence to no essence), and
consequently for its valid applicability in the given single case. In
description we employ the words perception, recollection, imaginative representation, enunciation, etc. What a wealth of immanent components does a single such word indicate, components
that we, "grasping" what is described, impose on it without
having found them in it analytically. Is it sufficient to use these
words in the popular sense, in the vague, completely chaotic
sense they have taken on, we know not how, in the "history"
of consciousness? And even if we were to know it, what good is
this history to do us, how is that to change the fact that vague
concepts are simply vague and, by virtue of this character proper
to them, obviously unscientific? So long as we have no better,
we may use them in the confidence that with them enough crude
distinctions for the practical aims of life have been attained. But
does a psychology that leaves the concepts that determine its
objects without scientific fixation, without methodical elaboration,
have a claim to "exactness"? No more, obviously, than would a
physics that would be satisfied with the everyday concepts of
heavy, warm, mass, etc. Modern psychology no longer wants to
be a science of the "soul" but rather of "psychical phenomena."
If that is what it wants, then it must be able to describe and determine these phenomena with conceptual rigor. It must have
acquired the necessary rigorous concepts by methodical work.
Where is this methodical work accomplished in "exact" psychology? We seek for it in vain throughout its vast literature.

The question as to how natural, "confused" experience can
become scientific experience, as to how one can arrive at the

determination of objectively valid empirical judgments, is the cardinal methodological question of every empirical science. It does not have to be put and answered in the abstract, and in any case it does not have to be answered purely philosophically. Historically it finds an answer in practice, in that the genial pioneers of empirical science grasp intuitively[35] and in the concrete the sense of the necessary empirical method and, by pursuing it faithfully in an accessible sphere of experience, realize a fragment of objectively valid empirical determination, thus getting the science started. The motive for their procedure they owe not to any revelation but to penetrating the sense of the experiences themselves, or the sense of the "being" in them. For, although already "given," in "vague" experience it is given only "confusedly." Consequently the question imposes itself: how are things really? How are they to be determined with objective validity? How, that is, by what better "experiences" and how are they to be improved—by what method? With regard to the knowledge of external nature, the decisive step from naïve to scientific experience, from vague everyday concepts to scientific concepts in full clarity, was, as is known, first realized by Galileo.[36] With regard to knowledge of the psychical, the sphere of consciousness, we have, it is true, "experimentally exact" psychology, which considers itself the fully justified "opposite number" of exact natural science—and yet, though it is scarcely aware of it, this science is still from the most important point of view pre-Galilean.

It can well seem strange that it is not aware of this. We do

---

[35] *Intuitiv:* not to be confused with the technical sense of that intuition that comes at the end of a prolonged phenomenological analysis. Still, this natural intuition of the genius has something in common with the laborious intuition of the phenomenologist—it penetrates to the unified "sense" of a multiplicity of experiences.

[36] For a detailed treatment of Galileo's contribution to the transformation of attitude among scientists—and of the "errors" that continue to influence scientists toward a merely "objectivistic" attitude—see *Krisis,* Nos. 8–12, pp. 18–68.

understand that prior to science naïve nature study lacked no natural experience, which is to say, nothing that could not in the ensemble of natural experience itself be expressed in naturally naïve empirical concepts. In its naïveté it was not aware that things have a "nature" which can be determined by means of certain exact concepts in an empirically logical procedure.[37] But psychology, with its institutes and apparatus of precision, with its keenly thought-out methods, justly feels that it is beyond the stage of the naïve empirical study of the soul belonging to former times. In addition, it has not failed to make careful, constantly renewed reflections on method. How could that which is in principle the most essential escape it? How could psychology fail to see that in its purely psychological concepts, with which it now cannot at all dispense, it necessarily gives a content that is not simply taken from what is actually given in experience but is applied to the latter? How fail to see that in so far as it approaches the sense of the psychical, it effects analyses of these conceptual contents and recognizes valid corresponding phenomenological connections, which it applies to experience but which in relation to experience are a priori? How could it miss the fact that the experimental method, to the extent that it will realize really psychological knowledge, cannot justify its own presuppositions, and that its procedure is radically distinct from that of physics precisely in so far as this latter excludes in principle the phenomenal in order to look for the nature that presents itself in the phenomenal, whereas psychology wanted precisely to be a science of phenomena themselves?

The phenomenal had to elude psychology because of its

---

[37] Cf. supra, p. 88, n. 22, on the "logic of experience." Husserl sees in all previous philosophy an effort to reason on the data of experience. His own efforts will be toward finding the "logos" (fundamental rationality; cf. *Form. u. trans. Log.,* p. 16) of experience itself. Experience can be thus rationalized only if it is itself constitutive of its own object—a theme treated at length in *Ideen III* and *Erfahrung und Urteil.* The upshot of all this is a dissatisfaction with the merely formal a priori of Kant and a demand for a material a priori (cf. Third Cartesian Meditation).

naturalistic point of view as well as its zeal to imitate the natural
sciences and to see experimental procedures as the main point.
In its laborious, frequently very keen considerations on the possibilities of psychophysical experiment, in proposing empirical
arrangements of experiments, in constructing the finest apparatus,
in discovering possible sources of error, etc., it has still neglected
to pursue the question more profoundly, i.e., how, by what
method, can those concepts that enter essentially into psychological judgments be brought from the state of confusion to that of
clarity and objective validity. It has neglected to consider to what
extent the psychical, rather than being the presentation of a
nature, has an essence proper to itself to be rigorously and in full
adequation investigated prior to any psychophysics.[38] It has not
considered what lies in the "sense" of psychological experience
and what "demands" being (in the sense of the psychical) of
itself makes on method.

What has constantly confused empirical psychology since its
beginnings in the eighteenth century is thus the deceptive image
of a scientific method modeled on that of the physicochemical
method. There is a sure conviction that the method of all empirical sciences, considered in its universal principles, is one and
the same, thus that it is the same in psychology as in the science
of physical nature. If metaphysics suffered so long a time from a
false imitation—whether of the geometrical or of the physical
method—the same procedure is now being repeated in psychology. It is not without significance that the fathers of experimentally exact psychology were physiologists and physicists. The
true method follows the nature of the things to be investigated
and not our prejudices and preconceptions.[39] From the vague

[38] Here Husserl later added the comment, "Not entirely correct." In the
second essay of this volume we shall find that he recognizes the impossibility
of adequately investigating the psychic without looking into the psychophysical. Cf. pp. 182–83, infra.

[39] Husserl's constant phenomenological battle-cry was "to things themselves!" Herein is expressed the conviction that things have an essence of
their own that is to guide the phenomenological investigation. It must be

subjectivity of things in their naïvely sensible appearance natural science laboriously brings out objective things with exact objective characteristics. Thus, they tell themselves, psychology must bring that which is psychologically vague in naïve interpretation to objectively valid determination. The objective method accomplishes this, and it is evident that this is the same as the experimental method brilliantly guaranteed in natural science by countless successes.

Nevertheless, questions such as how the data of experience came to be objectively determined and what sense "objectivity" and "determination of objectivity" have in each case, what function experimental method can in each case take over—these all depend on the proper sense of the data, i.e., on the sense given to them according to its essence by the empirical consciousness in question (as an intention of precisely this and no other being). To follow the model of the natural sciences almost inevitably means to reify consciousness—something that from the very beginning leads us into absurdity, whence stems the constantly renewed tendency toward the absurd problematizing and the false orientations of the investigation. Let us examine that more closely.

Only the spatiotemporal world of bodies is nature in the significant sense of that word.[40] All other individual being, i.e., the psychical, is nature in a secondary sense, a fact that determines basically essential differences between the methods of natural science and psychology. In principle, only corporeal being can be experienced in a number of direct experiences, i.e., perceptions,

---

remembered, however, that this essence is "constituted" in the experiencing of "things." But to say that it is constituted is not to deny that it is "discovered."

[40] It must be remembered that for Husserl, "nature" is itself a concept that must be phenomenologically constituted. Thus he does not say there is a spatiotemporal world but rather that when nature is present to consciousness, it is present as spatiotemporal. Nature is the intentional correlate of empirical experience (cf. *Ideen II*, No. 2), and the characteristics of nature (causality, identical repetition, etc.) are characteristics inseparable from the intention "nature." Husserl is not as far removed from Kant as he thinks!

as individually identical. Hence, only this being can, if the perceptions are thought of as distributed among various "subjects," be experienced by many subjects as individually identical and be described as intersubjectively the same.[41] The same realities (things, procedures, etc.) are present to the eyes of all and can be determined by all of us according to their "nature." Their "nature," however, denotes: presenting themselves in experience according to diversely varying "subjective appearances."

Nevertheless, they stand there as temporal unities of enduring or changing properties, and they stand there as incorporated in the totality of one corporeal world that binds them all together, with its one space and its one time. They are what they are only in this unity; only in the causal relation to or connection with each other do they retain their individual identity (substance), and this they retain as that which carries "real properties." All physically real properties are causal.[42] Every corporeal being is subject to laws of possible changes, and these laws concern the identical, the thing, not by itself but in the unified, actual, and possible totality of the one nature. Each physical thing has its nature (as the totality of what it, the identical, is) by virtue of being the union point of causalities within the one all-nature. Real properties (real after the manner of things, corporeal) are a title for the possibilities of transformation of something identical, possibilities preindicated according to the laws of causality. And thus this identical, with regard to what it is, is determinable only by recourse to these laws. Realities, however, are given as unities of immediate experience, as unities of diverse sensible ap-

---

[41] It is essential to nature that it remain identical, no matter how many times it is observed, either by the same subject or by many. The psychic, on the other hand, is unique; it never repeats iteslf identically. Cf. the second essay on the distinction between nature and spirit, pp. 183–84, infra.

[42] If causality belongs only to nature, then the causal and the material are inseparable. This seems to be a prejudice which Husserl inherited from Hume via Kant. Still, in *Ideen II* (pp. 161, 216, 226–27, 229, 259–60, 375) Husserl does speak of a "spiritual causality" that he calls "motivation." He will not, after all, accept Hume's mechanical "association of ideas."

pearances. Stabilities, changes, and relationships of change (all of which can be grasped sensibly) direct cognition everywhere, and function for it like a "vague" medium in which the true, objective, physically exact nature presents itself, a medium through which thought (as empirically scientific thought) determines and constructs what is true.[d]

All that is not something one attributes to the things of experience and to the experience of things. Rather it is something belonging inseparably to the essences of things in such a way that every intuitive and consistent investigation of what a thing in truth is (a thing which as experienced always appears as something, a being, determined and at the same time determinable, and which nevertheless, as appearances and their circumstances vary, is constantly appearing as a different being) necessarily leads to causal connections and terminates in the determination of corresponding objective properties subject to law. Natural science, then, simply follows consistently the sense of what the thing so to speak pretends to be as experienced, and calls this—vaguely enough— "elimination of secondary qualities," "elimination of the merely subjective in the appearance," while "retaining what is left, the primary qualities." And that is more than an obscure expression; it is a bad theory regarding a good procedure.

Let us now turn to the "world" of the "psychical," and let us confine ourselves to "psychical phenomena," which the new psychology looks upon as its field of objects—i.e., in beginning we leave out of consideration problems relative to the soul and to the ego. We ask, then, whether in every perception of the psychical, just as in the sense of every physical experience and of every perception of the real, there is included "nature"-objectivity? We soon see that the relationships in the sphere of the

[d] It should be noted that this medium of phenomenality, wherein the observation and thought of natural science constantly moves, is not treated as a scientific theme by the latter. It is the new sciences, psychology (to which belongs a good portion of physiology) and phenomenology, that are concerned with this theme.

psychical are totally different from those in the physical sphere. The psychical is divided (to speak metaphorically and not metaphysically) into monads that have no windows and are in communication only through empathy.[43] Psychical being, being as "phenomenon," is in principle not a unity that could be experienced in several separate perceptions as individually identical, not even in perceptions of the same subject. In the psychical sphere there is, in other words, no distinction between appearance and being, and if nature is a being that appears in appearances, still appearances themselves (which the psychologist certainly looks upon as psychical) do not constitute a being which itself appears by means of appearances lying behind it[44]— as every reflection on the perception of any appearance whatever makes evident. It is then clear: there is, properly speaking, only one nature, the one that appears in the appearances of things. Everything that in the broadest sense of psychology we call a psychical phenomenon, when looked at in and for itself, is precisely phenomenon and not nature.

A phenomenon, then, is no "substantial" unity; it has no "real properties," it knows no real parts, no real changes, and no causality; all these words are here understood in the sense proper to natural science. To attribute a nature to phenomena, to investigate their real component parts, their causal connections— that is pure absurdity, no better than if one wanted to ask about

---

[43] Husserl has no interest in the Leibnizian "monad" as an explanation of reality—no more than in any other "metaphysical" explanation. He simply borrows the image to emphasize the denial of any external causality in the realm of the psychic. Nothing was more distasteful to him than the mechanistic psychology of Locke.

[44] *So sind die Erscheinungen selbst . . . nicht selbst wieder ein Sein, das durch dahinterliegende Erscheinungen erscheint:* Husserl is violently opposed to the sort of naturalistic psychology that would simply make the spiritual epiphenomenal and only the material real. It is for this reason, perhaps, that he prefers "phenomenon" to "appearance"; it is difficult to separate the latter from a causal connection with that which appears, with the result that what appears becomes an unknown "thing-in-itself."

the causal properties, connections, etc. of numbers. It is the absurdity of naturalizing something whose essence excludes the kind of being that nature has. A thing is what it is, and it remains in its identity forever: nature is eternal. Whatever in the way of real properties or modifications of properties belongs in truth to a thing (to the thing of nature, not to the sensible thing of practical life, the thing "as it appears sensibly") can be determined with objective validity and confirmed or corrected in constantly new experiences. On the other hand, something psychical, a "phenomenon," comes and goes; it retains no enduring, identical being that would be objectively determinable as such in the sense of natural science, e.g., as objectively divisible into components, "analysable" in the proper sense.

What psychical being "is," experience cannot say in the same sense that it can with regard to the physical. The psychical is simply not experienced as something that appears; it is "vital experience" and vital experience seen in reflection; it appears as itself through itself, in an absolute flow,[45] as now and already "fading away," clearly recognizable as constantly sinking back into a "having been." The psychical can also be a "recalled," and thus in a certain modified way an "experienced"; and in the "recalled" lies a "having been perceived." It can also be a "repeatedly recalled," in recollections that are united in an act of consciousness which in turn is conscious of the recollections themselves as recalled or as still retained. In this connection, and in this alone, can the a priori psychical, in so far as it is the identical of such "repetitions," be "experienced" and identified as being. Everything psychical which is thus an "experienced" is, then, as we can say with equal evidence, ordered in an overall

---

[45] As time went on, the notion of "flow" assumed more and more importance in the thought of Husserl. Though the concept as Husserl employs it scarcely takes adequate account of process, it does describe what he considers to be an essential characteristic of the psychic (spiritual) in opposition to the natural. There is a unity and constancy to the phenomenal, but it is the unity and constancy of the "flow," not of identical repetition.

connection, in a "monadic" unity of consciousness, a unity that in itself has nothing at all to do with nature, with space and time or substantiality and causality, but has its thoroughly peculiar "forms." It is a flow of phenomena, unlimited at both ends, traversed by an intentional line that is, as it were, the index of the all-pervading unity. It is the line of an immanent "time" without beginning or end, a time that no chronometers measure.

Looking back over the flow of phenomena in an immanent view, we go from phenomenon to phenomenon (each a unity grasped in the flow and even in the flowing) and never to anything but phenomena. Only when immanent seeing and the experience of things come to synthesis, do viewed phenomenon and experienced thing enter into relation to each other. Through the medium of thing-experience empathy appears at the same time as a sort of mediate seeing of the psychical, characterized in itself as a reception into a second monadic connection.

Now, to what extent is something like rational investigation and valid statement possible in this sphere? To what extent, too, are only such statements possible which we have just now given as most crude descriptions (passing over in silence entire dimensions)? It goes without saying that research will be meaningful here precisely when it directs itself purely to the sense of the experiences, which are given as experiences of the "psychical," and when thereby it accepts and tries to determine the "psychical" exactly as it demands, as it were, to be accepted and determined, when it is seen[46]—above all where one admits no absurd naturalizings. One must, it was said, take phenomena as they give themselves, i.e., as this flowing "having consciousness," intending, appearing, as this foreground and background "having consciousness," a "having consciousness" as present or pre-present, as imagined or symbolic or copied, as intuitive or repre-

[46] "To things themselves!" Not, however, to things as they are "in themselves" (an sich), where their being is relative, but in the psychic flow, where their being is absolute, an essential being with the absoluteness of subjectivity; cf. Ideen I, p. 35.

sented emptily,[47] etc. Thus, too, we must take phenomena as they turn this way or that, transforming themselves, according as the point of view or mode of attention changes in one way or another. All that bears the title "consciousness-of" and that "has" a "meaning," "intends" something "objective," which latter—whether from one standpoint or other it is to be called "fiction" or "reality"—permits being described[48] as something "immanently objective," "intended as such," and intended in one or another mode of intending.

That one can here investigate and make statements, and do so on the basis of evidence, adapting oneself to the sense of this sphere of "experience," is absolutely evident. Admittedly, it is fidelity to the demands indicated above that constitutes the difficulty. On the single-mindedness and purity of the "phenomenological" attitude depends entirely the consistency or absurdity of the investigations that are here to be carried out. We do not easily overcome the inborn habit of living and thinking according to the naturalistic attitude, and thus of naturalistically adulterating the psychical. Furthermore, overcoming this habit depends to a great extent on the insight that in fact a "purely immanent" investigation of the psychical (using the term in its widest sense, which means the phenomenal as such) is possible, the kind of research that has just been generally characterized and that stands in contrast to any psychophysical investigation of the same, the latter being a kind of investigation we have not yet taken into consideration and which, of course, has its justification.

[47] An "intention" is intuitive when in the act of consciousness itself the object of the act is known to be validly posited. An intention is "empty" when its objective validity has not been determined.

[48] It is characteristic of any phenomenology that it "describe" rather than "explain." It is characteristic of Husserl's phenomenology that this description be aimed at an intuitive grasp of the "essences" contained in experience. "Descriptive concepts" are "concepts immediately expressing essences found in simple intuition" (*Ideen I*, p. 138). In the present context, of course, the implications of this "descriptive science" are barely sketched. The detailed explication was Husserl's life's work.

If the immanently psychical is not nature in itself but the respondent of nature, what are we seeking for in it as its "being"? If it is not determinable in "objective" identity as the substantial unity of real properties that must be grasped over and over again and be determined and confirmed in accordance with science and experience, if it is not to be withdrawn from the eternal flux, if it is incapable of becoming the object of an intersubjective evaluation—then what is there in it that we can seize upon, determine, and fix as an objective unity? This, however, is understood as meaning that we remain in the pure phenomenological sphere and leave out of account relationships to nature and to the body experienced as a thing. The answer, then, is that if phenomena have no nature, they still have an essence, which can be grasped and adequately determined in an immediate seeing. All the statements that describe the phenomena in direct concepts do so, to the degree that they are valid, by means of concepts of essence, that is, by conceptual significations of words that must permit of being redeemed in an essential intuition.

It is necessary to be accurate in our understanding of this ultimate foundation of all psychological method. The spell of the naturalistic point of view, to which all of us at the outset are subject and which makes us incapable of prescinding from nature and hence, too, of making the psychical an object of intuitive investigation from the pure rather than from the psychophysical point of view, has here blocked the road to a great science unparalleled in its fecundity, a science which is on the one hand the fundamental condition for a completely scientific psychology and on the other the field for the genuine critique of reason. The spell of inborn naturalism also consists in the fact that it makes it so difficult for all of us to see "essences," or "ideas"—or rather, since in fact we do, so to speak, constantly see them, for us to let them have the peculiar value which is theirs instead of absurdly naturalizing them. Intuiting essences conceals no more difficulties or "mystical" secrets than does perception. When we bring "color" to full intuitive clarity, to givenness for ourselves, then the datum is an "essence"; and when we likewise in pure intuition—looking, say, at one perception after another—bring to givenness for ourselves what "perception" is, perception in itself (this identical character of any number of flowing singular perceptions), then we have intuitively grasped the essence of perception. As far as intuition—i.e., having an intuitive consciousness—extends, so far extends the possibility of a corresponding "ideation" (as I called it in *Logische Untersuchungen*),[49] or of "seeing essence." To the extent that the intuition is a pure one that involves no transient connotations, to the same extent is the intuited essence an adequately intuited one, an absolutely given one. Thus the field dominated by pure intuition includes the entire sphere that the psychologist reserves to himself as the sphere of "psychical phenomena," provided that he takes them merely by themselves, in pure immanence. That the "essences" grasped in essential intuition permit, at least to a very great extent, of being fixed in definitive concepts and thereby afford possibilities of definitive and in their own way absolutely valid objective statements, is evident to anyone free of prejudice. The ultimate differences of color, its finest nuances, may defy fixation, but "color" as distinguished from "sound" provides a sure difference, than which there is in the world no surer.[50] And such absolutely distinguishable—better, fixable—essences are not only those whose very "content" is of the senses, appearances ("apparitions," phantoms, and the like), but also the essences of whatever is psychical in the pregnant sense, of all ego "acts" or ego states, which correspond to well-known headings such as perception, imagination, recollection, judgment, emotion, will—with all their countless particular forms. Herein remain excluded the ultimate "nuances,"

[49] *Log. Unt.,* Investigation 6, Nos. 40–62.

[50] The task is that of distinguishing essentially one immanent datum from another, not one "thing" from another. The objective distinction is contained in the subjective acts—with their objective correlates—properly grasped and described (cf. p. 114, n. 55, infra).

which belong to the indeterminable element of the "flow," although at the same time the describable typology of the flowing has its "ideas" which, when intuitively grasped and fixed, render possible absolute knowledge. Every psychological heading such as perception or will designates a most extensive area of "consciousness analyses," i.e., of investigations into essences. There is question here of a field that in extent can be compared only with natural science—however extraordinary this may sound.

Now, it is of decisive significance to know that essential intuition is in no way "experience" in the sense of perception, recollection, and equivalent acts;[51] further, that it is in no way an empirical generalization whose sense it is to posit existentially at the same time the individual being of empirical details. Intuition grasps essence as essential being, and in no way posits being-there. In accord with this, knowledge of essence is by no means matter-of-fact knowledge, including not the slightest shade of affirmation regarding an individual (e.g., natural) being-there. The foundation, or better, the point of departure for an essential intuition (e.g., of the essence of perception, recollection, judgment, etc.) can be a perception of a perception, of a recollection, of a judgment, etc., but it can also be a mere—but mere—imagination, so long as it is clear, even though obviously as such not an experience, that is, grasps no being-there. The grasp of essence is thereby in no way touched; as "grasp of essence" it is intuitive, and that is precisely an intuition of a different kind from experience. Obviously essences can also be vaguely represented, let us say represented in symbol and falsely posited; then they are merely conjectural essences, involving contradiction, as is shown by the transition to an intuition of their inconsistency. It is possible, however, that their vague position will be shown to be valid

[51] Not until *Erfahrung und Urteil* and *Cartesian Meditations* does Husserl identify "intuition" and "experience." This does not mean that only (sensual) experience is intuitive, à la Kant, but rather that experience in the fullest sense is an "essential intuition." Intuition is not narrowed; experience is broadened.

by a return to the intuition of the essence in its givenness.[52]

Every judgment which achieves in definitive, adequately constructed concepts an adequate experience of what is contained in essences, experiencing how essences of a certain genus or particularity are connected with others—how, for example, "intuition" and "empty intention," "imagination" and "perception," "concept" and "intuition" unite with each other; how they are on the basis of such and such essential components necessarily "unifiable," corresponding to each other (let us say) as "intention" and "fulfillment," or on the contrary cannot be united, founding as they do a "consciousness of deception," etc.—every judgment of this kind is an absolute, generally valid cognition, and as such it is a kind of essential judgment that it would be absurd to want to justify, confirm, or refute by experience. It fixes a "relation of idea," an a priori in the authentic sense that Hume, it is true, had before his eyes but which necessarily escaped him because of his positivistic confusion of essence and "idea"— as the opposite of "impression." Still, even his scepticism did not dare to be consistent here and to destroy itself on such a knowledge—to the extent that it sees it. Had his sensualism not blinded him to the whole sphere of intentionality, of "consciousness-of," had he grasped it in an investigation of essence, he would not have become the great sceptic, but instead the founder of a truly "positive" theory of reason.[53] All the problems that move him so passionately in the *Treatise* and drive him from confusion to confusion, problems that because of his attitude he can in no wise formulate suitably and purely—all these problems belong entirely

[52] This return to intuition is necessary because only in intuition is there "evidence," and the whole of transcendental phenomenology is, after all, the search for evidence.

[53] The thought here is not easy to follow. It would seem to mean that if Hume had followed out consistently the principles that led him to scepticism, they would have led him further, and he would have discovered transcendental consciousnes and therein a knowledge that would have made scepticism impossible.

to the area dominated by phenomenology.[54] Without exception they are to be solved by pursuing the essential connections of the forms of consciousness as well as of the intentionalities correlatively and essentially belonging to them, solved in a generally intuitive understanding that leaves no meaningful question open. Thus are solved the vast problems of the identity of the object in face of the various impressions or perceptions there are of it. As a matter of fact, how various perceptions or appearances come to the point of "bringing to appearance" one and the same object so that it can be "the same" for them and for the consciousness of unity or identity that unifies their variety, is a question that can be put clearly and answered only by phenomenological essential investigation (which, of course, our manner of formulating the problem has already preindicated). The desire to answer this question empirically on the basis of natural science means that the question has been misunderstood, has been misinterpreted in such a way as to make it an absurd question. That a perception, like any experience whatever, is precisely perception of this object oriented, colored, formed in precisely these ways is a matter of the perception's essence,[55] whatever the situation may be with regard to the "existence" of the object. Again, that this per-

[54] Here Husserl added the marginal comment: "Thus, too. the problem of genesis." Not every cognition is possible to every mind. There must be a growth, a "genesis" of cognition. By the same token, there is a growth of the transcendental ego, the ultimate a priori source of all cognition. In both senses genesis indicates a progressive complication in the process of intentional constitution (cf. Fourth Cartesian Meditation).

[55] Marginal note: "Relation to the determinate object is for the act a matter of its essence." The essence of the act has not been truly grasped until its determinate object relation has been grasped. At this point Husserl had not developed the noesis–noema structure of consciousness that becomes so important with *Ideen I*. The "act" of thinking is not merely the activity of thinking; the objective content, the noema, belongs to the very essence of the act. Thus, to know the thought is to know what is thought about, and only in the thought is the essence of the object discoverable. There is a sense in which the object "transcends" the act, but not as being "outside" of it.

ception is inserted in a continuity of perception, but not in an arbitrary one, in one wherein constantly "the same object presents itself in a constantly different orientation, etc.," that, too, is purely a matter of its essence. In short, here lie the great fields of "consciousness analysis," fields which, up to the present, are in the literature uncultivated, wherein the title consciousness (just as above the title psychical), whether it fits expressly or not, would have to be stretched so wide that it would have to designate everything immanent, and thus everything intended in consciousness, as so intended, and that in every sense. When freed from the false naturalism that absurdly misconstrues them, the problems of origin, for centuries so much discussed, are phenomenological problems. In like manner, the problems regarding the origin of "space representation," regarding representations of time, thing, number, "representations" of cause and effect, etc., are phenomenological problems. Only when these pure problems, meaningfully determined, are formulated and solved do the empirical problems regarding the occurrence of such representations as events of human consciousness acquire a sense that can be scientifically grasped and comprehended with a view to their solution.

The whole thing, however, depends on one's seeing and making entirely one's own the truth that just as immediately as one can hear a sound, so one can intuit an "essence"—the essence "sound," the essence "appearance of thing," the essence "apparition," the essence "pictorial representation," the essence "judgment" or "will," etc.—and in the intuition one can make an essential judgment. On the other hand, however, it depends on one's protecting himself from the Humean confusion and accordingly not confounding phenomenological intuition with "introspection,"[56] with interior experience—in short, with acts that posit not essences but individual details corresponding to them.[e]

[e] The *Logische Untersuchungen*, which in their fragments of a systematic
[56] "Introspection" looks only at the conscious activity, not at its objective correlate (*noema*). Only "reflection" does the latter.

Pure phenomenology as science, so long as it is pure and makes no use of the existential positing of nature, can only be essence investigation, and not at all an investigation of being-there; all "introspection" and every judgment based on such "experience" falls outside its framework. The particular can in its immanence be posited only as this—this disappearing perception, recollection, etc.—and if need be, can be brought under the strict essential concepts resulting from essential analysis. For the individual is not essence, it is true, but it "has" an essence, which can be said of it with evident validity. To fix this essence as an individual, however, to give it a position in a "world" of individual being-there, is something that such a mere subsumption under essential concepts cannot accomplish. For phenomenology, the singular is eternally the *apeiron*. Phenomenology can recognize with objective validity only essences and essential relations, and thereby it can accomplish and decisively accomplish whatever is necessary for a correct understanding of all empirical cognition and of all cognition whatsoever: the clarification of the "origin" of all formal-logical and natural-logical principles (and whatever other guiding "principles" there may be) and of all the problems involved in correlating "being" (being of nature, being of value, etc.) and consciousness, problems intimately connected with the aforementioned principles.ᶠ ⁵⁷

---

phenomenology for the first time employ essence analysis in the sense here characterized, have again and again been misunderstood as attempts to rehabilitate the method of introspection. Admittedly, part of the blame for this lies in the defective characterization of the method in the Introduction to the first investigation of the second volume, the designation of phenomenology as descriptive psychology. The necessary clarifications have already been brought out in my third "Bericht über deutsche Schriften zur Logik in den Jahren 1895–99," *Archiv für systematische Philosophie,* IX (1903), 397–400. [In *Ideen II,* pp. 313–14, Husserl explained in detail why phenomenology cannot be a "descriptive psychology." Even a "pure" psychology is only a preliminary step toward a transcendental phenomenology.—Tr.]

ᶠ The definiteness with which I express myself in an epoch when phenomenology is at best a title for specializations, for quite useful detail work in the sphere of introspection, rather than the systematic fundamental sci-

Let us now turn to the psychophysical attitude. Therein the "psychical," with the entire essence proper to it, receives an orientation to a body and to the unity of physical nature. What is grasped in immanent perception and interpreted as essentially so qualified, enters into relation to the sensibly perceived and consequently to nature. Only through this orientation does it gain an indirect natural objectivity, mediately a position in space and in nature's time (the kind we measure by clocks). To a certain but not more precisely determined extent, the experiential "dependence" on the physical provides a means of determining intersubjectively the psychical as individual being and at the same time of investigating psychophysical relationships to a progressively more thorough extent. That is the domain of "psychology as natural science," which according to the literal sense is psychophysical psychology, which is hence, obviously in contrast to phenomenology, an empirical science.

Not without misgivings, it is true, does one consider psychology, the science of the "psychical," merely as a science of "psychical phenomena" and of their connections with the body. But in fact psychology is everywhere accompanied by those inborn and inevitable objectivations whose correlates are the

ence of philosophy, the port of entry to a genuine metaphysics of nature, of spirit, of ideas, has its background throughout in the unceasing investigations of many years. upon whose progressive results my philosophical lectures in Göttingen since 1901 have been built. In view of the intimate functional connection of all phenomenological levels and consequently of the investigations related to them, and in view of the extraordinary difficulty the development of the pure methodology itself brings with it, I did not consider it advantageous to publish isolated results that are still problematical. In the not too distant future I hope to be able to present the wider public with researches in phenomenology and in phenomenological critique of reason that have in the meantime been confirmed on all sides and have turned into comprehensive systematic unities.

[57] Though "existentialism" may have been influenced by Husserl's phenomenology (as is frequently uncritically asserted), the latter remains a radical "essentialism." It has no concern for the individual, the unique, precisely because it could not do so and still be "scientific." There is, it is true, a concern on the intersubjective level with the individual subject, but for Husserl this concern is scarcely "existential."

empirical unities man and beast, and, on the other hand, soul, personality, or character, i.e., disposition of personality. Still, for our purposes it is not necessary to pursue the essential analysis of these unity constructions nor the problem of how they by themselves determine the task of psychology. After all, it immediately becomes sufficiently clear that these unities are of a kind that is in principle different from the realities of nature, realities that according to their essence are such as to be given through adumbrating[58] appearances, whereas this in no way applies to the unities in question. Only the basic substrate "human body," and not man himself, is a unity of real appearance; and above all, personality, character, etc. are not such unities. With all such unities we are evidently referred back to the immanent vital unity of the respective "consciousness flow" and to morphological peculiarities that distinguish the various immanent unities of this sort. Consequently, all psychological knowledge, too, even where it is related primarily to human individualities, characters, and dispositions, finds itself referred back to those unities of consciousness, and thereby to the study of the phenomena themselves and of their implications.

There is no need now, especially after all the explanations already given, of further refinements to enable us to see most clearly and for the most profound reasons what has already been presented above: that all psychological knowledge in the ordinary sense presupposes essential knowledge of the psychical, and that the hope of investigating the essence of recollection, judgment, will, etc. by means of casual inner perceptions or experiences, in order thereby to acquire the strict concepts that alone can give scientific value to the designation of the psychical in psychophysical statements and to these statements themselves—that such a hope would be the height of absurdity.

[58] *Abschattende:* The word has been variously translated. It points to the fact that things appear in multiple and varied ways, no appearance revealing the thing in its entirety. The succession of appearances, however, constitutes a unified "flow." Psychic unities, on the other hand, reveal themselves as they are, not in a succession of "adumbrating appearances."

It is the fundamental error of modern psychology, preventing it from being psychology in the true, fully scientific sense, that it has not recognized and developed this phenomenological method. Because of historical prejudices it allowed itself to be held back from using the predispositions to such a method that are contained in every clarifying analysis of concepts. Linked to this is the fact that the majority of psychologists have not understood the already present beginnings of phenomenology, that often, in fact, they have even considered essential investigation carried out from a purely intuitive standpoint to be metaphysical abstraction of the scholastic variety. What has been grasped from an intuitive point of view, however, can be understood and verified only from an intuitive point of view.

After the foregoing explanations it is clear, and it will, as I have good reason to hope, soon be more generally recognized, that a really adequate empirical science of the psychical in its relations to nature can be realized only when psychology is constructed on the base of a systematic phenomenology. It will be, when the essential forms of consciousness and of its immanent correlates, investigated and fixed in systematic connection on a basis of pure intuition, provide the norms for determining the scientific sense and content proper to the concepts of any phenomena whatever, and hence proper to the concepts whereby the empirical psychologist expresses the psychical itself in his psychophysical judgments. Only a really radical and systematic phenomenology, not carried on incidentally and in isolated reflections but in exclusive dedication to the extremely complex and confused problems of consciousness, and carried on with a completely free spirit blinded by no naturalistic prejudices, can give us an understanding of the "psychical"—in the sphere of social as well as of individual consciousness.[59] Only then will the gigan-

[59] It might be well here to paraphrase the argumentation. Psychology concerns itself with the psychophysical factors in consciousness. In studying the physical elements of this compound, psychology is justified in acting as a science of nature. Since, too, there is a connection between the psychic

tic experimental work of our times, the plenitude of empirical facts and in some cases very interesting laws that have been gathered, bear their rightful fruit as the result of a critical evaluation and psychological interpretation. Then, too, will we again be able to admit—what we can in no way admit with regard to present-day psychology—that psychology stands in close, even the closest, relation to philosophy. Then, too, the paradox of antipsychologism, according to which a theory of knowledge is not a psychological theory, will cease to scandalize, in so far as every real theory of knowledge must necessarily be based on phenomenology, which thus constitutes the common foundation for every philosophy and psychology. Finally, there will no longer be the possibility of that kind of specious philosophical literature that flowers so luxuriantly today and, with its claim to the most serious scientific character, offers us its theories of knowledge, logical theories, ethics, philosophies of nature, pedagogical theories, all based on a "foundation" of natural science and, above all, of "experimental psychology."[9] In fact, faced with this literature, one can only be amazed at the decline of the sense for the extremely profound problems and difficulties to which the greatest spirits of humanity have devoted their lives. Unfortunately one must also be amazed at the decline of the sense for genuine thoroughness, which thoroughness still demands from us

---

and physical elements, psychology should to this extent concern itself with the psychic also. Still, it will be able to do justice to this latter element only if it is supported by norms, that can be discovered only in an intuitive analysis that is strictly phenomenological. Hence, psychology is incomplete simply as psychology, without phenomenology.

[9] Not the least considerable reason for the progress of this sort of literature is the fact that the opinion according to which psychology—and obviously "exact" psychology—is the foundation of scientific philosophy has become a firm axiom at least among the groups of natural scientists in the philosophical faculties. These groups, succumbing to the pressure of the natural scientists, are very zealous in their efforts to give one chair of philosophy after another to scholars who in their own fields are perhaps outstanding but who have no more inner sympathy for philosophy than, let us say, chemists or physicists.

so much respect within experimental psychology itself—despite
the basic defects that (according to our interpretation) cling to it.
I am thoroughly convinced that the historical judgment of this
literature will one day be much more severe than that of the
much-decried popular philosophy of the eighteenth century.[*]

We now leave the controversial area of psychological naturalism. We may perhaps say that psychologism, which had been
progressing since the time of Locke, was only a muddy form in
which the only legitimate philosophical tendency had to work
through to a phenomenological foundation of philosophy. In
addition, in so far as phenomenological investigation is essence
investigation and is thus a priori in the authentic sense, it takes
into full account all the justified motives of apriorism. In any
case, it is hoped that our criticism will have made it clear that to
recognize naturalism as a fundamentally erroneous philosophy
still does not mean giving up the idea of a rigorously scientific

[*] By chance, as I write this article, there has come into my hands the excellent study by Dr. M. Geiger (Munich), "On the Essence and Meaning of
Empathy," *Bericht über den IV. Kongress für experimentelle Psychologie in
Innsbruck* (Leipzig, 1911). In a very instructive manner the author strives
to distinguish the genuine psychological problems that in previous efforts at
a description and theory of empathy have partly come clearly to light and
have partly been obscurely confused with each other, and he discusses what
has been attempted and accomplished with a view to their solution. As can
be seen in the account of the discussion (p. 66), his efforts were not well
received by the gathering. Amid loud applause Miss Martin says: "When I
came here, I expected to hear something about experiments in the field of
empathy. But what have I actually heard? Nothing but old—very old—
theories. Not a word about experiments in this field. *This is no philosophical
society.* It seemed to me that it is high time for anyone who wants to introduce such theories here to show whether they have been confirmed by
experiments. In the field of aesthetics such experiments have been made, e.g.,
Stratton's experiments on the aesthetic significance of ocular movements.
There are also my own investigations on this theory of inner perception."
Further, Marbe "sees the significance of the theory regarding empathy in the
impulse it gives to experimental investigations, such as have, in fact, already been conducted in this field. The method employed by the proponents
of the empathy theory is in many ways related to the experimentally psychological method in the way the method of the pre-Socratics is related to that
of modern natural science." To these facts I have nothing to add.

philosophy, a "philosophy from the ground up."[60] The critical separation of the psychological and phenomenological methods shows that the latter is the true way to a scientific theory of reason and, by the same token, to an adequate psychology.

In accord with our plan, we now turn to a critique of historicism and to a discussion of *Weltanschauung* philosophy.

HISTORICISM AND *WELTANSCHAUUNG* PHILOSOPHY

Historicism takes its position in the factual sphere of the empirical life of the spirit. To the extent that it posits this latter absolutely, without exactly naturalizing it (the specific sense of nature in particular lies far from historical thinking and in any event does not influence it by determining it in general), there arises a relativism that has a close affinity to naturalistic psychologism and runs into similar sceptical difficulties. Here we are interested only in what is characteristic of historical scepticism, and we want to familiarize ourselves more thoroughly with it.

Every spiritual formation—taking the term in its widest possible sense, which can include every kind of social unity, ultimately the unity of the individual itself and also every kind of cultural formation—has its intimate structure, its typology, its marvelous wealth of external and internal forms which in the stream of spirit-life itself grow and transform themselves, and in the very manner of the transformation again cause to come forward differences in structure and type. In the visible outer world the structure and typology of organic development afford us exact analogies. Therein there are no enduring species and no construc-

---

[60] *Philosophie von unten:* In opposition to a "system," which to Husserl means an imposition of principles from above. The notion is new enough: there is a tendency to look upon an a priori science as primarily deductive. There is reason, it would seem, to liken phenomenology's essential analysis to a process of induction—based, of course, on the conviction that there are ideal unities called "essences." The analysis, however, has none of the empirical character ordinarily associated with induction.

tion of the same out of enduring organic elements. Whatever seems to be enduring is but a stream of development. If by interior intuition we enter vitally into the unity of spirit-life, we can get a feeling for the motivations at play therein and consequently "understand" the essence and development of the spiritual structure in question, in its dependence on a spiritually motivated unity and development.[61] In this manner everything historical becomes for us "understandable," "explicable," in the "being" peculiar to it, which is precisely "spiritual being," a unity of interiorly self-questioning moments of a sense and at the same time a unity of intelligible structuration and development according to inner motivation. Thus in this manner also art, religion, morals, etc. can be intuitively investigated, and likewise the *Weltanschauung* that stands so close to them and at the same time is expressed in them. It is this *Weltanschauung* that, when it takes on the forms of science and after the manner of science lays claim to objective validity, is customarily called metaphysics, or even philosophy. With a view to such a philosophy there arises the enormous task of thoroughly investigating its morphological structure and typology as well as its developmental connections and of making historically understandable the spiritual motivations that determine its essence, by reliving them from within. That there are significant and in fact wonderful things to be accomplished from this point of view is shown by W. Dilthey's writings, especially the most recently published study on the types of *Weltanschauung.*[4]

Up to this point we have obviously been speaking of historical science, not of historicism. We shall grasp most easily the motives that impel toward the latter if in a few sentences we follow Dilthey's presentation. We read as follows: "Among the reasons

---

[4] Cf. W. Dilthey, et al., *Weltanschauung, Philosophie und Religion in Darstellungen* (Berlin: Reichel and Co., 1911).

[61] As will be seen in the second essay, Husserl had a very limited view of history. Here he gives a phenomenological analysis of the very concept of history as he sees it. It will change little with the years.

that constantly give new nourishment to scepticism, one of the most effective is the anarchy of philosophical systems" (p. 3). "Much deeper, however, than the sceptical conclusions based on the contradictoriness of human opinions go the doubts that have attached themselves to the progressive development of historical consciousness" (p. 4). "The theory of development (as a theory of evolution based on natural science, bound up with a knowledge of cultural structures based on developmental history) is necessarily linked to the knowledge of the relativity proper to the historical life form. In face of the view that embraces the earth and all past events, the absolute validity of any particular form of life-interpretation, of religion, and of philosophy disappears. Thus the formation of a historical consciousness destroys more thoroughly than does surveying the disagreement of systems a belief in the universal validity of any of the philosophies that have undertaken to express in a compelling manner the coherence of the world by an ensemble of concepts" (p. 6).

The factual truth of what is said here is obviously indubitable. The question is, however, whether it can be justified when taken as universal in principle.[62] Of course, *Weltanschauung* and *Weltanschauung* philosophy are cultural formations that come and go in the stream of human development, with the consequences that their spiritual content is definitely motivated in the given historical relationships. But the same is true of the strict sciences. Do they for that reason lack objective validity? A thoroughly extreme historicist will perhaps answer in the affirmative. In doing so he will point to changes in scientific views—how what is today accepted as a proved theory is recognized tomorrow as

[62] It is doubtful whether Dilthey was as "relativist," as Husserl makes him out to be, or that Husserl was as "absolutist," as Dilthey thought. Dilthey's main objection to Husserl was that he was a "Platonist," because he unduly objectified essences. In this connection there is a telling remark by Dilthey on Husserl's attempt to analyze the "flow" of consciousness: "A true Plato, who first of all fixes in concept things that become and flow and then supplements the fixed concept with a concept of flowing" (*Gesammelte Schriften,* V, 2nd edn. [Leipzig: Teubner, 1925], p. cxii).

worthless, how some call certain things laws that others call mere hypotheses and still others vague guesses, etc. Does that mean that in view of this constant change in scientific views we would actually have no right to speak of sciences as objectively valid unities instead of merely as cultural formations? It is easy to see that historicism, if consistently carried through, carries over into extreme sceptical subjectivism. The ideas of truth, theory, and science would then, like all ideas, lose their absolute validity. That an idea has validity would mean that it is a factual construction of spirit which is held as valid and which in its contingent validity determines thought. There would be no unqualified validity, or validity-in-itself, which is what it is even if no one has achieved it and though no historical humanity will ever achieve it.[63] Thus too there would then be no validity to the principle of contradiction nor to any logic, which latter is nevertheless still in full vigor in our time. The result, perhaps, will be that the logical principles of noncontradiction will be transformed into their opposites. And to go even further, all the propositions we have just enunciated and even the possibilities that we have weighed and claimed as constantly valid would in themselves have no validity, etc. It is not necessary to go further here and to repeat discussions already given in another place.[J] We shall certainly have said enough to obtain recognition that no matter what great difficulties the relation between a sort of fluid worth and objective validity, between science as a cultural phenomenon and science as a valid systematic theory, may offer an understanding concerned with clarifying them, the distinction and

[J] In the first volume of my *Logische Untersuchungen*.

[63] A superficial view finds it difficult to reconcile the eternal validity of the ideal with its being constituted in consciousness. The difficulty, however, is not peculiar to Husserl; it haunts every idealism, with the possible exception of Hegel's "absolute idealism." In regard to Hegel, it is interesting to speculate how much more plausible Husserl might have been if he had not rejected out of hand the Hegelian dialectic development. In Hegel's *Phenomenology of Spirit* the identity of thought and being is a "result" in a way it is not in Husserl's phenomenology.

opposition must be recognized. If, however, we have admitted science as a valid idea, what reason would we still have not to consider similar differences between the historically worthwhile and the historically valid as at least an open possibility—whether or not we can understand this idea in the light of a critique of reason? The science of history, or simply empirical humanistic science in general, can of itself decide nothing, either in a positive or in a negative sense, as to whether a distinction is to be made between art as a cultural formation and valid art, between historical and valid law, and finally between historical and valid philosophy. It cannot decide whether or not there exists, to speak Platonically, between one and the other the relation between the idea and the dim form in which it appears.[64] And even if spiritual formations can in truth be considered and judged from the standpoint of such contraries of validity, still the scientific decision regarding validity itself and regarding its ideal normative principles is in no way the affair of empirical science. Certainly the mathematician too will not turn to historical science to be taught about the truth of mathematical theories. It will not occur to him to relate the historical development of mathematical representations with the question of truth. How, then, is it to be the historian's task to decide as to the truth of given philosophical systems and, above all, as to the very possibility of a philosophical science that is valid in itself? And what would he have to add that could make the philosopher uncertain with regard to his idea, i.e., that of a true philosophy? Whoever denies a determined system, and even more, whoever denies the ideal possibility of a philosophical system as such, must advance reasons. Historical facts of development, even the most general facts concerning the manner of development proper to systems as such, may be reasons, good reasons. Still, historical reasons can produce only historical consequences. The desire either to

[64] The distinction between the various forms of cultural manifestation and the essential reality that they manifest is reminiscent of Plato's "Forms" and precisely as an argument against relativism.

prove or to refute ideas on the basis of facts is nonsense—according to the quotation Kant used: *ex pumice aquam*.[k]

Consequently, just as historical science can advance nothing relevant against the possibility of absolute validities in general, so it can advance nothing in particular against the possibility of an absolute (i.e. scientific) metaphysics or any other philosophy. It can as historical science in no way prove even the affirmation that up to the present there has been no scientific philosophy; it can do so only from other sources of knowledge, and they are clearly philosophical sources. For it is clear that philosophical criticism, too, in so far as it is really to lay claim to validity, is philosophy and that its sense implies the ideal possibility of a systematic philosophy as a strict science. The unconditional affirmation that any scientific philosophy is a chimaera, based on the argument that the alleged efforts of millennia make probable the intrinsic impossibility of such a philosophy, is erroneous not merely because to draw a conclusion regarding an unlimited future from a few millennia of higher culture would not be a good induction, but erroneous as an absolute absurdity, like $2 \times 2 = 5$. And this is for the indicated reason: if there is something there whose objective validity philosophical criticism can refute, then there is also an area within which something can be grounded as objectively valid. If problems have demonstrably been posed "awry," then it must be possible to rectify this and pose straight problems. If criticism proves that philosophy in its historical growth has operated with confused concepts, has been guilty of mixed concepts and specious conclusions, then

[k] Dilthey too (op. cit.) rejects historic scepticism. I do not understand, however, how he thinks that from his so instructive analysis of the structure and typology of *Weltanschauungen* he has obtained decisive arguments against scepticism. For as has been explained in the text, a humanistic science that is at the same time empirical can argue neither for nor against anything laying claim to objective validity. The question changes—and that seems to be the inner movement of his thought—when the empirical point of view, directed as it is toward empirical understanding, is replaced by the phenomenological essential point of view.

if one does not wish to fall into nonsense, that very fact makes it undeniable that, ideally speaking, the concepts are capable of being pointed, clarified, distinguished, that in the given area correct conclusions can be drawn. Any correct, profoundly penetrating criticism itself provides means for advancing and ideally points to correct goals, thereby indicating an objectively valid science. To this would obviously be added that the historical untenableness of a spiritual formation as a fact has nothing to do with its untenableness from the standpoint of validity.[65] And this applies both to all that has been discussed so far and to all spheres whatever where validity is claimed.

What may still lead the historicist astray is the circumstance that by entering vitally into a historically reconstructed spiritual formation, into the intention or signification that is dominant in it as well as into the ensembles of motivations that belong to it, we not only can understand its intrinsic sense but also can judge its relative worth. If by a sort of assumption we make use of the premises a past philosopher had at his disposition, then we can eventually recognize and even marvel at the relative "consistency" of his philosophy. From another point of view, we can excuse the inconsistencies along with shifts and transformations of problems that were inevitable at that stage of the problematic and of the analysis of signification. We can esteem as a great accomplishment the successful solution of a scientific

[65] Husserl's attitude toward the history of ideas is peculiar: he may find in it a stimulus to his own thoughts; he may even find truths that he can accept (once they have been phenomenologically justified; cf. p. 147, *infra*); he finds, however, no objective development at all. Even in later years, when he speaks much of the history of ideas (cf. *Krisis* and the second essay in this volume), his point of view is rather negative. There is a teleological development toward a scientific philosophy, a pure phenomenology. In achieving this goal, thought passes through many inferior stages, but the progress is a question of fact, not a development in which each stage has its necessary place in the whole. In the terms of the Fourth Cartesian Meditation, we might say that Husserl recognizes in history a subjective, but no objective, "genesis." Cf. "Die Frage nach dem Ursprung der Geometrie," *Revue internationale de philosophie*, I (1938–39), 220.

problem that would today belong to a class of problems easily mastered by a high-school student. And the same holds true in all fields. In this regard we obviously still maintain that the principles of even such relative evaluations lie in the ideal sphere, which the evaluating historian who will understand more than mere developments can only presuppose and not—as historian—justify. The norm for the mathematical lies in mathematics, for the logical in logic, for the ethical in ethics, etc. He would have to seek reasons and methods of verification in these disciplines if he also wanted to be really scientific in his evaluation. If from this standpoint there are no strictly developed sciences, then he evaluates on his own responsibility—let us say, as an ethical or as a religious man, but in any case not as a scientific historian.

If, then, I look upon historicism as an epistemological mistake that because of its consequences must be just as unceremoniously rejected as was naturalism, I should still like to emphasize expressly that I fully recognize the extraordinary value of history in the broadest sense for the philosopher. For him the discovery of the common spirit is just as significant as the discovery of nature. In fact, a deeper penetration into the general life of the spirit offers the philosopher a more original and hence more fundamental research material than does penetration into nature. For the realm of phenomenology, as a theory of essence, extends immediately from the individual spirit over the whole area of the general spirit; and if Dilthey has established in such an impressive way that psychophysical psychology is not the one that can serve as the "foundation for the humanistic sciences," I would say that it is the phenomenological theory of essence alone that is capable of providing a foundation for a philosophy of the spirit.

We pass now to evaluating the sense and justification of *Weltanschauung* philosophy,[66] in order thereafter to compare it with

[66] To do this is to institute a phenomenological investigation whose function will be to show that the very essence of *Weltanschauung* prohibits it from being a scientific philosophy.

philosophy as a rigorous science. Modern *Weltanschauung* philosophy is, as has already been indicated, a child of historical scepticism. Normally the latter stops short of the positive sciences, to which, with the inconsistency characteristic of every kind of scepticism, it accords real validity. Accordingly, *Weltanschauung* philosophy presupposes all the particular sciences as treasuries of objective truth, and in so far as it has as its goal to satisfy as far as possible our need for thoroughgoing and unifying, all-embracing and all-penetrating knowledge, it looks on all particular sciences as its basis. In view of this, by the way, it calls itself scientific philosophy precisely because it builds on solid sciences. Nevertheless since, properly understood, the scientific character of a discipline contains the scientific character not only of its foundation but also of the aim-providing problems and of its methods, as also a certain logical harmony between the guiding problems on the one hand and, on the other, precisely such foundations and methods, then the designation "scientific philosophy" still says little. And in fact this title is not generally understood as being completely serious. The majority of *Weltanschauung* philosophers feel quite sure that their philosophy with its claim to scientific rigor does not have a very good case, and quite a few of them admit openly and honestly at least the inferior scientific rank of its results. Still, they esteem very highly the worth of this sort of philosophy, which wants precisely to be rather *Weltanschauung* than science of the world, and they esteem it all the more highly the more, precisely under the influence of historicism, they look sceptically at the orientation toward strict philosophical world science. Their motives, that at the same time more exactly determined the sense of *Weltanschauung* philosophy, are approximately the following:

Every great philosophy is not only a historical fact, but in the development of humanity's life of the spirit it has a great, even unique teleological function, that of being the highest elevation of the life experience, education, and wisdom of its time. Let us linger awhile over the clarification of these concepts.

Experience as a personal habitus is the residue of acts belonging to a natural experimental attitude, acts that have occurred during the course of life. This habitus is essentially conditioned by the manner in which the personality, as this particular individuality, lets itself be motivated by acts of its own experience, and not less by the manner in which it lets experiences transmitted by others work on it by agreeing with it or rejecting it. With regard to cognitive acts included under the heading of experience, they can be cognitions of natural existence of every kind, either simple perceptions or other acts of immediately intuitive cognition, or the acts of thought based on these at different levels of logical elaboration and confirmation. But that does not go far enough. We also have experiences of art works and of other beauty values, and no less of ethical values, whether on the basis of our own ethical conduct or of looking into that of others; and likewise of real goods, practical utilities, technical applications. In short, we have not only theoretical but also axiological and practical experiences. Analysis shows that these latter refer back to vital experiences of evaluating and willing as their intuitive foundation. On such experiences too are constructed experiential cognitions of a higher, logical dignity. In accord with this, the man of many-sided experience, or as we also say, the "cultivated man," has not only experience of the world but also religious, aesthetic, ethical, political, practico-technical, and other kinds of experience, or "culture." Nevertheless, we use this admitted cliché "culture," in so far as we have its contrary "unculture," only for the relatively superior forms of the described habitus. With regard to particularly high levels of value, there is the old-fashioned word "wisdom" (wisdom of the world, wisdom of world and life), and most of all, the now-beloved expressions "world view" and "life view," or simply *Weltanschauung*.

We shall have to look upon wisdom, or *Weltanschauung,* in this sense as an essential component of that still more valuable human habitus that comes before us in the idea of perfect virtue and designates habitual ability with regard to all the orientations of human attitudes, whether cognitional, evaluational, or volitional. For evidently hand in hand with this ability goes the well-developed capacity to judge rationally regarding the objectivities proper to these attitudes, regarding the world about us,[67] regarding values, real goods, deeds, etc., or the capacity to justify expressly one's attitudes. That, however, presupposes wisdom and belongs to its higher forms.

Wisdom, or *Weltanschauung,* in this determined sense, which includes a variety of types and grades of value, is—and this needs no further explanation—no mere accomplishment of the isolated personality (this latter would moreover be an abstraction); rather it belongs to the cultural community and to the time, and with regard to its most pronounced forms there is a good sense in which one can speak not only of the culture and *Weltanschauung* of a determined individual but also of that of the time. This is particularly true of the forms we are now to treat.

To grasp in thought the wisdom that in a great philosophical personality is vital, interiorly most rich, but for this personality itself still vague and unconceptualized, is to open out the possibilities of logical elaboration; on higher levels it permits the application of the logical methodology developed in the strict sciences. It is evident that the collective content of these sciences, which in fact confront the individual as valid demands of the collective spirit, belongs on this level to the substructure of a full-valued culture, or *Weltanschauung.* In so far, then, as the vital and hence most persuasive cultural motives of the time are not only conceptually grasped but also logically unfolded and otherwise elaborated in thought, in so far as the results thus obtained are brought, in interplay with additional intuitions and insights,

[67] *Umwelt:* The word does not have the technical sense here that it will have in the second essay, a sense developed in the Fourth Cartesian Meditation: a particular world correlative to a subject (monadic or intersubjective) according to the subject's degree of genetic development.

to scientific unification and consistent completion, there develops an extraordinary extension and elevation of the originally unconceptualized wisdom. There develops a *Weltanschauung* philosophy, which in the great systems gives relatively the most perfect answer to the riddles of life and the world, which is to say, it affords as well as possible a solution and satisfactory explanation to the theoretical, axiological, and practical inconsistencies of life that experience, wisdom, mere world and life view, can only imperfectly overcome.[68] The spirit-life of humanity, with its plenitude of new connections, new spiritual struggles, new experiences, evaluations, and orientations, progresses constantly; with the broadened horizon of life into which all the new spiritual formations enter, culture, wisdom, and *Weltanschauung* change, philosophy changes, mounting to higher and ever higher peaks.

In so far as the value of *Weltanschauung* philosophy (and thereby also the value of striving toward such a philosophy) is primarily conditioned by the value of wisdom and the striving for wisdom, it is hardly necessary to consider in particular the goal it sets itself. If one makes the concept of wisdom as wide as we have made it, then it certainly expresses an essential component in the ideal of that perfect ability achievable in accord with the measure proper to the respective phase in humanity's life, in other words, a relatively perfect adumbration of the idea of humanity. It is clear, then, how each one should strive to be as universally able a personality as possible, able in all the fundamental orientations of life, which for their part correspond to the fundamental types of possible attitudes. It is clear, too, how each should strive to be in each of these orientations as

---

[68] One wonders if even Husserl's "rigorous science" of philosophy escapes this imperfection. Frequently the impression is inescapable that the phenomenological analysis gives the only explanation that "makes sense." This, however, is no guarantee that the sense it "makes" is the true sense. Nor does it touch the thornier problem as to whether everything should make sense the way Husserl wants it to.

"experienced," as "wise," and hence also as much a "lover of wisdom" as possible. According to this idea, every man who strives is necessarily a "philosopher," in the most original sense of the word.

From the natural reflections on the best ways to achieve the lofty goal of humanity and consequently at the same time the lofty goal of perfect wisdom, there has grown up, as is known, a technique—that of the virtuous or able man. If it is as usual defined as the art of correct conduct, it obviously comes to the same thing. For consistently able conduct, which is certainly meant, leads back to the able, practical character, and this presupposes habitual perfection from the intellectual and axiological point of view. Again, conscious striving for perfection presupposes striving for universal wisdom. In regard to content, this discipline directs the one striving to the various groups of values, those present in the sciences, the arts, religion, etc. that every individual in his conduct has to recognize as intersubjective and unifying validities; and one of the highest of these values is the idea of this wisdom and perfect ability itself. Of course, this theory of ethical conduct, whether considered more as popular or as scientific, enters into the framework of a *Weltanschauung* philosophy that for its part, with all its fields, in the way it has developed in the collective consciousness of its time and comes persuasively before the individual as an objective validity, must become a most significant cultural force, a point of radiation for the most worthwhile personalities of the time.

Now that we have seen to it that full justice has been accorded to the high value of *Weltanschauung* philosophy, it might seem that nothing should keep us from unconditionally recommending the striving toward such a philosophy.

Still, perhaps it can be shown that in regard to the idea of philosophy, other values—and from certain points of view,[69]

---

[69] *Von gewissen Gesichtspunkten:* It is important to remember this qualification. From his later writings one can get the impression that scientific truth is the only value Husserl recognizes. Having dedicated his life to the

higher ones—must be satisfied, which is to say, those of a philosophical science. The following should be taken into account. Our consideration takes place from the standpoint of the high scientific culture of our time, which is a time for mighty forces of objectified strict sciences. For modern consciousness the ideas of culture, or *Weltanschauung,* and science—understood as practical ideas—have been sharply separated, and from now on they remain separated for all eternity. We may bemoan it, but we must accept it as a progressively effective fact that is to determine correspondingly our practical attitude. The historical philosophies were certainly *Weltanschauung* philosophies, in so far as the wisdom drive ruled their creators; but they were just as much scientific philosophies, in so far as the goal of scientific philosophy was also alive in them. The two goals were either not at all or not sharply distinguished. In the practical striving they flowed together; they lay, too, infinitely far away, no matter what lofty experiences the aspirant may have had in their regard. Since the constitution of a supratemporal universality of strict sciences, that situation has fundamentally changed. Generations upon generations work enthusiastically on the mighty structure of science and add to it their modest building blocks, always conscious that the structure is endless, by no means ever to be finished. *Weltanschauung,* too, is an "idea," but of a goal lying in the finite, in principle to be realized in an individual life by way of constant approach, just like morality, which would certainly lose its sense if it were the idea of an eternal that would be in principle transfinite.[70] The "idea" of *Weltanschauung* is consequently a different one for each time, a fact that can be seen without difficulty from the preceding analysis of its con-

---

promotion of this value, Husserl denied himself others, but he did not deny that they are values nor that there are ways in which they are superior to the values for which he himself has opted.

[70] For ethics Husserl will recognize a certain *Verworfenheit* (a being determined in and by one's situation), but he will reject it for theoretical philosophy. Heidegger and the "philosophers of existence" will introduce the same notion into the very essence of philosophical thinking.

cept. The "idea" of science, on the contrary, is a supratemporal one, and here that means limited by no relatedness to the spirit of one time. Now, along with these differences go essential differences of practical orientations. After all, our life goals are in general of two kinds, some temporal, others eternal, some serving our own perfection and that of our contemporaries, others the perfection of posterity, too, down to the most remote generations. Science is a title standing for absolute, timeless values. Every such value, once discovered, belongs thereafter to the treasure trove of all succeeding humanity and obviously determines likewise the material content of the idea of culture, wisdom, *Weltanschauung,* as well as of *Weltanschauung* philosophy.

Thus *Weltanschauung* philosophy and scientific philosophy are sharply distinguished as two ideas, related in a certain manner to each other but not to be confused. Herein it is also to be observed that the former is not, so to speak, the imperfect temporal realization of the latter. For if our interpretation is correct, then up to the present there has been no realization at all of that idea, i.e., no philosophy actually in existence is a rigorous science; there is no "system of doctrines," even an incomplete one, objectively set forth in the unified spirit of the research community of our time.[71] On the other hand, there were already *Weltanschauung* philosophies thousands of years ago. Nevertheless, it can be said that the realization of these ideas (presupposing realizations of both) would approach each other asymptotically in the infinite and coincide, should we want to represent to ourselves the infinite of science metaphorically as an "infinitely distant point." The concept of philosophy would thereby have to be taken in a correspondingly broad sense, so broad that along with the specifically philosophical sciences it

---

[71] Here a new characteristic of the scientific ideal in philosophy is introduced. Not only must it produce objectively valid results, but like the positive sciences it must create a community of philosophers who, basing their investigations on the same principles, can share a community of scientific truths that accumulate as scientific investigation advances.

would embrace all particular sciences, after they had been turned into philosophies by a rationally critical explanation and evaluation.

If we take the two distinct ideas as contents of life goals, then accordingly, in opposition to the aspiration proper to *Weltanschauung,* an entirely different research aspiration is possible. This latter, though fully conscious that science can in no wise be the complete creation of the individual, still devotes its fullest energies to promoting, in cooperation with men of like mind, the break-through and gradual progress of a scientific philosophy. The big problem at present is, apart from clearly distinguishing them, to make a relative evaluation of these goals and thereby of their practical unifiability.

Let it be admitted from the beginning that on the basis of the individuals who philosophize no definitive practical decision for the one or the other kind of philosophizing can be given. Some are pre-eminently theoretical men inclined by nature to seek their vocation in strictly scientific research, provided the field that attracts them offers prospects for such research. Herein it may well be that the interest, even passionate interest, in this field comes from temperamental needs, let us say from needs rooted in a *Weltanschauung.* On the other hand, the situation is different for aesthetic and practical natures (for artists, theologians, jurists, etc.). They see their vocation in the realization of aesthetic or practical ideals, thus of ideals belonging to a nontheoretical sphere. In this class we likewise put theological, juristic, and in the broadest sense technical scholars and writers, to the extent that by their writings they do not seek to promote pure theory but primarily to influence practice. In the actuality of life, of course, the separation is not entirely sharp; precisely at a time when practical motives are making such a powerful upsurge, even a theoretical nature will be capable of giving in to the force of such motives more thoroughly than its theoretical vocation would permit. Here, however, particularly for the philosophy of our time, lies a great danger.

We must ask, however, not only from the standpoint of the individual but also from that of humanity and of history (in so far, that is, as we take history into account), what it means for the development of culture, for the possibility of a constantly progressive realization of humanity as an eternal idea—not of the individual man—that the question be decided predominantly in the one or the other sense. In other words, whether the tendency toward one type of philosophy entirely dominates the time and brings it about that the opposite tendency—say, the one toward scientific philosophy—dies out. That, too, is a practical question. For the influences we exert upon history, and with them our ethical responsibilities, extend to the utmost reaches of the ethical ideal called for by the idea of human development.

How the decision in question would present itself to a theoretical nature, if there already existed indubitable beginnings of a philosophical doctrine, is clear. Let us take a look at other sciences. All "wisdom" or wisdom doctrine whose origin is mathematical or in the realm of the natural sciences has, to the extent that the corresponding theoretical doctrine has been given an objectively valid foundation, forfeited its rights. Science has spoken; from now on, it is for wisdom to learn. The striving toward wisdom in the realm of natural science was not, so to speak, unjustified before the existence of strict science; it is not retroactively discredited for its own time. In the urgency of life that in practice necessitates adopting a position, man could not wait until—say, after thousands of years—science would be there, even supposing that he already knew the idea of strict science at all.

Now, on the other hand, every science, however exact, offers only a partially developed system of doctrine surrounded by a limitless horizon of what has not yet become science. What, then, is to be considered the correct goal for this horizon? Further development of strict doctrine, or *Anschauung,* "wisdom"? The theoretical man, the investigator of nature, will not hesitate in answering. Where science can speak, even though only centuries from now, he will disdainfully reject vague *Anschauungen*. He would hold it a sin against science to "recommend" projects of nature—*Anschauungen*. In this he certainly represents a right of future humanity. The strict sciences owe their greatness, the continuity and full force of their progressive development, in very large measure precisely to the radicalism of such a mentality. Of course, every exact scholar constructs for himself *Anschauungen;* by his views, his guesses, his opinions, he looks beyond what has been firmly established, but only with methodical intent, in order to plan new fragments of strict doctrine. This attitude does not preclude, as the investigator of nature himself knows quite well, that experience in the prescientific sense— though[72] in connection with scientific insights—plays an important role within the technique proper to natural science. Technical tasks want to be done, the house, the machine is to be built; there can be no waiting until natural science can give exact information on all that concerns them. The technician, therefore, as a practical man, decides otherwise than the theoretician of natural science. From the latter he takes doctrine, from life he takes "experience."

The situation is not quite the same in regard to scientific philosophy, precisely because as yet not even a beginning of scientifically rigorous doctrine has been developed, and the philosophy handed down historically as well as that conceived in a living development, each representing itself as such a doctrine, are at most scientific half-fabrications, or indistinguished mixtures of *Weltanschauung* and theoretical knowledge. On the other hand, here too we unfortunately cannot wait. Philosophical necessity as a need for *Weltanschauung* forces us. This need becomes constantly greater the wider the circle of positive sciences is extended. The extraordinary fullness of scientifically "explained" facts that they bestow on us cannot help us, since in principle, along with

---

[72] *Obschon:* The word is embarrassing in the context. The meaning seems to be: "Empirical experience plays a role only when connected with scientific intuitions, nevertheless it does play an important role."

all the sciences, they bring in a dimension of riddles whose solutions become for us a vital question. The natural sciences have not in a single instance unraveled for us actual reality, the reality in which we live, move, and are. The general belief that it is their function to accomplish this and that they are merely not yet far enough advanced, the opinion that they can accomplish this—in principle—has revealed itself to those with more profound insight as a superstition. The necessary separation between natural science and philosophy—in principle, a differently oriented science, though in some fields essentially related to natural science—is in process of being established and clarified. As Lotze puts it, "To calculate the course of the world does not mean to understand it."[73] In this direction, however, we are no better off with the humanistic sciences. To "understand" humanity's spirit-life is certainly a great and beautiful thing. But unfortunately even this understanding cannot help us, and it must not be confused with the philosophical understanding that is to unravel for us the riddles of the world and of life.

The spiritual need of our time has, in fact, become unbearable. Would that it were only theoretical lack of clarity regarding the sense of the "reality" investigated in the natural and humanistic sciences that disturbed our peace—e.g., to what extent is being in the ultimate sense understood in them, what is to be looked on as such "absolute" being, and whether this sort of thing is knowable at all. Far more than this, it is the most radical vital need that afflicts us, a need that leaves no point of our lives untouched. All life is taking a position, and all taking of position is subject to a must—that of doing justice to validity and invalidity according to alleged norms of absolute validation. So long as these norms were not attacked, were threatened and

[73] Husserl will not have us think that the attitude of the philosopher is one of indifference to life's problems—truth for its own sake. The philosopher is to "understand" for the true needs of life that which "science" presents in a manner adequate to its own needs. It is not the scientist, as scientist, but the philosopher who sits in judgment on the results of science.

ridiculed by no scepticism, there was only one vital question: how best to satisfy these norms in practice. But how is it now, when any and every norm is controverted or empirically falsified and robbed of its ideal validity? Naturalists and historicists fight about *Weltanschauung,* and yet both are at work on different sides to misinterpret ideas as facts and to transform all reality, all life, into an incomprehensible, idealess confusion of "facts." The superstition of the fact is common to them all.

It is certain that we cannot wait. We have to take a position, we must bestir ourselves to harmonize the disharmonies in our attitude to reality—to the reality of life, which has significance for us and in which we should have significance—into a rational, even though unscientific, "world-and-life-view." And if the *Weltanschauung* philosopher helps us greatly in this, should we not thank him?

No matter how much truth there is in what has just been asserted, no matter how little we should like to miss the exaltation and consolation old and new philosophies offer us, still it must be insisted that we remain aware of the responsibility we have in regard to humanity. For the sake of time we must not sacrifice eternity; in order to alleviate our need, we have no right to bequeath to our posterity need upon need as an eventually ineradicable evil. The need here has its source in science. But only science can definitively overcome the need that has its source in science. If the sceptical criticism of naturalists and historicists dissolves genuine objective validity in all fields of obligation into nonsense, if unclear and disagreeing, even though naturally developed, reflective concepts and consequently equivocal and erroneous problems impede the understanding of actuality and the possibility of a rational attitude toward it, if a special but (for a large class of sciences) required methodical attitude becomes a matter of routine so that it is incapable of being transformed into other attitudes, and if depressing absurdities in the interpretation of the world are connected with such prejudices, then there is only one remedy for these and all similar evils: a scientific critique and in addition a radical science, rising from below, based on sure foundations, and progressing according to the most rigorous methods—the philosophical science for which we speak here. *Weltanschauungen* can engage in controversy; only science can decide, and its decision bears the stamp of eternity.

And so whatever be the direction the new transformation of philosophy may take, without question it must not give up its will to be rigorous science. Rather as theoretical science it must oppose itself to the practical aspiration toward *Weltanschauung* and quite consciously separate itself from this aspiration. For here all attempts at reconciliation must likewise be rejected. The proponents of the new *Weltanschauung* philosophy will perhaps object that to follow this philosophy need not mean letting go the idea of rigorous science. The right kind of *Weltanschauung* philosopher, they will say, will not only be scientific in laying his foundations, i.e., using all the data of the rigorous particular sciences as solid building blocks, but he will also put into practice scientific method and will willingly seize upon every possibility of advancing philosophical problems in a rigorously scientific manner. But in contrast to the metaphysical irresolution and scepticism of the age just past, he will courageously pursue even the loftiest metaphysical problems in order to achieve the goal of a *Weltanschauung* that, according to the situation of the time, harmoniously satisfies both intellect and feeling.

To the extent that this is intended as a reconciliation calculated to erase the line of demarcation between *Weltanschauung* philosophy and scientific philosophy, we must throw up our defense against it. It can only lead to a softening and weakening of the scientific impulse and to promoting a specious scientific literature destitute of intellectual honesty. There are no compromises here, no more here than in any other science. We could no longer hope for theoretical results if the *Weltanschauung* impulse were to become predominant and were to deceive even theoretical natures by its scientific forms. When over thousands of years the greatest scientific spirits, passionately dominated by the will to science, have achieved not a single fragment of pure doctrine in philosophy and have accomplished all the great things they have accomplished (even though imperfectly matured) only as a result of this will to science, the *Weltanschauung* philosophers will certainly not be able to think that they can merely by the way promote and definitively establish philosophical science. These men who set the goal in the finite, who want to have their system and want it soon enough to be able to live by it, are in no way called to this task. Here there is only one thing to do: *Weltanschauung* philosophy itself must in all honesty relinquish the claim to be a science, and thereby at the same time cease confusing minds and impeding the progress of scientific philosophy —which, after all, is certainly contrary to its intentions.

Let its ideal goal remain *Weltanschauung,* which above all is essentially not science. It must not allow itself to be led into error here by that scientific fanaticism only too widespread in our time that discredits all that is not to be demonstrated with "scientific exactitude" as "unscientific."[74] Science is one value among other equally justified values. That in particular the value of *Weltanschauung* stands with utmost firmness on its own foundation, that it is to be judged as the habitus and accomplishment of the individual personality whereas science is to be judged as the collective accomplishment of generations of scholars, we have made quite clear above.[75] And just as both have their distinct sources of value, so they also have their distinct functions, their distinct manners of working and teaching. Thus *Weltanschauung* philos-

[74] Where the object involved is somehow static, as it is in mathematics and to a certain extent in the science of nature, one can speak of "exactitude" as a necessary characteristic of rigorous science. It is not, however, of the essence of rigorous science as such. What is here required is an indubitable knowledge (submitted to the kind of verification it demands), which, where the object is "flowing," cannot be "exact."

[75] Husserl was constantly opposed to looking upon phenomenologists as forming a "school." But he did hope to promote a cooperative effort of investigators, all employing the phenomenological method (cf. p. 136, n. 71, supra).

ophy teaches the way wisdom does: personality directs itself to personality. As a teacher in the style of such a philosophy, then, he alone may direct himself to a wider public who is called thereto because of a particularly significant character and characteristic wisdom—or he may be called as the servant of lofty practical interests, religious, ethical, legal, etc. Science, however, is impersonal. Its collaborator requires not wisdom but theoretical talent. What he contributes increases a treasure of eternal validities that must prove a blessing to humanity. And as we saw above, this is true to an extraordinarily high degree of philosophical science.

Only when the decisive separation of the one philosophy from the other has become a fact in the consciousness of the time is it proper to think of philosophy's adopting the form and language of genuine science and of its recognizing as an imperfection one of its much-praised and even imitated qualities, profundity. Profundity is a mark of the chaos that genuine science wants to transform into a cosmos, into a simple, completely clear, lucid order. Genuine science, so far as its real doctrine extends, knows no profundity. Every bit of completed science is a whole composed of "thought steps" each of which is immediately understood,[76] and so not at all profound. Profundity is an affair of wisdom; conceptual distinctness and clarity is an affair of rigorous theory. To recast the conjectures of profundity into unequivocal rational forms—that is the essential process in constituting anew the rigorous sciences. The exact sciences, too, had their long periods of profundity, and just as they did in the struggles of the Renaissance, so too, in the present-day struggles, I dare to hope, will philosophy fight through from the level of profundity to that of scientific clarity. For that, however, it needs only a correct assurance regarding its goal and a great will directed with full con-

[76] In the light of Husserl's theory of intuition this characteristic of science takes on added meaning. At the same time it is a convenient limitation of the philosophical problematic—one simply excludes what does not fulfill this condition.

sciousness toward this goal and a putting forth of all available scientific energies. Our age is called an age of decadence. I cannot consider this complaint justified. You will scarcely find in history an age in which such a sum of working forces was set in motion and worked with such success. Perhaps we do not always approve the goals; we may also complain that in more tranquil epochs, when life passed more peacefully, flowers of the spirit's life grew whose like we cannot find or hope for in our age. And too, sometimes that which is so constantly desired in our age may repel the aesthetic sense, which finds so much more appeal in the naïve beauty of that which grows freely, just as extraordinary values are present in the sphere of the will only so long as great wills find the correct goals. It would mean doing our age a great injustice, however, if one wanted to impute to it the desire for what is inferior. He who is capable of awakening faith in, of inspiring understanding of and enthusiasm for the greatness of a goal, will easily find the forces that are applied to this goal. I mean, our age is according to its vocation a great age—only it suffers from the scepticism that has disintegrated the old, unclarified ideals. And for that very reason it suffers from the too negligible development and force of philosophy, which has not yet progressed enough, is not scientific enough to overcome sceptical negativism (which calls itself positivism) by means of true positivism.[77] Our age wants to believe only in "realities." Now, its strongest reality is science, and thus what our age most needs is philosophical science.

If, however, in specifying the sense of our age we apply ourselves to this great goal, we must also make clear to ourselves that we can achieve it in only one way, which is to say, if with the radicalism belonging to the essence of genuine philosophical science we accept nothing given in advance, allow nothing traditional to pass as a beginning, nor ourselves to be dazzled by any

[77] Husserl is playing on the word "positivism." Here it signifies an attitude of will that affirms a scientific aim and rejects "negative" scepticism as a lack of confidence in human reason.

names however great, but rather seek to attain the beginnings in a free dedication to the problems themselves and to the demands stemming from them.

Of course, we need history too. Not, it is true, as the historian does, in order to lose ourselves in the developmental relations in which the great philosophies have grown up, but in order to let the philosophies themselves, in accord with their spiritual content, work on us as an inspiration. In fact, out of these historical philosophies there flows to us philosophical life—if we understand how to peer into them, to penetrate to the soul of their words and theories—philosophical life with all the wealth and strength of living motivations. But it is not through philosophies that we become philosophers. Remaining immersed in the historical, forcing oneself to work therein in historico-critical activity, and wanting to attain philosophical science by means of eclectic elaboration or anachronistic renaissance—all that leads to nothing but hopeless efforts. The impulse to research must proceed not from philosophies but from things and from the problems connected with them. Philosophy, however, is essentially a science of true beginnings, or origins, of *rizōmata pantōn*. The science concerned with what is radical must from every point of view be radical itself in its procedure. Above all it must not rest until it has attained its own absolutely clear beginnings,[78] i.e., its absolutely clear problems, the methods preindicated in the proper sense of these problems, and the most basic field of work wherein things are given with absolute clarity. But one must in no instance abandon one's radical lack of prejudice, prematurely identifying, so to speak, such "things" with empirical "facts." To do this is to stand like a blind man before ideas, which are, after all, to such a great extent absolutely given in immediate intuition. We are too subject to the prejudices that still come from the Renais-

---

[78] We must insist on the notion of "beginnings," as does Husserl. There is question not merely of renewing philosophy but of approaching each problem anew, without prejudice or presupposition. It might legitimately be asked whether this is humanly possible, or for that matter desirable.

sance. To one truly without prejudice it is immaterial whether a certainty comes to us from Kant or Thomas Aquinas, from Darwin or Aristotle, from Helmholtz or Paracelsus. What is needed is not the insistence that one see with his own eyes; rather it is that he not explain away under the pressure of prejudice what has been seen. Because in the most impressive of the modern sciences, the mathematico-physical, that which is exteriorly the largest part of their work, results from indirect methods, we are only too inclined to overestimate indirect methods and to misunderstand the value of direct comprehensions. However, to the extent that philosophy goes back to ultimate origins, it belongs precisely to its very essence that its scientific work move in spheres of direct intuition. Thus the greatest step our age has to make is to recognize that with the philosophical intuition in the correct sense, the phenomenological grasp of essences, a limitless field of work opens out, a science that without all indirectly symbolical and mathematical methods, without the apparatus of premises and conclusions, still attains a plenitude of the most rigorous and, for all further philosophy, decisive cognitions.

Philosophy and the Crisis of European Man

In this lecture I will venture an attempt to awaken new interest in the oft-treated theme of the European crisis by developing the philosophico-historical idea (or the teleological sense) of European man.[1] In so far as in thus developing the topic I bring out the essential function that philosophy and its ramifications in our sciences have to perform in this process, the European crisis will also be given added clarification.

We can illustrate this in terms of the well-known distinction between scientific medicine and "naturopathy." Just as in the common life of peoples the latter derives from naïve experience and tradition, so scientific medicine results from the utilization of insights belonging to purely theoretical sciences concerned with the human body, primarily anatomy and physiology. These in turn are based on those fundamental sciences that seek a universal explanation of nature as such, physics and chemistry.

Now let us turn our gaze from man's body to his spirit, the

---

[1] It is unquestionable that "Western man" would be a happier expression in the context. Husserl, however, speaks of *europäischen Menschentums,* which, as will be seen later, must be translated as "European man" if the rest of the text is to make sense.

theme of the so-called humanistic sciences.[2] In these sciences
theoretical interest is directed exclusively to human beings as
persons, to their personal life and activity, as also correlatively to
the concrete results of this activity. To live as a person is to live in
a social framework, wherein I and we live together in community
and have the community as a horizon.[3] Now, communities are
structured in various simple or complex forms, such as family,
nation, or international community. Here the word "live" is not
to be taken in a physiological sense but rather as signifying purposeful living, manifesting spiritual creativity—in the broadest
sense, creating culture within historical continuity. It is this that
forms the theme of various humanistic sciences. Now, there is an
obvious difference between healthy growth and decline, or to put
it another way, between health and sickness, even for societies,
for peoples, for states. In consequence there arises the not so far-
fetched question: how is it that in this connection there has never
arisen a medical science concerned with nations and with international communities? The European nations are sick; Europe
itself, they say, is in critical condition. Nor in this situation are
there lacking all sorts of nature therapies. We are, in fact, quite
overwhelmed with a torrent of naïve and extravagant suggestions
for reform. But why is it that so luxuriantly developed human-

---

[2] *Geisteswissenschaften:* In certain contexts it will be necessary to translate this term more literally as "sciences of the spirit." This will be particularly true where the term occurs in the singular. cf. p. 154 n. 1 and n.
10 infra.

[3] The notion of "horizon," which played such an important part in
Husserl's earlier writings, has here taken on a somewhat broader connotation. Formerly it signified primarily those concomitant elements in consciousness that are given, without being the direct object of the act of consciousness under consideration. In every act of consciousness there are aspects of
the object that are not directly intended but which are recognized, either
by recall or anticipation, as belonging to the object intended. These aspects
constitute its horizon. In the present essay "the community as a horizon"
signifies the framework in which experience occurs, conditioning that experience and supplying the diverse aspects of objectivity that are not directly
intended in any one act of consciousness.

istic sciences here fail to perform the service that in their own sphere the natural sciences perform so competently?

Those who are familiar with the spirit of modern science will not be embarrassed for an answer. The greatness of the natural sciences consists in their refusal to be content with an observational empiricism, since for them all descriptions of nature are but methodical procedures for arriving at exact explanations, ultimately physico-chemical explanations. They are of the opinion that "merely descriptive" sciences tie us to the finitudes of our earthly environing world.[4] Mathematically exact natural science, however, embraces with its method the infinities contained in its actualities and real possibilities. It sees in the intuitively given a merely subjective appearance, and it teaches how to investigate intersubjective ("objective")[5] nature itself with systematic approximation on the basis of elements and laws that are unconditionally universal. At the same time, such exact science teaches how to explain all intuitively pre-given concretions, whether men, or animals, or heavenly bodies, by an appeal to what is ultimate, i.e., how to induce from the appearances, which are the data in any factual case, future possibilities and probabilities, and to do this with a universality and exactitude that surpasses any empiricism limited to intuition.[6] The consistent development of exact sciences in modern times has been a true revolution in the technical mastery of nature.

[4] I am using an expression borrowed from Dewey to translate the Husserlian *Umwelt,* a term Husserl uses frequently only in his last period. In the light of the *Cartesian Meditations* we must remember that though such a world is subjectively "constituted," it is still not a private world, since its constitution is ultimately "intersubjective."

[5] Like Kant, Husserl saw "necessity" and "universality" as the notes that characterize genuinely valid objectivity. Not until his later works (*Ideen II* and *Cartesian Meditations*), however, does he explicitly see "intersubjective constitution" as the ultimate concrete foundation for universal objectivity.

[6] Here Husserl is giving to the term "intuition" the limited meaning of sense intuition that it has for Kant.

In the humanistic sciences the methodological situation (in the sense already quite intelligible to us) is unfortunately quite different, and this for internal reasons. Human spirituality[7] is, it is true, based on the human *physis,* each individually human soul-life is founded on corporeality, and thus too each community on the bodies of the individual human beings who are its members. If, then, as is done in the sphere of nature, a really exact explanation and consequently a similarly extensive scientific practical application is to become possible for the phenomena belonging to the humanistic sciences, then must the practitioners of the humanistic sciences consider not only the spirit as spirit but must also go back to its bodily foundations, and by employing the exact sciences of physics and chemistry, carry through their explanations. The attempt to do this, however, has been unsuccessful (and in the foreseeable future there is no remedy to be had) due to the complexity of the exact psycho-physical research needed in the case of individual human beings, to say nothing of the great historical communities. If the world were constructed of two, so to speak, equal spheres of reality—nature and spirit—neither with a preferential position methodologically and factually, the situation would be different. But only nature can be handled as a self-contained world; only natural science can with complete consistency abstract from all that is spirit and consider nature purely as nature. On the other side such a consistent abstraction from nature does not, for the practitioner of humanistic science who is interested purely in the spiritual, lead to a self-contained "world," a world whose interrelationships are purely spiritual, that could be the theme of a pure and universal humanistic science, parallel to pure natural science. Animal spirituality,[8] that of the human and animal "souls," to which all other spirituality

---

[7] *Geistigkeit:* Following a decision to translate "Geist" as "spirit" rather than as "mind," we are forced into a somewhat uncomfortable translation of the present abstraction. The embarrassment becomes acute when reference is made to the "spirituality" of animals (cf. n. 8 infra), but it is not likely that "mentality" would be any less embarrassing.

[8] Where there is consciousness, there is spirit, and in animals there is

is referred, is in each individual instance causally based on corpo-reality. It is thus understandable that the practitioner of human-istic science, interested solely in the spiritual as such, gets no further than the descriptive, than a historical record of spirit, and thus remains tied to intuitive finitudes. Every example mani-fests this. A historian, for example, cannot, after all, treat the history of ancient Greece without taking into consideration the physical geography of ancient Greece; he cannot treat its archi-tecture without considering the materiality of its buildings, etc., etc. That seems clear enough.

What is to be said, then, if the whole mode of thought that reveals itself in this presentation rests on fatal prejudices and is in its results partly responsible for Europe's sickness? I am con-vinced that this is the case, and in this way I hope to make under-standable that herein lies an essential source for the conviction which the modern scientist has that the possibility of grounding a purely self-contained and universal science of the spirit is not even worth mentioning, with the result that he flatly rejects it.

It is in the interests of our Europe-problem to penetrate a bit more deeply into this question and to expose the above, at first glance lucidly clear, argumentation. The historian, the investi-gator of spirit, of culture, constantly has of course physical nature too among the phenomena with which he is concerned; in our example, nature in ancient Greece. But this is not nature in the sense understood by natural science; rather it is nature as it was for the ancient Greeks, natural reality present to their eyes in the world that surrounded them. To state it more fully; the historical environing world of the Greeks is not the objective world in our sense; rather it is their "representation of the world," i.e., their own subjective evaluation, with all the realities therein that were valid for them, for example the gods, the daemons, etc.

Environing world is a concept that has its place exclusively in the spiritual sphere. That we live in our own particular environ-

consciousness. For Husserl, self-consciousness is a mark of "personality" rather than "spirituality."

ing world, to which all our concerns and efforts are directed, points to an event that takes place purely in the spiritual order. Our environing world is a spiritual structure in us and in our historical life.[9] Here, then, there is no reason for one who makes his theme the spirit as spirit to demand for it any but a purely spiritual explanation. And this has general validity: to look upon environing nature as in itself alien to spirit, and consequently to desire to support humanistic science with natural science and thus presumably to make the former exact, is nonsense.

Obviously, too, it is forgotten that natural science (like all sciences as such) is a title for spiritual activities, those of natural scientists in cooperation with each other; as such these activities belong, as do all spiritual occurrences, to the realm of what should be explained by means of a science of the spirit.[10] Is it not, then, nonsensical and circular, to desire to explain by means of natural science the historical event "natural science," to explain it by invoking natural science and its laws of nature, both of which, as produced by spirit,[11] are themselves part of the problem?

Blinded by naturalism (no matter how much they themselves

[9] In this connection one should consult the Second Cartesian Meditation, where Husserl insists that the only reality that the world can have for one who would approach it scientifically is a phenomenal reality. If we are to understand it scientifically, our analysis of it must be purely phenomenological, i.e., it is the phenomenon "world" that we must analyze. "We shall direct our attention to the fact that phenomenological *epochē* lays open (to me, the meditating philosopher) an infinite realm of being of a new kind, as the sphere of a new kind of experience: transcendental experience" (*Cartesian Meditations,* p. 66). Cf. ibid., p. 69: "Now, however, we are envisaging a science that is, so to speak, absolutely subjective, whose thematic object exists whether or not the world exists."

[10] Because of the context here, it is imperative that "Geisteswissenschaft" not be translated as "humanistic science."

[11] From his earliest days Husserl never tired of insisting that there can be no "natural science" of science itself. It is the theme of *Logische Untersuchungen* and is perhaps most eloquently expressed in *Formale und transzendentale Logik,* whose purpose is to develop a "science of science," which, Husserl holds, can be only a transcendental (constitutive) phenomenology.

may verbally oppose it), the practitioners of humanistic science have completely neglected even to pose the problem of a universal and pure science of the spirit and to seek a theory of the essence of spirit as spirit, a theory that pursues what is unconditionally universal in the spiritual order with its own elements and its own laws. Yet this last should be done with a view to gaining thereby scientific explanations in an absolutely conclusive sense.

The preceding reflections proper to a science of the spirit provide us with the right attitude for grasping and handling our theme of spiritual Europe as a problem belonging purely to science of the spirit, first of all from the point of view of spirit's history. As has already been stated in the introductory remarks, in following this path we should reveal an extraordinary teleology, which is, so to speak, innate only in our Europe. This, moreover, is most intimately connected with the eruption (or the invasion) of philosophy and of its ramifications, the sciences, in the ancient Greek spirit. We already suspect that there will be question of clarifying the profoundest reasons for the origin of fatal naturalism, or—and this is of equal importance—of modern dualism in interpreting the world. Ultimately the proper sense of European man's crisis should thereby come to light.

We may ask, "How is the spiritual image of Europe to be characterized?" This does not mean Europe geographically, as it appears on maps, as though European man were to be in this way confined to the circle of those who live together in this territory. In the spiritual sense it is clear that to Europe belong the English dominions, the United States, etc., but not, however, the Eskimos or Indians of the country fairs, or the Gypsies, who are constantly wandering about Europe. Clearly the title Europe designates the unity of a spiritual life and a creative activity—with all its aims, interests, cares, and troubles, with its plans, its establishments, its institutions. Therein individual human beings work in a variety of societies, on different levels, in families, races,[12] nations, all

[12] *Stämmen:* Literally the term means "stocks," but the English word could scarcely be unambiguous in the context.

intimately joined together in spirit and, as I said, in the unity of one spiritual image. This should stamp on persons, groups, and all their cultural accomplishments an all-unifying character.

"The spiritual image of Europe"—what is it? It is exhibiting the philosophical idea immanent in the history of Europe (of spiritual Europe). To put it another way, it is its immanent teleology, which, if we consider mankind in general, manifests itself as a new human epoch emerging and beginning to grow, the epoch of a humanity that from now on will and can live only in the free fashioning of its being and its historical life out of rational ideas and infinite tasks.[13]

Every spiritual image has its place essentially in a universal historical space or in a particular unity of historical time in terms of coexistence or succession—it has its history. If, then, we follow historical connections, beginning as we must with ourselves and our own nation, historical continuity leads us ever further away from our own to neighboring nations, and so from nation to nation, from age to age. Ultimately we come to ancient times and go from the Romans to the Greeks, to the Egyptians, the Persians, etc.; in this there is clearly no end. We go back to primeval times, and we must perforce turn to Menghin's significant and genial work *The History of the Stone Age*.[14] To an investigation of this type mankind manifests itself as a single life of men and of peoples, bound together by spiritual relationships alone, filled with all types of human beings and of cultures, but constantly flowing each into the other. It is like a sea in which human beings, peoples, are the waves constantly forming, changing, and disappearing, some more richly, more complexly involved, others more simply.

---

[13] Not only is Europe, according to Husserl, the birthplace of philosophy and the sciences, but it is philosophy and the sciences that more than anything else have made European culture unique, have given it its most distinguishing characteristic.

[14] Oswald Menghin, *Weltgeschichte der Steinzeit* (Vienna: A. Schroll, 1931).

In this process consistent, penetrating observation reveals new, characteristic compositions and distinctions. No matter how inimical the European nations may be toward each other, still they have a special inner affinity of spirit that permeates all of them and transcends their national differences. It is a sort of fraternal relationship that gives us the consciousness of being at home in this circle. This becomes immediately evident as soon as, for example, we penetrate sympathetically into the historical process of India, with its many peoples and cultural forms. In this circle there is again the unity of a family-like relationship, but one that is strange to us. On the other hand, Indians find us strangers and find only in each other their fellows. Still, this essential distinction between fellowship and strangeness, which is relativized on many levels and is a basic category of all historicity, cannot suffice. Historical humanity does not always divide itself in the same way according to this category. We get a hint of that right in our own Europe. Therein lies something unique, which all other human groups, too, feel with regard to us, something that, apart from all considerations of expediency, becomes a motivation for them—despite their determination to retain their spiritual autonomy—constantly to Europeanize themselves, whereas we, if we understand ourselves properly, will never, for example, Indianize ourselves.[15] I mean we feel (and with all its vagueness this feeling is correct) that in our European humanity there is an innate entelechy that thoroughly controls the changes in the European image and gives to it the sense of a development in the direction of an ideal image of life and of being, as moving toward an eternal pole. It is not as though there were question here of one of those known orientations that give to the physical realm of organic beings its character—not a question, therefore, of something like biological development in stages from seminal

---

[15] The tacit beginning of all Husserl's philosophizing is the value judgment that the rational life, in the sense in which he understands it, is the best life. But unlike Hegel, he has not excogitated a philosophy of history to justify this judgment.

form up to maturity followed by aging and dying out. There is essentially no zoology of peoples. They are spiritual unities. They have not, and above all the supernationality Europe has not, a mature form that has been or can be reached, no form of regular repetition. From the point of view of soul, humanity has never been a finished product, nor will it be, nor can it ever repeat itself.[16] The spiritual *telos* of European Man, in which is included the particular *telos* of separate nations and of individual human beings, lies in infinity; it is an infinite idea, toward which in secret the collective spiritual becoming, so to speak, strives. Just as in the development it becomes a conscious *telos*, so too it becomes necessarily practical as a goal of the will, and thereby is introduced a new, a higher stage of development that is guided by norms, by normative ideas.

All of this, however, is not intended as a speculative interpretation of our historicity but rather as the expression of a vital anticipation arising out of unprejudiced reflection. But this anticipation serves as intentional guidance[17] toward seeing in European history extraordinarily significant connections, in the pursuit of which the anticipated becomes for us guaranteed certainty. Anticipation is the emotional guide to all discoveries.

Let us develop this. Spiritually Europe has a birthplace. By this I do not mean a geographical place, in some one land, though this too is true. I refer, rather, to a spiritual birthplace in a nation or in certain men or groups of men belonging to this nation. It is the ancient Greek nation[18] in the seventh and sixth

[16] Nature is precisely that which does repeat constantly (despite evolution). It is characteristic of natural species that their members follow each other in the same identifiable form. Spirit, however, is an ongoing totality, never reaching maturity, never reproducing itself in the same form.

[17] This notion of "intentional guide," or "clue," is developed in No. 21 of the Second Cartesian Meditation. Husserl recognizes a subjective factor—here "anticipation"—as guiding the manner in which objects—here history itself—are intentionally "constituted."

[18] Husserl was never particularly concerned with historical accuracy, even in his choice of terminology. Apart from the anachronism involved in applying the term "nation" to the loose unities of the ancient world, "Greek"

centuries B.C. In it there grows up a new kind of attitude[19] of individuals toward their environing world. Consequent upon this emerges a completely new type of spiritual structure, rapidly growing into a systematically rounded (*geschlossen*) cultural form that the Greeks called philosophy. Correctly translated, in its original sense, this bespeaks nothing but universal science, science of the world as a whole, of the universal unity of all being. Very soon the interest in the totality and, by the same token, the question regarding the all-embracing becoming and the resulting being begin to particularize themselves in accord with the general forms and regions of being.[20] Thus philosophy, the one science, is ramified into the various particular sciences.

In the emergence of philosophy in this sense, a sense, that is, which includes all sciences, I see—no matter how paradoxical this may seem—the original phenomenon of spiritual Europe. The elucidations that follow, however brief they must be kept, will soon eliminate the seeming paradox.

Philosophy-science[21] is the title for a special class of cultural structures. The historical movement that has taken on the form of European supernationality goes back to an ideal image whose dimension is the infinite; not, however, to an image that could be

---

itself is a term that covers a somewhat heterogeneous grouping in the seventh and sixth centuries B.C.

[19] Despite the embarrasments involved in certain contexts, I have chosen to translate *Einstellung* for the most part by "attitude." The German term indicates a focusing of attention in a particular way. There is no way in English of rendering the play on words involved in the opposition of *Einstellung–Umstellung,* which latter is more than a mere "change" of attitude; "reorientation" of attitude is more like it.

[20] This is Husserl's somewhat unwieldy way of indicating that the overall interest in being breaks down into particular interests in types or classes of being—which are the objects of particular sciences.

[21] Here, near the end of his life, Husserl retains the theme he had developed so many years earlier in "Philosophy as Rigorous Science." The ideal of philosophy and the particular sciences is the same; differences are to be traced to the degree of universality involved in the one and the other. The entire book *Die Krisis der europäischen Wissenschaften* is devoted to developing this theme historically.

recognized in a merely external morphological examination of changing forms. To have a norm constantly in view is something intimately a part of the intentional life of individual persons and consequently of nations and of particular societies within the latter, and ultimately of the organism formed by the nations united together as Europe. This, of course, is not true of all persons and, therefore, is not fully developed in the higher-level personalites constituted by intersubjective acts. Still, it is present in them in the form of a necessary progressive development and extension in the spirit of universally valid norms. This spirit, however, signifies at the same time the progressive transformation of collective humanity beginning with the effective formation of ideas in small and even in the smallest circles. Ideas, conceived within individual persons as sense-structures that in a wonderfully new manner secrete within themselves intentional infinities, are not in space like real things, which latter, entering as they do into the field of human experiences, do not by that very fact as yet signify anything for the human being as a person. With the first conception of ideas man gradually becomes a new man. His spiritual being enters into the movement of a progressive re-formation. This movement from the very beginning involves communication and awakens a new style of personal existence in its vital circle by a better understanding of a correspondingly new becoming. In this movement first of all (and subsequently even beyond it) a special type of humanity spreads out, living in finitude but oriented toward poles of infinity. By the very same token there grows up a new mode of sociality and a new form of enduring society, whose spiritual life, cemented together by a common love of and creation of ideas and by the setting of ideal norms for life, carries within itself a horizon of infinity for the future—an infinity of generations finding constant spiritual renewal in ideas. This takes place first of all in the spiritual territory of a single nation, the Greeks, as a development of philosophy and of philosophical communities. Along with this there grows, first in this nation, a general cultural spirit that draws the whole of mankind under its sway and is therefore a progressive transformation in the shape of a new historicity.[22]

This rough sketch will gain in completeness and intelligibility as we examine more closely the historical origin of philosophical and scientific man and thereby clarify the sense of Europe and, consequently, the new type of historicity that through this sort of development distinguishes itself from history in general.[23]

First, let us elucidate the remarkable character of philosophy as it unfolds in ever-new special sciences. Let us contrast it with other forms of culture already present in prescientific man, in his artefacts, his agriculture, his architecture, etc. All manifest classes of cultural products along with the proper methods for insuring their successful production. Still, they have a transitory existence in their environing world. Scientific achievements, on the other hand, once the method of insuring their successful creation has been attained, have an entirely different mode of being, an entirely different temporality. They do not wear out, they are imperishable. Repeated creation does not produce something similar, at best something similarly useful. Rather, no matter how many times the same person or any number of persons repeat these achievements, they remain exactly identical, identical in sense and in value. Persons united together in actual mutual understanding can only experience what their respective fellows have produced in the same manner as identical with what they

[22] Under the verbiage of this extremely difficult paragraph is hidden a profound insight into the transformation that takes place in men when they begin to look beyond facts to ideas. The only way to describe the horizon thus opened is to call it "infinite." Whether this began only with the Greeks is, of course, open to dispute. Still, the Greeks are the intellectual first parents of Western man.

[23] With the advent of philosophical and scientific ideals history itself becomes historical in a new and more profound sense. It is unfortunate, however, that Husserl fails to see history as the progressive concretization of the ideal.

have produced themselves.[24] In a word, what scientific activity achieves is not real but ideal.

What is more, however, whatever validity or truth has been gained in this way serves as material for the production of higher-level idealities; and this goes on and on. Now, in the developed theoretical interest, each interest receives ahead of time the sense of a merely relative goal; it becomes a transition to constantly new, higher-level goals in an infinity preindicated as science's universal field of endeavor, its "domain." Thus science designates the idea of an infinity of tasks, of which at any time a finite number have already been accomplished and are retained in their enduring validity. These constitute at the same time the fund of premises for an endless horizon of tasks united into one all-embracing task.

Here, however, an important supplementary remark should be made. In science the ideality of what is produced in any particular instance means more than the mere capacity for repetition based on a sense that has been guaranteed as identical; the idea of truth in the scientific sense is set apart (and of this we have still to speak) from the truth proper to pre-scientific life. Scientific truth claims to be unconditioned truth, which involves infinity, giving to each factually guaranteed truth a merely relative character, making it only an approach oriented, in fact, toward the infinite horizon, wherein the truth in itself is, so to speak, looked on as an infinitely distant point.[25] By the same token this infinity belongs also to what in the scientific sense "really is." A fortiori, there is infinity involved in "universal" validity for "everyone," as the subject of whatever rational foundations are to be secured;

[24] It would seem that in terms of ideas the world scientific community is far more closely knit than is the philosophical community. The type of unity, however, is analogous in both cases. Husserl would not like to admit that the differences are due to essential differences in the disciplines themselves. It is questionable that the sort of unity achieved in science is even desirable in philosophy.

[25] For Husserl, truth is, so to speak, a Platonic Idea, in relation to which any particular truth is but a participation.

nor is this any longer everyone in the finite sense the term has in prescientific life.[26]

Having thus characterized the ideality peculiar to science, with the ideal infinities variously implied in the very sense of science, we are faced, as we survey the historical situation, with a contrast that we express in the following proposition: no other cultural form in the pre-philosophical historical horizon is a culture of ideas in the above-mentioned sense; none knows any infinite tasks—none knows of such universes of idealities that as wholes and in all their details, as also in their methods of production, bear within themselves an essential infinity.

Extra-scientific culture, not yet touched by science, is a task accomplished by man in finitude. The openly endless horizon around him is not made available to him. His aims and activities, his commerce and his travel, his personal, social, national, mythical motivation—all this moves about in an environing world whose finite dimensions can be viewed. Here there are no infinite tasks, no ideal attainments whose very infinity is man's field of endeavor—a field of endeavor such that those who work in it are conscious that it has the mode of being proper to such an infinite sphere of tasks.

With the appearance of Greek philosophy, however, and with its first definitive formulation in a consistent idealizing of the new sense of infinity, there occurs, from this point of view, a progressive transformation that ultimately draws into its orbit all ideas proper to finitude and with them the entire spiritual culture of mankind. For us Europeans there are, consequently, even outside the philosophico-scientific sphere, any number of infinite ideas (if we may use the expression), but the analogous character of infinity that they have (infinite tasks, goals, verifications, truths,

<hr/>

[26] If "everyone" simply includes the sum total of all existing subjects, it does not have the universal significance that Husserl demands. In the sense in which he understands it, "universal" is inseparable from "essential." One is reminded of the critics who accuse Husserl of being "scholastic." Cf. p. 82 supra.

"true values," "genuine goods," "absolutely" valid norms) is due primarily to the transformation of man through philosophy and its idealities. Scientific culture in accord with ideas of infinity means, then, a revolutionizing of all culture, a revolution that affects man's whole manner of being as a creator of culture. It means also a revolutionizing of historicity, which is now the history of finite humanity's disappearance, to the extent that it grows into a humanity with infinite tasks.

Here we meet the obvious objection that philosophy, the science of the Greeks, is not, after all, distinctive of them, something which with them first came into the world. They themselves tell of the wise Egyptians, Babylonians, etc.; and they did in fact learn much from these latter. Today we possess all sorts of studies on Indian, Chinese, and other philosophies, studies that place these philosophies on the same level with Greek philosophy, considering them merely as different historical formulations of one and the same cultural idea. Of course, there is not lacking something in common. Still, one must not allow intentional depths to be covered over by what is merely morphologically common and be blind to the most essential differences of principle.

Before anything else, the attitude of these two kinds of "philosophers," the overall orientation of their interests, is thoroughly different. Here and there one may observe a world-embracing interest that on both sides (including, therefore, the Indian, Chinese, and other like "philosophies") leads to universal cognition of the world, everywhere developing after the manner of a sort of practical vocational interest and for quite intelligible reasons leading to vocational groups, in which from generation to generation common results are transmitted and even developed. Only with the Greeks, however, do we find a universal ("cosmological") vital interest in the essentially new form of a purely "theoretical" attitude.[27] This is true, too, of the com-

[27] The attitude that pursues "knowledge for its own sake." It is pre-

munal form in which the interest works itself out, the corresponding, essentially new attitude of the philosophers and the scientists
(mathematicians, astronomers, etc.). These are the men who, not
isolated but with each other and for each other, i.e., bound together in a common interpersonal endeavor, strive for and carry
into effect *theoria* and only *theoria*. These are the ones whose
growth and constant improvement ultimately, as the circle of
cooperators extends and the generations of investigators succeed
each other, become a will oriented in the direction of an infinite
and completely universal task. The theoretical attitude has its historical origin in the Greeks.

Speaking generally, attitude bespeaks a habitually determined
manner of vital willing, wherein the will's directions or interests,
its aims and its cultural accomplishments, are preindicated and
thus the overall orientation determined. In this enduring orientation taken as a norm, the individual life is lived. The concrete
cultural contents change in a relatively enclosed historicity. In its
historical situation mankind (or the closed community, such as a
nation, a race, etc.) always lives within the framework of some
sort of attitude. Its life always has a normative orientation and
within this a steady historicity or development.

Thus if the theoretical attitude in its newness is referred back
to a previous, more primitive normative attitude, the theoretical
is characterized as a transformed attitude.[28] Looking at the historicity of human existence universally in all its communal forms
and in its historical stages, we find, then, that essentially a certain
style of human existence (taken in formal universality) points to
a primary historicity, within which the actual normative style of
culture-creating existence at any time, no matter what its rise or
fall or stagnation, remains formally the same. In this regard we
are speaking of the natural, the native attitude, of originally

cisely in this that the "infinity" of the horizon consists: there is no assign-
able practical goal in which its interest can terminate.

[28] Here the play on words involved in *Einstellung* and *Umstellung* is impossible to render in English.

natural life, of the first primitively natural form of cultures—be they higher or lower, uninhibitedly developing or stagnating. All other attitudes, then, refer back to these natural ones as transformations of them.[29] To put it more concretely, in an attitude natural to one of the actual human groups in history there must arise at a point in time motives that for the first time impel individual men and groups having this attitude to transform it.

How are we, then, to characterize the essentially primitive attitude, the fundamental historical mode of human existence?[30] The answer: on the basis of generation men naturally live in communities—in a family, a race, a nation—and these communities are in themselves more or less abundantly subdivided into particular social units. Now, life on the level of nature is characterized as a naïvely direct living immersed in the world, in the world that in a certain sense is constantly there consciously as a universal horizon but is not, merely by that fact, thematic. Thematic is that toward which man's attention is turned. Being genuinely alive is always having one's attention turned to this or that, turned to something as to an end or a means, as relevant or irrelevant, interesting or indifferent, private or public, to something that is in daily demand or to something that is startlingly new. All this belongs to the world horizon, but there is need of special motives if the one who is caught up in such a life in the world is to transform himself and is to come to the point where he some-

[29] In Husserl's view, the beginning of a philosophical (or scientific) focusing of attention on the environing world—as opposed to a naïve, mythical, or poetic attitude—represents the most important revolution in the history of human thought. At the same time, he sees this revolution as continuous with previous attitudes, since it is a transformation of them—not an elimination—something is common to the old and the new.

[30] That man's *Einstellung* in regard to the world about him should, for Husserl, be the mode of human existence seems to imply some affinity between this position and that which Heidegger expresses by *In-der-Welt-sein*. Whether Husserl was influenced by his own student in this cannot be determined (cf. Spiegelberg, *The Phenomenological Movement,* I, p. 300). It may or may not be significant that this theme appears in Husserl's writings only after the publication of Heidegger's *Sein und Zeit* (1927; tr. *Being and Time,* New York: Harper & Row, 1962).

how makes this world itself his theme, where he conceives an enduring interest in it.

But here more detailed explanations are needed. Individual human beings who change their attitudes as human beings belonging to their own general vital community (their nation), have their particular natural interests (each his own). These they can by no change in attitude simply lose; that would mean for each ceasing to be the individual he is, the one he has been since birth. No matter what the circumstances, then, the transformed attitude can only be a temporary one. It can take on a lasting character that will endure as a habit throughout an entire life only in the form of an unconditional determination of will to take up again the selfsame attitudes in a series of periods that are temporary but intimately bound together. It will mean that by virtue of a continuity that bridges intentionally the discreteness involved, men will hold on to the new type of interests as worth being realized and will embody them in corresponding cultural forms.[31]

We are familiar with this sort of thing in the occupations that make their appearance even in a naturally primitive form of cultural life, where there are temporary periods devoted to the occupation, periods that interrupt the rest of life with its concrete temporality (e.g., the working hours of a functionary, etc.).

Now, there are two possibilities. On the one hand, the interests of the new attitude will be made subservient to the natural interests of life, or what is essentially the same, to natural practicality. In this case the new attitude is itself a practical one. This, then, can have a sense similar to the practical attitude of the politician, who as a state functionary is attentive to the common good and whose attitude, therefore, is to serve the practical interests of all (and incidentally his own). This sort of thing ad-

[31] Neither philosophy nor science nor, for that matter, any professional interest can become the exclusive interest in any man's life. But it is true that one is designated philosopher, scientist, etc., by the predominant interest which has an intentional continuity throughout all the occupations of his daily life.

mittedly still belongs to the domain of the natural attitude, which is, of course, different for different types of community members and is in fact one thing for the leaders of the community and another for the "citizens"—both obviously understood in the broadest sense. In any event, the analogy makes it clear that the universality of a practical attitude, in this case one that embraces a whole world, need in no way signify being interested in and occupied with all the details and particularities of that world—it would obviously be unthinkable.

In contrast to the higher-level practical attitude there exists, however, still another essential possibility of a change in the universal natural attitude (with which we shall soon become acquainted in its type, the mythical-religious attitude), which is to say, the theoretical attitude—a name being given to it, of course, only provisionally, because in this attitude philosophical *theoria* must undergo a development and so become its proper aim or field of interest. The theoretical attitude, even though it too is a professional attitude, is thoroughly unpractical. Thus it is based on a deliberate *epochē* from all practical interests,[32] and consequently even those of a higher level, that serve natural needs within the framework of a life's occupation governed by such practical interests.

Still, it must at the same time be said that there is no question here of a definitive "cutting off" of the theoretical life from the practical. We are not saying that the concrete life of the theoretical thinker falls into two disconnected vital continuities partitioned off from each other, which would mean, socially speaking, that two spiritually unconnected spheres would come into existence. For there is still a third form of universal attitude possible (in contrast both to the mythical-religious, which is based on the

---

[32] In a somewhat different context the meaning of *epochē* here parallels its technical meaning as employed, for example, in *Ideen I*. It is neither an elimination of nor a prescinding from other interests. Rather, it simply "puts them in brackets," thus retaining them, but allowing them in no way to influence theoretical considerations.

natural, and to the theoretical attitudes). It is the synthesis of opposing interests that occurs in the transition from the theoretical to the practical attitude. In this way *theoria* (the universal science), whose growth has manifested a tight unity through an *epochē* from all practical considerations, is called upon (and even proves in a theoretical insight[33] that it is called upon) to serve humanity in a new way, first of all in its concrete existence as it continues to live naturally. This takes place in the form of a new kind of practical outlook, a universal critique of all life and of its goals, of all the forms and systems of culture that have already grown up in the life of mankind. This brings with it a critique of mankind itself and of those values that explicitly or implicitly guide it. Carrying it to a further consequence, it is a practical outlook whose aim is to elevate mankind through universal scientific reason in accord with norms of truth in every form, and thus to transform it into a radically new humanity made capable of an absolute responsibility to itself on the basis of absolute theoretical insights.[34] Still, prior to this synthesis of theoretical universality and a practical outlook with universal interests, there is obviously another synthesis of theory and practice—the utilization of the limited results of theory, of those special sciences that are limited to the practical aspects of natural life, having relinquished by their very specialization the universality of theoretical interest. Here the primitively natural attitude and the theoretical are joined together in an orientation toward finite goals.

For a profounder understanding of Greco-European science (universally speaking, this means philosophy) in its fundamental difference from the equally notable oriental "philosophies," it is now necessary to consider in more detail the practically universal

[33] I.e., in a phenomenological essential intuition.

[34] Since Husserl's philosophical life was devoted almost exclusively to the programmatic aspects of phenomenology—getting it "off the ground," so to speak—he found little time himself for the sort of thing he describes here. But many of his students did. Much of the contemporary interest in Husserl, manifested in a wide variety of areas, is due to a desire to learn how to do what Husserl suggests.

attitude, and to explain it as mythical-religious, an attitude that, prior to European science, brings those other philosophies into being. It is a well-known fact, to say nothing of an essentially obvious necessity, that mythical-religious motives and a mythical-religious practice together belong to a humanity living naturally —before Greek philosophy, and with it a scientific world view, entered on the scene and matured. A mythical-religious attitude is one that takes as its theme the world as a totality—a practical theme. The world in this case is, of course, one that has a concrete, traditional significance for the men in question (let us say, a nation) and is thus mythically apperceived. This sort of mythical-natural attitude embraces from the very first not only men and animals and other infrahuman and infra-animal beings (*Wesen*) but also the suprahuman. The view that embraces them as a totality is a practical one; not, however, as though man, whose natural life, after all, is such that he is actually interested only in certain realities, could ever have come to the point where everything together would suddenly and in equal degree take on practical relevance. Rather, to the extent that the whole world is looked upon as dominated by mythical powers and to the extent that human destiny depends immediately or mediately on the way these powers rule in the world, a universally mythical world view may have its source in practicality and is, then, itself a world view whose interests are practical. It is understandable that priests belonging to a priesthood in charge of both mythical-religious interests and of the traditions belonging to them should have motives for such a mythical-religious attitude. With this priesthood there arises and spreads the linguistically solidified "knowledge" of these mythical powers (in the broadest sense thought of as personal). This knowledge quasi-automatically takes on the form of a mystical speculation which, by setting itself up as a naïvely convincing interpretation, transforms the mythos itself. At the same time, obviously, attention is constantly directed also to the ordinary world ruled by these mythical powers and to the human and infrahuman beings belonging to it (these, incidentally, unsettled in their own essential being, are also open to the influence of mythical factors). This attention looks to the ways in which the powers control the events of this world, the manner in which they themselves must be subject to a unified supreme order of power, the manner in which they with regard to individual functions and functioners intervene by initiating and carrying out, by handing down decrees of fate. All this speculative knowledge, however, has as its purpose to serve man toward his human aims, to enable him to live the happiest possible life on earth, to protect that life from sickness, from misfortune, need, and death. It is understandable that in this mythico-practical approach to knowing the world there can arise not a little knowledge of the actual world, of the world known in a sort of scientific experience, a knowledge subsequently to be subjected to a scientific evaluation. Still, this sort of knowledge is and remains mythico-practical in its logical connections, and it is a mistake for someone brought up in the scientific modes of thought initiated in Greece and progressively developed in modern times to speak of Indian and Chinese philosophy (astronomy, mathematics) and thus to interpret India, Babylonia, and China in a European way.[35]

There is a sharp cleavage, then, between the universal but mythico-practical attitude and the "theoretical," which by every previous standard is unpractical, the attitude of *thaumazein* [Gr. = to wonder], to which the great men of Greek philosophy's first culminating period, Plato and Aristotle, trace the origin of philosophy. Men are gripped by a passion for observing and knowing the world, a passion that turns from all practical interests and in the closed circle of its own knowing activities, in the time

[35] Aside from the fact that he knows little or nothing of Eastern thought, Husserl here repeats the arbitrariness of "Philosophy as Rigorous Science," where he simply decides what philosophy is (in an essential intuition, of course) and refuses to dignify with that name whatever does not measure up.

devoted to this sort of investigation, accomplishes and wants to accomplish only pure *theoria*.[36] In other words, man becomes the disinterested spectator, overseer of the world, he becomes a philosopher. More than that, from this point forward his life gains a sensitivity for motives which are possible only to this attitude, for novel goals and methods of thought, in the framework of which philosophy finally comes into being and man becomes philosopher.

Like everything that occurs in history, of course, the introduction of the theoretical attitude has its factual motivation in the concrete circumstances of historical events. Therefore it is worthwhile to explain in this connection how, considering the manner of life and the horizon of Greek man in the seventh century B.C., in his intercourse with the great and already highly cultivated nations surrounding him, that *thaumazein* could introduce itself and at first become established in individuals. Regarding this we shall not enter into greater detail; it is more important for us to understand the path of motivation, with its sense-giving and sense-creating, which leads from mere conversion (or from mere *thaumazein*) to *theoria*—a historical fact, that nevertheless must have in it something essential. It is important to explain the change from original *theoria*, from the completely "disinterested" (consequent upon the *epoché* from all practical interests) world view (knowledge of the world based only on universal contemplation) to the *theoria* proper to science—both stages exemplifying the contrast between *doxa* [Gr. = opinion] and *epistēmē* [Gr. = knowledge]. The theoretical interest that comes on the scene as that *thaumazein,* is clearly a modification of curiosity that has its original place in natural life as an interruption in the course of "earnest living," as a working out of originally effected vital interests, or as a playful looking about when the specific needs of

[36] Despite Husserl's insistence here and elsewhere that this is Plato's attitude, there is little justification for his failing to recognize that Plato's purpose, even in his most "theoretical" investigations, is eminently practical. In a somewhat different meaning, the same can be said for Aristotle.

actual life have been satisfied or working hours are past. Curiosity, too (not in the sense of an habitual "vice"), is a modification, an interest raised above merely vital interests and prescinding from them.

With an attitude such as this, man observes first of all the variety of nations, his own and others, each with its own environing world, which with its traditions, its gods and demigods, with its mythical powers, constitutes for each nation the self-evident, real world. In the face of this extraordinary contrast there arises the distinction between the represented and the real world, and a new question is raised concerning the truth—not everyday truth bound as it is to tradition but a truth that for all those who are not blinded by attachment to tradition is identical and universally valid, a truth in itself. Thus it is proper to the theoretical attitude of the philosopher that he is more and more predetermined to devote his whole future life, in the sense of a universal life, to the task of *theoria*, to build theoretical knowledge upon theoretical knowledge *in infinitum*.[37]

In isolated personalities, like Thales, et al., there thus grows up a new humanity—men whose profession it is to create a philosophical life, philosophy as a novel form of culture. Understandably there grows up at the same time a correspondingly novel form of community living. These ideal forms are, as others understand them and make them their own, simply taken up and made part of life. In like manner they lead to cooperative endeavor and to mutual help through criticism. Even the outsiders, the non-philosophers, have their attention drawn to the unusual activity that is going on. As they come to understand, they either become philosophers themselves, or if they are too much taken up with

[37] To characterize "essentially" the "path of motivation" from mere curiosity about the world to a universal philosophical science of the world is, of course, extremely aprioristic. We are simply told how it must have been (the danger of all "essential" intuition). It remains true, however, that there is no better introduction to philosophy than a history of the pre-Socratic attempts to know the secrets of the world—without doing anything about it.

their own work, they become pupils. Thus philosophy spreads in a twofold manner, as a widening community of professional philosophers and as a common educational movement growing along with the former. Here also, however, lies the origin of the subsequent, so unfortunate internal split in the unity of the people into educated and uneducated. Still, it is clear that this tendency to spread is not confined to the limits of the originating nation. Unlike all other cultural products, this is not a movement of interests bound to the soil of national traditions. Even foreigners learn in their turn to understand and in general to share in the gigantic cultural change which streams forth from philosophy. Now precisely this must be further characterized.

As philosophy spreads in the form of research and training, it produces a twofold effect. On the one hand, most essential to the theoretical attitude of philosophical man is the characteristic universality of the critical standpoint, which its determination not to accept without question any pregiven opinion, any tradition, and thus to seek out, with regard to the entire universe handed down in tradition, the true in itself—which is ideal. Yet this is not merely a new way of looking at knowledge. By virtue of the demand to subject the whole of experience to ideal norms, i.e., those of unconditional truth, there results at the same time an all-embracing change in the practical order of human existence and thus of cultural life in its entirety. The practical must no longer take its norms from naïve everyday experience and from tradition but from the objective truth. In this way ideal truth becomes an absolute value that in the movement of education and in its constant application in the training of children carries with it a universal revision of practice. If we consider somewhat more in detail the manner of this transformation, we shall immediately understand the inevitable: if the general idea of truth in itself becomes the universal norm of all the relative truths that play a role in human life—actual and conjectural situation truths—then this fact affects all traditional norms, those of right, of beauty, of purpose, of dominant values in persons, values having a personal character, etc.

Thus there grows up a special type of man and a special vocation in life correlative to the attainment of a new culture. Philosophical knowledge of the world produces not only these special types of result but also a human conduct that immediately influences the rest of practical living with all its demands and its aims, aims of the historical tradition according to which one is educated, thus giving these aims their own validity. A new and intimate community, we might say a community of ideal interests, is cultivated among men—men who live for philosophy, united in their dedication to ideas, which ideas are not only of use to all but are identically the property of all. Inevitably there develops a particular kind of cooperation whereby men work with each other and for each other, helping each other by mutual criticism, with the result that the pure and unconditioned validity of truth grows as a common possession. In addition there is the necessary tendency toward the promotion of interest, because others understand what is herein desired and accomplished; and this is a tendency to include more and more as yet unphilosophical persons in the community of those who philosophize. This occurs first of all among members of the same nation. Nor can this expansion be confined to professional scientific research; rather its success goes far beyond the professional circle, becoming an educational movement.

Now, if this educational movement spreads to ever wider circles of the people, and naturally to the superior, dominant types, to those who are less involved in the cares of life, the results are of what sort? Obviously it does not simply bring about a homogeneous change in the normal, on the whole satisfactory national life; rather in all probability it leads to great cleavages, wherein the national life and the entire national culture go into an upheaval. The conservatives, content with tradition, and the philosophical circle will struggle against each other, and without doubt the battle will carry over into the sphere of political power. At the very beginning of philosophy, persecution sets in. The men dedicated to those ideas are outlawed. And yet ideas are stronger than any forces rooted in experience.[38]

A further point to be taken into consideration here is that philosophy, having grown out of a critical attitude to each and every traditional predisposition, is limited in its spread by no national boundaries. All that must be present is the capacity for a universal critical attitude, which too, of course, presupposes a certain level of prescientific culture. Thus can the upheaval in the national culture propagate itself, first of all because the progressing universal science becomes a common possession of nations that were at first strangers to each other, and then because a unified community, both scientific and educational, extends to the majority of nations.

Still another important point must be adduced; it concerns philosophy's position in regard to traditions. There are in fact two possibilities to observe here. Either the traditionally accepted is completely rejected, or its content is taken over philosophically, and thereby it too is reformed in the spirit of philosophical ideality. An outstanding case in point is that of religion—from which I should like to exclude the "polytheistic religions." Gods in the plural, mythical powers of every kind, are objects belonging to the environing world, on the same level of reality as animal or man. In the concept of God, the singular is essential.[39] Looking at this from the side of man, moreover, it is proper that the reality of God, both as being and as value, should be experienced as binding man interiorly. There results, then, an understandable blending of this absoluteness with that of philosophical ideality. In the overall process of idealization that philosophy undertakes,

---

[38] One is reminded of the contrast made by Aristotle between "men of experience" and "men of science" (*Metaph.* A 981a). In a more striking way Socrates met this in his conflict with the "practical" politicians of his day.

[39] Again, a phenomenological essential intuition, that says nothing regarding the "existence" of God.

God is, so to speak, logicized and becomes even the bearer of the absolute logos. I should like, moreover, to see a logic in the very fact that theologically religion invokes faith itself as evidence and thus as a proper and most profound mode of grounding true being.[40] National gods, however, are simply there as real facts of the environing world, without anyone confronting philosophy with questions stemming from a critique of cognition, with questions of evidence.

Substantially, though in a somewhat sketchy fashion, we have now described the historical movement that makes understandable how, beginning with a few Greek exceptions, a transformation of human existence and of man's entire cultural life could be set in motion, beginning in Greece and its nearest neighbors. Moreover, now it is also discernible how, following upon this, a supernationality of a completely new kind could arise. I am referring, of course, to the spiritual form of Europe. It is now no longer a number of different nations bordering on each other, influencing each other only by commercial competition and war. Rather a new spirit stemming from philosophy and the sciences based on it, a spirit of free criticism providing norms for infinite tasks, dominates man, creating new, infinite ideals. These are ideals for individual men of each nation and for the nations themselves. Ultimately, however, the expanding synthesis of nations too has its infinite ideals, wherein each of these nations, by the very fact that it strives to accomplish its own ideal task in the spirit of infinity,[41] contributes its best to the community of nations. In this give and take the supernational totality with its

[40] Nowhere, it seems, has Husserl developed this profound insight wherein he sees faith as a special kind of evidence, permitting theology, too, to be a science. In different ways this is developed by Scheler in his philosophy of religion, by Van der Leeuw and Hering in their phenomenology of religion, and by Otto in his investigations of "the sacred."

[41] *Im Geiste der Unendlichkeit:* The expression, scarcely translatable into English, bespeaks a spirit that refuses to stop short of infinity in its pursuit of truth. In Husserl himself, one hesitates to see it as a plea for a metaphysics, but in a Scheler, a Heidegger, a Conrad-Martius, it becomes just that; cf. Peter Wust, *Die Auferstehung der Metaphysik* (Leipzig, 1920).

graded structure of societies grows apace, filled with the spirit of one all-inclusive task, infinite in the variety of its branches yet unique in its infinity. In this total society with its ideal orientation, philosophy itself retains the role of guide, which is its special infinite task.[42] Philosophy has the role of a free and universal theoretical disposition that embraces at once all ideals and the one overall ideal—in short, the universe of all norms. Philosophy has constantly to exercise through European man its role of leadership for the whole of mankind.

II

It is now time that there be voiced misunderstandings and doubts that are certainly very importunate and which, it seems to me, derive their suggestive force from the language of popular prejudice.

Is not what is here being advocated something rather out of place in our times—saving the honor of rationalism, of enlightenment, of an intellectualism that, lost in theory, is isolated from the world, with the necessarily bad result that the quest for learning becomes empty, becomes intellectual snobbishness? Does it not mean falling back into the fatal error of thinking that science makes men wise, that science is called upon to create a genuine humanity, superior to destiny and finding satisfaction in itself? Who is going to take such thoughts seriously today?

This objection certainly is relatively justified in regard to the state of development in Europe from the seventeenth up to the end of the nineteenth century. But it does not touch the precise sense of what I am saying. I should like to think that I, seemingly a reactionary, am far more revolutionary than those who today in word strike so radical a pose.

[42] In *Formale und transzendentale Logik* Husserl calls philosophy the "science of all sciences," which is to say, it provides the norms whereby any science can be worthy of the name.

I, too, am quite sure that the European crisis has its roots in a mistaken rationalism.[43] That, however, must not be interpreted as meaning that rationality as such is an evil or that in the totality of human existence it is of minor importance. The rationality of which alone we are speaking is rationality in that noble and genuine sense, the original Greek sense, that became an ideal in the classical period of Greek philosophy—though of course it still needed considerable clarification through self-examination. It is its vocation, however, to serve as a guide to mature development. On the other hand, we readily grant (and in this regard German idealism has spoken long before us) that the form of development given to *ratio* in the rationalism of the Enlightenment was an aberration, but nevertheless an understandable aberration.

Reason is a broad title. According to the good old definition, man is the rational living being, a sense in which even the Papuan is man and not beast. He has his aims, and he acts with reflection, considering practical possibilities. As products and methods grow, they enter into a tradition that is ever intelligible in its rationality. Still, just as man (and even the Papuan) represents a new level of animality—in comparison with the beast—so with regard to humanity and its reason does philosophical reason represent a new level. The level of human existence with its ideal norms for infinite tasks, the level of existence *sub specie aeternitatis,* is, however, possible only in the form of absolute universality, precisely that which is a priori included in the idea of philosophy. It is true that universal philosophy, along with all the particular sciences, constitutes only a partial manifestation of European culture. Contained, however, in the sense of my entire presentation is the claim that this part is, so to speak, the

[43] Husserl's constant plea has been for a return to the "rationalism" of Socrates and Plato (cf. "Philosophy as Rigorous Science," p. 76 supra), not to the rationalism of seventeenth- and eighteenth-century Europe. His own inspiration, however, is traceable far more to Descartes, Hume, and Kant than to Socrates and Plato.

functioning brain upon whose normal functioning the genuine, healthy spirit of Europe depends. The humanity of higher man, of reason, demands, therefore, a genuine philosophy.

But at this very point there lurks a danger. "Philosophy"—in that we must certainly distinguish philosophy as a historical fact belonging to this or that time from philosophy as idea, idea of an infinite task.[44] The philosophy that at any particular time is historically actual is the more or less successful attempt to realize the guiding idea of the infinity, and thereby the totality, of truths. Practical ideals, viewed as external poles from the line of which one cannot stray during the whole of life without regret, without being untrue to oneself and thus unhappy, are in this view by no means yet clear and determined; they are anticipated in an equivocal generality. Determination comes only with concrete pursuit and with at least relatively successful action. Here the constant danger is that of falling into one-sidedness and premature satisfaction, which are punished in subsequent contradictions. Thence the contrast between the grand claims of philosophical systems, that are all the while incompatible with each other. Added to this are the necessity and yet the danger of specialization.

In this way, of course, one-sided rationality can become an evil. It can also be said that it belongs to the very essence of reason that philosophers can at first understand and accomplish their infinite task only on the basis of an absolutely necessary one-sidedness.[45] In itself there is no absurdity here, no error. Rather, as has been remarked, the direct and necessary path for reason allows it initially to grasp only one aspect of the task, at first without recognizing that a thorough knowledge of the entire infinite

[44] The *philosophia perennis* that, like a Platonic Idea, is eternally changeless amid the varying participations that we can call "philosophies."

[45] One is reminded of Husserl's insistence in the *Cartesian Meditations* (pp. 121–35) that a successful phenomenological philosophy must begin as solipsism, moving on to an intersubjectivity only after it has been established on a solipsistic basis. In this Husserl once more derives his inspiration from seventeenth- and eighteenth-century rationalism.

task, the totality of being, involves still other aspects. When inadequacy reveals itself in obscurities and contradiction, then this becomes a motive to engage in a universal reflection. Thus the philosopher must always have as his purpose to master the true and full sense of philosophy, the totality of its infinite horizons. No one line of knowledge, no individual truth must be absolutized. Only in such a supreme consciousness of self, which itself becomes a branch of the infinite task, can philosophy fulfill its function of putting itself, and therewith a genuine humanity, on the right track. To know that this is the case, however, also involves once more entering the field of knowledge proper to philosophy on the highest level of reflection upon itself. Only on the basis of this constant reflectiveness is a philosophy a universal knowledge.

I have said that the course of philosophy goes through a period of naïveté. This, then, is the place for a critique of the so renowned irrationalism, or it is the place to uncover the naïveté of that rationalism that passes as genuine philosophical rationality, and that admittedly is characteristic of philosophy in the whole modern period since the Renaissance, looking upon itself as the real and hence universal rationalism. Now, as they begin, all the sciences, even those whose beginnings go back to ancient times, are unavoidably caught up in this naïveté. To put it more exactly, the most general title for this naïveté is objectivism, which is given a structure in the various types of naturalism, wherein the spirit is naturalized.[46] Old and new philosophies were and remain naïvely objectivistic. It is only right, however, to add that German idealism, beginning with Kant, was passionately concerned with overcoming the naïveté that had already become very sensitive. Still, it was incapable of really attaining to the level of superior reflectiveness that is decisive for the new image of philosophy and of European man.

What I have just said I can make intelligible only by a few

[46] The theme is familiar from the whole first part of "Philosophy as Rigorous Science."

sketchy indications. Natural man (let us assume, in the pre-philosophical period) is oriented toward the world in all his concerns and activities. The area in which he lives and works is the environing world which in its spatiotemporal dimensions surrounds him and of which he considers himself a part. This continues to be true in the theoretical attitude, which at first can be nothing but that of the disinterested spectator of a world that is demythologized before his eyes. Philosophy sees in the world the universe of what is, and world becomes objective world over against representations of the world—which latter change subjectively, whether on a national or an individual scale—and thus truth becomes objective truth. Thus philosophy begins as cosmology. At first, as is self-evident, it is oriented in its theoretical interest to corporeal nature, since in fact all spatiotemporal data do have, at least basically, the form of corporeality. Men and beasts are not merely bodies, but to the view oriented to the environing world they appear as some sort of corporeal being and thus as realities included in the universal spatiotemporality. In this way all psychic events, those of this or that ego, such as experience, thinking, willing, have a certain objectivity. Community life, that of families, of peoples, and the like, seems then to resolve itself into the life of particular individuals, who are psychophysical objects. In the light of psychophysical causality there is no purely spiritual continuity in spiritual grouping; physical nature envelops everything.

The historical process of development is definitively marked out through this focus on the environing world. Even the hastiest glance at the corporeality present in the environing world shows that nature is a homogeneous, unified totality, a world for itself, so to speak, surrounded by a homogeneous spatiotemporality and divided into individual things, all similar in being *res extensae* and each determining the other causally. Very quickly comes a first and greatest step in the process of discovery: overcoming the finitude of nature that has been thought of as objective-in-itself, finitude in spite of the open infinity of it. Infinity is discovered, and first of all in form of idealized quantities, masses, numbers, figures, straight lines, poles, surfaces, etc. Nature, space, and time become capable of stretching ideally into infinity and also of being infinitely divided ideally. From the art of surveying develops geometry; from counting, arithmetic; from everyday mechanics, mathematical mechanics; etc. Now, without anyone forming a hypothesis in this regard, the world of perceived nature is changed into a mathematical world, the world of mathematical natural sciences. As ancient times moved forward, with the mathematics proper to that stage, the first discovery of infinite ideals and of infinite tasks was accomplished simultaneously. That discovery becomes for all subsequent times the guiding star of the sciences.

How, then, did the intoxicating success of this discovery of physical infinity affect the scientific mastery of the realm of spirit? In the focus on the environing world, a constantly objective attitude, everything spiritual appeared to be based on physical corporeality. Thus an application of the mode of thought proper to natural science was obvious. For this reason we already find in the early stages Democritean materialism and determinism.[47] However, the greatest minds recoiled from this and also from any newer style of psychophysics. Since Socrates, man is made thematic precisely as human, man with his spiritual life in society. Man retains an orientation to the objective world, but with the advent of Plato and Aristotle this world becomes the great theme of investigations. At this point a remarkable cleavage makes itself felt: the human belongs to the universe of objective facts, but as persons, as egos, men have goals, aims. They have norms for tradition, truth norms—eternal norms. Though the development proceeded haltingly in ancient times, still it was not lost. Let us make the leap to so-called "modern" times. With glowing enthusiasm the infinite task of a mathematical knowledge of nature

[47] Democritus, who flourished two hundred years after Thales, was a contemporary of Socrates. Thus he belongs more properly to the "golden age" of Greek philosophy than to the "early stages."

and in general of a world knowledge is undertaken. The extraordinary successes of natural knowledge are now to be extended to knowledge of the spirit. Reason had proved its power in nature. "As the sun is one all-illuminating and warming sun, so too is reason one" (Descartes).[48] The method of natural science must also embrace the mysteries of spirit. The spirit is real[49] and objectively in the world, founded as such in corporeality. With this the interpretation of the world immediately takes on a predominantly dualistic, i.e., psychophysical, form. The same causality—only split in two—embraces the one world; the sense of rational explanation is everywhere the same, but in such a way that all explanation of spirit, in the only way in which it can be universal, involves the physical. There can be no pure, self-contained search for an explanation of the spiritual, no purely inner-oriented psychology or theory of spirit beginning with the ego in psychical self-experience and extending to the other psyche.[50] The way that must be traveled is the external one, the path of physics and chemistry. All the fond talk of common spirit, of the common will of a people, of nations' ideal political goals, and the like, are romanticism and mythology, derived from an analogous application of concepts that have a proper sense only in the individual personal sphere. Spiritual being is fragmentary. To the question regarding the source of all these difficulties the following answer is to be given: this objectivism or this psychophysical interpretation of the world, despite its seeming self-evidence, is a naïve one-sidedness that never was understood to be such. To speak of the spirit as reality (*Realität*), presumably a real (*realen*) annex

[48] *Regulae ad directionem ingenii,* Rule 1. The quotation is verbally inaccurate (probably from memory), but the sense is the same.

[49] For Husserl, *real* has a distinctively different meaning from *reell*. The former is applied only to the material world of facts; the latter belongs to the ideal world of intentionality. Cf. *Ideen I,* pp. 218–20.

[50] Cf. Husserl's *Encyclopaedia Britannica* article, "Phenomenology," where he develops the notion of a "pure" psychology independent of psychophysical considerations.

to bodies and having its supposedly spatiotemporal being within nature, is an absurdity.

At this point, however, it is important for our problem of the crisis to show how it is that the "modern age," that has for centuries been so proud of its successes in theory and practice, has itself finally fallen into a growing dissatisfaction and must even look upon its own situation as distressful. Want has invaded all the sciences, most recently as a want of method. Moreover, the want that grips us Europeans, even though it is not understood, involves very many persons.[51]

There are all sorts of problems that stem from naïveté, according to which objectivistic science holds what it calls the objective world to be the totality of what is, without paying any attention to the fact that no objective science can do justice to the subjectivity that achieves science. One who has been trained in the natural sciences finds it self-evident that whatever is merely subjective must be eliminated and that the method of natural science, formulated according to a subjective mode of representation, is objectively determined. In the same manner he seeks what is objectively true for the psychic too. By the same token, it is taken for granted that the subjective, eliminated by the physical scientist, is, precisely as psychic, to be investigated in psychology and of course in psychophysical psychology. The investigator of nature, however, does not make it clear to himself that the constant foundation of his admittedly subjective thinking activity is the environing world of life. This latter is constantly presupposed as the basic working area, in which alone his questions and his methodology make sense. Where, at the present time, is that powerful bit of method that leads from the intuitive environing world to the idealizing of mathematics and its interpreta-

51 The play upon the word *Not* is impossible to render here. The situation of modern science is described as a *Notlage,* which can be translated as a "situation of distress." By itself *Not* can mean "need," "want," "suffering," etc. The word is used three times, and there is a shade of difference in meaning each time it is used.

tion as objective being, subjected to criticism and clarification? Einstein's revolutionary changes concern the formulas wherein idealized and naïvely objectivized nature (*physis*) is treated. But regarding the question of how formulas or mathematical objectification in general are given a sense based on life and the intuitive environing world, of this we hear nothing. Thus Einstein does nothing to reformulate the space and time in which our actual life takes place.

Mathematical science of nature is a technical marvel for the purpose of accomplishing inductions whose fruitfulness, probability, exactitude, and calculability could previously not even be suspected. As an accomplishment it is a triumph of the human spirit. With regard to the rationality of its methods and theories, however, it is a thoroughly relative science. It presupposes as data principles that are themselves thoroughly lacking in actual rationality. In so far as the intuitive environing world, purely subjective as it is, is forgotten in the scientific thematic, the working subject is also forgotten, and the scientist is not studied.[52] (Thus from this point of view the rationality of the exact sciences is on a level with the rationality of the Egyptian pyramids.)

It is true, of course, that since Kant we have a special theory of knowledge, and on the other hand there is psychology, which with its claims to scientific exactitude wants to be the universal fundamental science of the spirit. Still, our hope for real rationality, i.e., for real insight,[53] is disappointed here as elsewhere. The psychologists simply fail to see that they too study neither themselves nor the scientists who are doing the investigating nor their own vital environing world. They do not see that from the very

[52] The work of Werner Heisenberg and Niels Bohr has shown how quantum mechanics and nuclear physics have high-lighted precisely the problem Husserl brings out here.

[53] It is axiomatic for Husserl that only insight can reveal "essences" and that only a knowledge of essences can be ultimately scientific. That this insight should be at once intuitive and constitutive is peculiar to the Husserlian theory of intentionality; cf. my *La phénoménologie de Husserl,* pp. 31–34.

beginning they necessarily presuppose themselves as a group of men belonging to their own environing world and historical period. By the same token, they do not see that in pursuing their aims they are seeking a truth in itself, universally valid for everyone. By its objectivism psychology simply cannot make a study of the soul in its properly essential sense, which is to say, the ego that acts and is acted upon. Though by determining the bodily function involved in an experience of evaluating or willing, it may objectify the experience and handle it inductively, can it do the same for purposes, values, norms? Can it study reason as some sort of "disposition"? Completely ignored is the fact that objectivism, as the genuine work of the investigator intent upon finding true norms, presupposes just such norms; that objectivism refuses to be inferred from facts, since in the process facts are already intended as truths and not as illusions. It is true, of course, that there exists a feeling for the difficulties present here, with the result that the dispute over psychologism is fanned into a flame. Nothing is accomplished, however, by rejecting a psychological grounding of norms, above all of norms for truth in itself. More and more perceptible becomes the overall need for a reform of modern psychology in its entirety. As yet, however, it is not understood that psychology through its objectivism has been found wanting; that it simply fails to get at the proper essence of spirit; that in isolating the soul and making it an object of thought, that in reinterpreting psychophysically being-in-community, it is being absurd. True, it has not labored in vain, and it has established many empirical rules, even practically worthwhile ones. Yet it is no more a real psychology than moral statistics with its no less worthwhile knowledge is a moral science.[54]

In our time we everywhere meet the burning need for an understanding of spirit, while the unclarity of the methodological and factual connection between the natural sciences and the

[54] Husserl's judgment of "psychologism" was no less severe at the end of his life than it was when he wrote "Philosophy as Rigorous Science."

sciences of the spirit has become almost unbearable. Dilthey, one of the greatest scientists of the spirit, has directed his whole vital energy to clarifying the connection between nature and spirit, to clarifying the role of psychophysical psychology, which he thinks is to be complemented by a new, descriptive and analytic psychology. Efforts by Windelband and Rickert have likewise, unfortunately, not brought the desired insight. Like everyone else, these men are still committed to objectivism. Worst of all are the new psychological reformers, who are of the opinion that the entire fault lies in the long-dominant atomistic prejudice, that a new era has been introduced with wholistic psychology (*Ganzheitspsychologie*) There can, however, never be any improvement so long as an objectivism based on a naturalistic focusing on the environing world is not seen in all its naïveté, until men recognize thoroughly the absurdity of the dualistic interpretation of the world, according to which nature and spirit are to be looked upon as realities (*Realitäten*) in the same sense. In all seriousness my opinion is this: there never has nor ever will be an objective science of spirit, an objective theory of the soul, objective in the sense that it permits the attribution of an existence under the forms of spatio-temporality to souls or to communities of persons.

The spirit and in fact only the spirit is a being in itself and for itself; it is autonomous and is capable of being handled in a genuinely rational, genuinely and thoroughly scientific way only in this autonomy.[55] In regard to nature and scientific truth con-

---

[55] "Dualism" and "monism" are terms whose meanings are not easily determined. As a convinced "idealist" Husserl considered himself a monist, and he criticized Kant strongly for remaining a dualist. Hegel, on the other hand, criticizes Fichte (whom Husserl resembles closely in this) for not having escaped dualism. One might well make a case for designating as monism a theory that accepts only one kind of reality, to which both matter and spirit (or the "factual" and the "ideal") belong. By this criterion Husserl's distinction would be "dualistic." Perhaps the best that can be said is that Husserl is, in intention at least, epistemologically a monist. Spirit alone is being in the full sense, because only of spirit can there be science in the full sense. One conclusion from all this, it would seem, is that the terminology involved bears revision.

cerning it, however, the natural sciences give merely the appearance of having brought nature to a point where for itself it is rationally known. For true nature in its proper scientific sense is a product of the spirit that investigates nature, and thus the science of nature presupposes the science of the spirit. The spirit is essentially qualified to exercise self-knowledge, and as scientific spirit to exercise scientific self-knowledge, and that over and over again. Only in the kind of pure knowledge proper to science of the spirit is the scientist unaffected by the objection that his accomplishment is self-concealing.[56] As a consequence, it is absurd for the sciences of the spirit to dispute with the sciences of nature for equal rights. To the extent that the former concede to the latter that their objectivity is an autonomy, they are themselves victims of objectivism. Moreover, in the way the sciences of the spirit are at present developed, with their manifold disciplines, they forfeit the ultimate, actual rationality which the spiritual *Weltanschauung* makes possible. Precisely this lack of genuine rationality on all sides is the source of what has become for man an unbearable unclarity regarding his own existence and his infinite tasks. These last are inseparably united in one task: only if the spirit returns to itself from its naïve exteriorization, clinging to itself and purely to itself, can it be adequate to itself.[57]

Now, how did the beginning of such a self-examination come about? A beginning was impossible so long as sensualism, or better, a psychology of data, a *tabula rasa* psychology, held the field. Only when Brentano promoted psychology to being a science of vital intentional experiences was an impulse given that could lead further—though Brentano himself had not yet over-

[56] If the proper function of true science is to know "essences," there seems little question that the sciences of nature neither perform nor pretend to perform this function. If, in addition, essences are, only insofar as they are "constituted" in consciousnes (ultimately spirit), then only a science of spirit can legitimately lay claim to the title.

[57] One is reminded of Hegel's dictum that when reason is conscious to itself of being all reality, it is spirit. The difference in the paths by which Hegel and Husserl arrive at this conclusion should be obvious.

come objectivism and psychological naturalism.[58] The development of a real method of grasping the fundamental essence of spirit in its intentionalities and consequently of instituting an analysis of spirit with a consistency reaching to the infinite, led to transcendental phenomenology. It was this that overcame naturalistic objectivism, and for that matter any form of objectivism, in the only possible way, by beginning one's philosophizing from one's own ego; and that purely as the author of all one accepts, becoming in this regard a purely theoretical spectator. This attitude brings about the successful institution of an absolutely autonomous science of spirit in the form of a consistent understanding of self and of the world as a spiritual accomplishment. Spirit is not looked upon here as part of nature or parallel to it; rather nature belongs to the sphere of spirit. Then, too, the ego is no longer an isolated thing alongside other such things in a pregiven world. The serious problem of personal egos external to or alongside of each other comes to an end in favor of an intimate relation of beings in each other and for each other.

Regarding this question of interpersonal relations, nothing can be said here; no one lecture could exhaust the topic. I do hope, however, to have shown that we are not renewing here the old rationalism, which was an absurd naturalism, utterly incapable of grasping the problems of spirit that concern us most. The *ratio* now in question is none other than spirit understanding itself in a really universal, really radical manner, in the form of a science whose scope is universal, wherein an entirely new scientific thinking is established in which every conceivable question, whether of being, of norm, or of so-called "existence,"[59] finds its place. It is my conviction that intentional phenomenology has for the first time made spirit as spirit the field of systematic, scien-

---

[58] For his part, Brentano complained that his theory of intentionality had been transformed by Husserl into an a priori idealism.

[59] *Existenz:* Husserl was never particularly sympathetic to "existentialism." To him it smacked too much of irrationalism. A rational science of philosophy could only be an essentialism. In such a science, existence could be significant only as "possible existence."

tific experience, thus effecting a total transformation of the task of knowledge. The universality of the absolute spirit embraces all being in an absolute historicity, into which nature fits as a product of spirit. It is intentional, which is to say transcendental, phenomenology that sheds light on the subject by virtue of its point of departure and its methods. Only when seen from the phenomenological point of view is naturalistic objectivism, along with the profoundest reasons for it, to be understood. Above all, phenomenology makes clear that, because of its naturalism, psychology simply could not come to terms with the activity and the properly radical problem of spirit's life.

III

Let us summarize the fundamental notions of what we have sketched here. The "crisis of European existence," which manifests itself in countless symptoms of a corrupted life, is no obscure fate, no impenetrable destiny. Instead, it becomes manifestly understandable against the background of the philosophically discoverable "teleology of European history." As a presupposition of this understanding, however, the phenomenon "Europe" is to be grasped in its essential core. To get the concept of what is contra-essential in the present "crisis," the concept "Europe" would have to be developed as the historical teleology of infinite goals of reason; it would have to be shown how the European "world" was born from ideas of reason, i.e., from the spirit of philosophy.[60] The "crisis" could then become clear as the "seeming collapse of rationalism." Still, as we said, the reason for the downfall of a rational culture does not lie in the essence of rationalism itself but only in its exteriorization, its absorption in "naturalism" and "objectivism."

[60] Though Husserl's "historical erudition" frequently leaves much to be desired, there is a profound insight here. It is the spirit of philosophy conceived in ancient Greece that throughout the centuries has guided the intellectual life of the West.

The crisis of European existence can end in only one of two ways: in the ruin of a Europe alienated from its rational sense of life, fallen into a barbarian hatred of spirit; or in the rebirth of Europe from the spirit of philosophy, through a heroism of reason that will definitively overcome naturalism. Europe's greatest danger is weariness. Let us as "good Europeans" do battle with this danger of dangers with the sort of courage that does not shirk even the endless battle. If we do, then from the annihilating conflagration of disbelief, from the fiery torrent of despair regarding the West's mission to humanity, from the ashes of the great weariness, the phoenix of a new inner life of the spirit will arise as the underpinning of a great and distant human future, for the spirit alone is immortal.

HARPER PAPERBACKS / PHILOSOPHY

W. ARTHUR LEWIS: Economic Survey, 1919-1939 TB/1446

W. ARTHUR LEWIS: The Principles of Economic Planning. *New Introduction by the Author°* TB/1436

ROBERT GREEN MC CLOSKEY: American Conservatism in the Age of Enterprise TB/1137

PAUL MANTOUX: The Industrial Revolution in the Eighteenth Century: *An Outline of the Beginnings of the Modern Factory System in England°* TB/1079

WILLIAM MILLER, Ed.: Men in Business: *Essays on the Historical Role of the Entrepreneur* TB/1081

GUNNAR MYRDAL: An International Economy. *New Introduction by the Author* TB/1445

RICHARD S. WECKSTEIN, Ed.: Expansion of World Trade and the Growth of National Economies ** TB/1373

Historiography and History of Ideas

HERSCHEL BAKER: The Image of Man: *A Study of the Idea of Human Dignity in Classical Antiquity, the Middle Ages, and the Renaissance* TB/1047

J. BRONOWSKI & BRUCE MAZLISH: The Western Intellectual Tradition: *From Leonardo to Hegel* TB/3001

EDMUND BURKE: On Revolution. Ed. by Robert A. Smith TB/1401

WILHELM DILTHEY: Pattern and Meaning in History: *Thoughts on History and Society.° Edited with an Intro. by H. P. Rickman* TB/1075

ALEXANDER GRAY: The Socialist Tradition: *Moses to Lenin °* TB/1375

J. H. HEXTER: More's Utopia: *The Biography of an Idea. Epilogue by the Author* TB/1195

H. STUART HUGHES: History as Art and as Science: *Twin Vistas on the Past* TB/1207

ARTHUR O. LOVEJOY: The Great Chain of Being: *A Study of the History of an Idea* TB/1009

JOSE ORTEGA Y GASSET: The Modern Theme. *Introduction by Jose Ferrater Mora* TB/1038

RICHARD H. POPKIN: The History of Scenticism from Erasmus to Descartes. *Revised Edition* TB/1391

G. J. RENIER: History: *Its Purpose and Method* TB/1209

MASSIMO SALVADORI, Ed.: Modern Socialism # HR/1374

BRUNO SNELL: The Discovery of the Mind: *The Greek Origins of European Thought* TB/1018

W. WARREN WAGER, ed.: European Intellectual History Since Darwin and Marx TB/1297

W. H. WALSH: Philosophy of History: In Introduction TB/1020

History: General

HANS KOHN: The Age of Nationalism: *The First Era of Global History* TB/1380

BERNARD LEWIS: The Arabs in History TB/1029

BERNARD LEWIS: The Middle East and the West ° TB/1274

History: Ancient

A. ANDREWS: The Greek Tyrants TB/1103

ERNST LUDWIG EHRLICH: A Concise History of Israel: *From the Earliest Times to the Destruction of the Temple in A.D. 70°* TB/128

THEODOR H. GASTER: Thespis: *Ritual Myth and Drama in the Ancient Near East* TB/1281

MICHAEL GRANT: Ancient History ° TB/1190

A. H. M. JONES, Ed.: A History of Rome through the Fifgth Century # *Vol. I: The Republic* HR/1364

Vol. II The Empire: HR/1460

SAMUEL NOAH KRAMER: Sumerian Mythology TB/1055

NAPHTALI LEWIS & MEYER REINHOLD, Eds.: Roman Civilization *Vol. I: The Republic* TB/1231

Vol. II: The Empire TB/1232

History: Medieval

MARSHALL W. BALDWIN, Ed.: Christianity Through the 13th Century # HR/1468

MARC BLOCH: Land and Work in Medieval Europe. *Translated by J. E. Anderson* TB/1452

HELEN CAM: England Before Elizabeth TB/1026

NORMAN COHN: The Pursuit of the Millennium: *Revolutionary Messianism in Medieval and Reformation Europe* TB/1037

G. G. COULTON: Medieval Village, Manor, and Monastery HR/1022

HEINRICH FICHTENAU: The Carolingian Empire: *The Age of Charlemagne. Translated with an Introduction by Peter Munz* TB/1142

GALBERT OF BRUGES: The Murder of Charles the Good: *A Contemporary Record of Revolutionary Change in 12th Century Flanders. Translated with an Introduction by James Bruce Ross* TB/1311

F. L. GANSHOF: Feudalism TB/1058

F. L. GANSHOF: The Middle Ages: *A History of International Relations. Translated by Rémy Hall* TB/1411

DENYS HAY: The Medieval Centuries ° TB/1192

DAVID HERLIHY, Ed.: Medieval Culture and Society # HR/1340

J. M. HUSSEY: The Byzantine World TB/1057

ROBERT LATOUCHE: The Birth of Western Economy: *Economic Aspects of the Dark Ages °* TB/1290

HENRY CHARLES LEA: The Inquisition of the Middle Ages. || *Introduction by Walter Ullmann* TB/1456

FERDINARD LOT: The End of the Ancient World and the Beginnings of the Middle Ages. *Introduction by Glanville Downey* TB/1044

H. R. LOYN: The Norman Conquest TB/1457

GUIBERT DE NOGENT: Self and Society in Medieval France: *The Memoirs of Guilbert de Nogent.* || *Edited by John F. Benton* TB/1471

MARSILIUS OF PADUA: The Defender of Peace. *The Defensor Pacis. Translated with an Introduction by Alan Gewirth* TB/1310

CHARLES PETET-DUTAILLIS: The Feudal Monarchy in France and England: *From the Tenth to the Thirteenth Century °* TB/1165

STEVEN RUNCIMAN: A History of the Crusades *Vol. I: The First Crusade and the Foundation of the Kingdom of Jerusalem. Illus.* TB/1143

Vol. II: The Kingdom of Jerusalem and the Frankish East 1100-1187. Illus. TB/1243

Vol. III: The Kingdom of Acre and the Later Crusades. Illus. TB/1298

J. M. WALLACE-HADRILL: The Barbarian West: *The Early Middle Ages, A.D. 400-1000* TB/1061

4

History: Renaissance & Reformation

JACOB BURCKHARDT: The Civilization of the Renaissance in Italy. *Introduction by Benjamin Nelson and Charles Trinkaus. Illus.* Vol. I TB/40; Vol. II TB/41

JOHN CALVIN & JACOPO SADOLETO: A Reformation Debate. *Edited by John C. Olin* TB/1239

FEDERICO CHABOD: Machiavelli and the Renaissance TB/1193

THOMAS CROMWELL: Thomas Cromwell. *Selected Letters on Church and Commonwealth, 1523-1540. ¶ Ed. with an Intro. by Arthur J. Slavin* TB/1462

R. TREVOR DAVIES: The Golden Century of Spain, 1501-1621 ° TB/1194

J. H. ELLIOTT: Europe Divided, 1559-1598 a ° TB/1414

G. R. ELTON: Reformation Europe, 1517-1559 ° a TB/1270

DESIDERIUS ERASMUS: Christian Humanism and the Reformation: *Selected Writings. Edited and Translated by John C. Olin* TB/1166

DESIDERIUS ERASMUS: Erasmus and His Age: *Selected Letters. Edited with an Introduction by Hans J. Hillerbrand. Translated by Marcus A. Haworth* TB/1461

WALLACE K. FERGUSON et al.: Facets of the Renaissance TB/1098

WALLACE K. FERGUSON et al.: The Renaissance: *Six Essays. Illus.* TB/1084

FRANCESCO GUICCIARDINI: History of Florence. *Translated with an Introduction and Notes by Mario Domandi* TB/1470

WERNER L. GUNDERSHEIMER, Ed.: French Humanism, 1470-1600. * *Illus.* TB/1473

MARIE BOAS HALL, Ed.: Nature and Nature's Laws: *Documents of the Scientific Revolution #* HR/1420

HANS J. HILLERBRAND, Ed., The Protestant Reformation HR/1342

JOHAN HUIZINGA: Erasmus and the Age of Reformation. *Illus.* TB/19

JOEL HURSTFIELD: The Elizabethan Nation TB/1312

JOEL HURSTFIELD, Ed.: The Reformation Crisis TB/1267

PAUL OSKAR KRISTELLER: Renaissance Thought: *The Classic, Scholastic, and Humanist Strains* TB/1048

PAUL OSKAR KRISTELLER: Renaissance Thought II: *Papers on Humanism and the Arts* TB/1163

PAUL O. KRISTELLER & PHILIP P. WIENER, Eds.: Renaissance Essays TB/1392

DAVID LITTLE: Religion, Order and Law: *A Study in Pre-Revolutionary England. § Preface by R. Bellah* TB/1418

NICCOLO MACHIAVELLI: History of Florence and of the Affairs of Italy: *From the Earliest Times to the Death of Lorenzo the Magnificent. Introduction by Felix Gilbert* TB/1027

ALFRED VON MARTIN: Sociology of the Renaissance. ° *Introduction by W. K. Ferguson* TB/1099

GARRETT MATTINGLY et al.: Renaissance Profiles. *Edited by J. H. Plumb* TB/1162

J. E. NEALE: The Age of Catherine de Medici ° TB/1085

J. H. PARRY: The Establishment of the European Hegemony: 1415-1715: *Trade and Exploration in the Age of the Renaissance* TB/1045

J. H. PARRY, Ed.: The European Reconnaissance: *Selected Documents #* HR/1345

BUONACCORSO PITTI & GREGORIO DATI: Two Memoirs of Renaissance Florence: *The Diaries of Buonaccorso Pitti and Gregorio Dati. Edited with Intro. by Gene Brucker. Trans. by Julia Martines* TB/1333

J. H. PLUMB: The Italian Renaissance: *A Concise Survey of Its History and Culture* TB/1161

A. F. POLLARD: Henry VIII. *Introduction by A. G. Dickens.* ° TB/1249

RICHARD H. POPKIN: The History of Scepticism from Erasmus to Descartes TB/1391

PAOLO ROSSI: Philosophy, Technology, and the Arts, in the Early Modern Era 1400-1700. || *Edited by Benjamin Nelson. Translated by Salvator Attanasio* TB/1458

FERDINAND SCHEVILL: The Medici. *Illus.* TB/1010

FERDINAND SCHEVILL: Medieval and Renaissance Florence. *Illus. Vol. I: Medieval Florence* TB/1090

Vol. II: The Coming of Humanism and the Age of the Medici TB/1091

R. H. TAWNEY: The Agrarian Problem in the Sixteenth Century. *Intro. by Lawrence Stone* TB/1315

H. R. TREVOR-ROPER: The European Witch-craze of the Sixteenth and Seventeenth Centuries and Other Essays ° TB/1416

VESPASIANO: Rennaissance Princes, Popes, and XVth Century: *The Vespasiano Memoirs. Introduction by Myron P. Gilmore. Illus.* TB/1111

History: Modern European

RENE ALBRECHT-CARRIE, Ed.: The Concert of Europe # HR/1341

MAX BELOFF: The Age of Absolutism, 1660-1815 TB/1062

OTTO VON BISMARCK: Reflections and Reminiscences. *Ed. with Intro. by Theodore S. Hamerow* ¶ TB/1357

EUGENE C. BLACK, Ed.: British Politics in the Nineteenth Century # HR/1427

EUGENE C. BLACK, Ed.: European Political History, 1815-1870: *Aspects of Liberalism* ¶ TB/1331

ASA BRIGGS: The Making of Modern England, 1783-1867: *The Age of Improvement* ° TB/1203

ALAN BULLOCK: Hitler, A Study in Tyranny. ° *Revised Edition. Illus.* TB/1123

EDMUND BURKE: On Revolution. *Ed. by Robert A. Smith* TB/1401

E. R. CARR: International Relations Between the Two World Wars. 1919-1939 ° TB/1279

E. H. CARR: The Twenty Years' Crisis, 1919-1939: *An Introduction to the Study of International Relations* ° TB/1122

GORDON A. CRAIG: From Bismarck to Adenauer: *Aspects of German Statecraft. Revised Edition* TB/1171

LESTER G. CROCKER, Ed.: The Age of Enlightenment # HR/1423

DENIS DIDEROT: The Encyclopedia: *Selections. Edited and Translated with Introduction by Stephen Gendzier* TB/1299

JACQUES DROZ: Europe between Revolutions, 1815-1848. ° *a Trans. by Robert Baldick* TB/1346

JOHANN GOTTLIEB FICHTE: Addresses to the German Nation. *Ed. with Intro. by George A. Kelly* ¶ TB/1366

ROBERT & ELBORG FORSTER, Eds.: European Society in the Eighteenth Century # HR/1404

C. C. GILLISPIE: Genesis and Geology: *The Decades before Darwin* § TB/51

ALBERT GOODWIN, Ed.: The European Nobility in the Enghteenth Century   TB/1313
ALBERT GOODWIN: The French Revolution   TB/1064
ALBERT GUERARD: France in the Classical Age: *The Life and Death of an Ideal*   TB/1183
JOHN B. HALSTED, Ed.: Romanticism #   HR/1387
J. H. HEXTER: Reappraisals in History: *New Views on History and Society in Early Modern Europe* °   TB/1100
STANLEY HOFFMANN et al.: In Search of France: *The Economy, Society and Political System In the Twentieth Century*   TB/1219
H. STUART HUGHES: The Obstructed Path: *French Social Thought in the Years of Desperation*   TB/1451
JOHAN HUIZINGA: Dutch Civilisation in the 17th Century and Other Essays   TB/1453
LIONAL KOCHAN: The Struggle for Germany: *1914-45*   TB/1304
HANS KOHN: The Mind of Germany: *The Education of a Nation*   TB/1204
HANS KOHN, Ed.: The Mind of Modern Russia: *Historical and Political Thought of Russia's Great Age*   TB/1065
WALTER LAQUEUR & GEORGE L. MOSSE, Eds.: Education and Social Structure in the 20th Century. ° *Volume 6 of the* Journal of Contemporary History   TB/1339
WALTER LAQUEUR & GEORGE L. MOSSE, Ed.: International Fascism, 1920-1945. ° *Volume 1 of the* Journal of Contemporary History   TB/1276
WALTER LAQUEUR & GEORGE L. MOSSE, Eds.: Literature and Politics in the 20th Century. ° *Volume 5 of the* Journal of Contemporary History.   TB/1328
WALTER LAQUEUR & GEORGE L. MOSSE, Eds.: The New History: *Trends in Historical Research and Writing Since World War II.* ° *Volume 4 of the* Journal of Contemporary History   TB/1327
WALTER LAQUEUR & GEORGE L. MOSSE, Eds.: 1914: *The Coming of the First World War.* ° *Volume3 of the* Journal of Contemporary History   TB/1306
C. A. MACARTNEY, Ed.: The Habsburg and Hohenzollern Dynasties in the Seventeenth and Eighteenth Centuries #   HR/1400
JOHN MCMANNERS: European History, 1789-1914: *Men, Machines and Freedom*   TB/1419
PAUL MANTOUX: The Industrial Revolution in the Eighteenth Century: *An Outline of the Beginnings of the Modern Factory System in England*   TB/1079
FRANK E. MANUEL: The Prophets of Paris: *Turgot, Condorcet, Saint-Simon, Fourier, and Comte*   TB/1218
KINGSLEY MARTIN: French Liberal Thought in the Eighteenth Century: *A Study of Political Ideas from Bayle to Condorcet*   TB/1114
NAPOLEON III: Napoleonic Ideas: *Des Idées Napoléoniennes, par le Prince Napoléon-Louis Bonaparte. Ed. by Brison D. Gooch* ¶   TB/1336
FRANZ NEUMANN: Behemoth: *The Structure and Practice of National Socialism, 1933-1944*   TB/1289
DAVID OGG: Europe of the Ancien Régime, 1715-1783 ° *a*   TB/1271
GEORGE RUDE: Revolutionary Europe, 1783-1815 ° *a*   TB/1272
MASSIMO SALVADORI, Ed.: Modern Socialism #   TB/1374
HUGH SETON-WATSON: Eastern Europe Between the Wars, 1918-1941   TB/1330

DENIS MACK SMITH, Ed.: The Making of Italy, 1796-1870 #   HR/1356
ALBERT SOREL: Europe Under the Old Regime. *Translated by Francis H. Herrick*   TB/1121
ROLAND N. STROMBERG, Ed.: Realism, Naturalism, and Symbolism: *Modes of Thought and Expression in Europe, 1848-1914* #   HR/1355
A. J. P. TAYLOR: From Napoleon to Lenin: *Historical Essays* °   TB/1268
A. J. P. TAYLOR: The Habsburg Monarchy, 1809-1918: *A History of the Austrian Empire and Austria-Hungary* °   TB/1187
J. M. THOMPSON: European History, 1494-1789   TB/1431
DAVID THOMSON, Ed.: France: Empire and Republic, 1850-1940 #   HR/1387
ALEXIS DE TOCQUEVILLE & GUSTAVE DE BEAUMONT: Tocqueville and Beaumont on Social Reform. *Ed. and trans. with Intro. by Seymour Drescher*   TB/1343
G. M. TREVELYAN: British History in the Nineteenth Century and After: 1792-1919 °   TB/1251
H. R. TREVOR-ROPER: Historical Essays   TB/1269
W. WARREN WAGAR, Ed.: Science, Faith, and MAN: *European Thought Since 1914* #   HR/1362
MACK WALKER, Ed.: Metternich's Europe, 1813-1848 #   HR/1361
ELIZABETH WISKEMANN: Europe of the Dictators, 1919-1945 ° *a*   TB/1273
JOHN B. WOLF: France: 1814-1919: *The Rise of a Liberal-Democratic Society*   TB/3019

Literature & Literary Criticism

JACQUES BARZUN: The House of Intellect   TB/1051
W. J. BATE: From Classic to Romantic: *Premises of Taste in Eighteenth Century England*   TB/1036
VAN WYCK BROOKS: Van Wyck Brooks: The Early Years: *A Selection from his Works, 1908-1921 Ed. with Intro. by Claire Sprague*   TB/3082
ERNST R. CURTIUS: European Literature and the Latin Middle Ages. *Trans. by Willard Trask*   TB/2015
RICHMOND LATTIMORE, Translator: The Odyssey of Homer   TB/1389
SAMUEL PEPYS: The Diary of Samual Pepys. ° *Edited by O. F. Morshead. 60 illus. by Ernest Shepard*   TB/1007
ROBERT PREYER, Ed.: Victorian Literature **   TB/1302
ALBION W. TOURGEE: A Fool's Errand: *A Novel of the South during Reconstruction. Intro. by George Fredrickson*   TB/3074
BASIL WILEY: Nineteenth Century Studies: *Coleridge to Matthew Arnold* °   TB/1261

Philosophy

HENRI BERGSON: Time and Free Will: *An Essay on the Immediate Data of Consciousness* °   TB/1021
LUDWIG BINSWANGER: Being-in-the-World: *Selected Papers. Trans. with Intro. by Jacob Needleman*   TB/1365
H. J. BLACKHAM: Six Existentialist Thinkers: *Kierkegaard, Nietzsche, Jaspers, Marcel, Heidegger, Sartre* °   TB/1002
J. M. BOCHENSKI: The Methods of Contemporary Thought. *Trans. by Peter Caws* #   TB/1377
CRANE BRINTON: Nietzsche. *Preface, Bibliography, and Epilogue by the Author*   TB/1197

ERNST CASSIRER: Rousseau, Kant and Goethe. *Intro. by Peter Gay* TB/1092
FREDERICK COPLESTON, S. J.: Medieval Philosophy TB/376
F. M. CORNFORD: From Religion to Philosophy: *A Study in the Origins of Western Speculation* § TB/20
WILFRID DESAN: The Tragic Finale: *An Essay on the Philosophy of Jean-Paul Sartre* TB/1030
MARVIN FARBER: The Aims of Phenomenology: *The Motives, Methods, and Impact of Husserl's Thought* TB/1291
MARVIN FARBER: Basic Issues of Philosophy: *Experience, Reality, and Human Values* TB/1344
MARVIN FARBERS: Phenomenology and Existence: *Towards a Philosophy within Nature* TB/1295
PAUL FRIEDLANDER: `Plato: *An Introduction* TB/2017
MICHAEL GELVEN: A Commentary on Heidegger's "Being and Time" TB/1464
J. GLENN GRAY: Hegel and Greek Thought TB/1409
W. K. C. GUTHRIE: The Greek Philosophers: *From Thales to Aristotle* ° TB/1008
G. W. F. HEGEL: On Art, Religion Philosophy: *Introductory Lectures to the Realm of Absolute Spirit.* || *Edited with an Introduction by J. Glenn Gray* TB/1463
G. W. F. HEGEL: Phenomenology of Mind. ° || *Introduction by George Lichtheim* TB/1303
MARTIN HEIDEGGER: Discourse on Thinking. *Translated with a Preface by John M. Anderson and E. Hans Freund. Introduction by John M. Anderson* TB/1459
F. H. HEINEMANN: Existentialism and the Modern Predicament TB/28
WERER HEISENBERG: Physics and Philosophy: *The Revolution in Modern Science. Intro. by F. S. C. Northrop* TB/549
EDMUND HUSSERL: Phenomenology and the Crisis of Philosophy. § *Translated with an Introduction by Quentin Lauer* TB/1170
IMMANUEL KANT: Groundwork of the Metaphysic of Morals. *Translated and Analyzed by H. J. Paton* TB/1159
IMMANUEL KANT: Lectures on Ethics. § *Introduction by Lewis White Beck* TB/105
WALTER KAUFMANN, Ed.: Religion From Tolstoy to Camus: *Basic Writings on Religious Truth and Morals* TB/123
QUENTIN LAUER: Phenomenology: *Its Genesis and Prospect. Preface by Aron Gurwitsch* TB/1169
MAURICE MANDELBAUM: The Problem of Historical Knowledge: *An Answer to Relativism* TB/1198
H. J. PATON: The Categorical Imperative: *A Study in Kant's Moral Philosophy* TB/1325
MICHAEL POLANYI: Personal Knowledge: *Towards a Post-Critical Philosophy* TB/1158
KARL R. POPPER: Conjectures and Refutations: *The Growth of Scientific Knowledge* TB/1376
WILLARD VAN ORMAN QUINE: Elementary Logic *Revised Edition* TB/577
WILLARD VAN ORMAN QUINE: From a Logical Point of View: *Logico-Philosophical Essays* TB/566
JOHN E. SMITH: Themes in American Philosophy: *Purpose, Experience and Community* TB/1466
MORTON WHITE: Foundations of Historical Knowledge TB/1440
WILHELM WINDELBAND: A History of Philosophy *Vol. I: Greek, Roman, Medieval* TB/38
Vol. II: Renaissance, Enlightenment, Modern TB/39

LUDWIG WITTGENSTEIN: The Blue and Brown Books ° TB/1211
LUDWIG WITTGENSTEIN: Notebooks, 1914-1916 TB/1441

Political Science & Government

C. E. BLACK: The Dynamics of Modernization: *A Study in Comparative History* TB/1321
DENIS W. BROGAN: Politics in America. *New Introduction by the Author* TB/1469
CRANE BRINTON: English Political Thought in the Nineteenth Century TB/1071
ROBERT CONQUEST: Power and Policy in the USSR: *The Study of Soviet Dynastics* ° TB/1307
ROBERT A. DAHL & CHARLES E. LINDBLOM: Politics, Economics, and Welfare: *Planning and Politico-Economic Systems Resolved into Basic Social Processes* TB/1277
HANS KOHN: Political Ideologies of the 20th Century TB/1277
ROY C. MACRIDIS, Ed.: Political Parties: *Contemporary Trends and Ideas* ** TB/1322
ROBERT GREEN MC CLOSKEY: American Conservatism in the Age of Enterprise, 1865-1910 TB/1137
MARSILIUS OF PADUA: The Defender of Peace. *The Defensor Pacis. Translated with an Introduction by Alan Gewirth* TB/1310
KINGSLEY MARTIN: French Liberal Thought in the Eighteenth Century: *A Study of Political Ideas from Bayle to Condorcet* TB/1114
BARRINGTON MOORE, JR.:Political Power and Social Theory: *Seven Studies* || TB/1221
BARRINGTON MOORE, JR.: Soviet Politics—The Dilemma of Power: *The Role of Ideas in Social Change* || TB/1222
BARRINGTON MOORE, JR.: Terror and Progress—USSR: *Some Sources of Change and Stability*
JOHN B. MORRALL: Political Thought in Medieval Times TB/1076
KARL R. POPPER: The Open Society and Its Enemies *Vol. I: The Spell of Plato* TB/1101
Vol. II: The High Tide of Prophecy: Hegel, Marx, and the Aftermath TB/1102
CONYERS READ, Ed.: The Constitution Reconsidered. *Revised Edition, Preface by Richard B. Morris* TB/1384
JOHN P. ROCHE, Ed.: Origins of American Political Thought: *Selected Readings* TB/1301
JOHN P. ROCHE, Ed.: American Political Thought: *From Jefferson to Progressivism* TB/1332
HENRI DE SAINT-SIMON: Social Organization, The Science of Man, and Other Writings. || *Edited and Translated with an Introduction by Felix Markham* TB/1152
CHARLES SCHOTTLAND, Ed.: The Welfare State ** TB/1323
JOSEPH A. SCHUMPETER: Capitalism, Socialism and Democracy TB/3008

Psychology

ALFRED ADLER: The Individual Psychology of Alfred Adler: *A Systematic Presentation in Selections from His Writings. Edited by Heinz L. & Rowena R. Ansbacher* TB/1154
LUDWIG BINSWANGER: Being-in-the-World: *Selected Papers.* || *Trans. with Intro. by Jacob Needleman* TB/1365
HADLEY CANTRIL: The Invasion from Mars: *A Study in the Psychology of Panic* || TB/1282
MIRCEA ELIADE: Cosmos and History: *The Myth of the Eternal Return* § TB/2050
MIRCEA ELIADE: Myth and Reality TB/1369

7

MIRCEA ELIADE: Myths, Dreams and Mysteries: *The Encounter Between Contemporary Faiths and Archaic Realities* § TB/1320
MIRCEA ELIADE: Rites and Symbols of Initiation: *The Mysteries of Birth and Rebirth* § TB/1236
HERBERT FINGARETTE: The Self in Transformation: *Psychoanalysis, Philosophy and the Life of the Spirit* || ɪʙ/1177
SIGMUND FREUD: On Creativity and the Unconscious: *Papers on the Psychology of Art, Literature, Love, Religion.* § *Intro. by Benjamin Nelson* TB/45
J. GLENN GRAY: The Warriors: *Reflections on Men in Battle. Introduction by Hannah Arendt* TB/1294
WILLIAM JAMES: Psychology: *The Briefer Course. Edited with an Intro. by Gordon Allport* TB/1034
C. G. JUNG: Psychological Reflections. *Ed. by J. Jacobi* TB/2001
KARL MENNINGER, M.D.: Theory of Psychoanalytic Technique TB/1144
JOHN H. SCHAAR: Escape from Authority: *The Perspectives of Erich Fromm* TB/1155
MUZAFER SHERIF: The Psychology of Social Norms. *Introduction by Gardner Murphy* TB/3072
HELLMUT WILHELM: Change: *Eight Lectures on the* I *Ching* TB/2019

Religion: Ancient and Classical, Biblical and Judaic Traditions

W. F. ALBRIGHT: The Biblical Period from Abraham to Ezra TB/102
SALO W. BARON: Modern Nationalism and Religion TB/818
C. K. BARRETT, Ed.: The New Testament Background: *Selected Documents* TB/86
MARTIN BUBER: Eclipse of God: *Studies in the Relation Between Religion and Philosophy* TB/12
MARTIN BUBER: Hasidism and Modern Man. *Edited and Translated by Maurice Friedman* TB/839
MARTIN BUBER: The Knowledge of Man. *Edited with an Introduction by Maurice Friedman. Translated by Maurice Friedman and Ronald Gregor Smith* TB/135
MARTIN BUBER: Moses. *The Revelation and the Covenant* TB/837
MARTIN BUBER: The Origin and Meaning of Hasidism. *Edited and Translated by Maurice Friedman* TB/835
MARTIN BUBER: The Prophetic Faith TB/73
MARTIN BUBER: Two Types of Faith: *Interpenetration of Judaism and Christianity* ° TB/75
MALCOLM L. DIAMOND: Martin Buber: *Jewish Existentialist* TB/840
M. S. ENSLIN: Christian Beginnings TB/5
M. S. ENSLIN: The Literature of the Christian Movement TB/6
ERNST LUDWIG EHRLICH: A Concise History of Israel: *From the Earliest Times to the Destruction of the Temple in A.D. 70* ° TB/128
HENRI FRANKFORT: Ancient Egyptian Religion: *An Interpretation* TB/77
ABRAHAM HESCHEL: The Earth Is the Lord's & The Sabbath. *Two Essays* TB/828
ABRAHAM HESCHEL: God in Search of Man: *A Philosophy of Judaism* TB/807
ABRAHAM HESCHEL: Man Is not Alone: *A Philosophy of Religion* TB/838
ABRAHAM HESCHEL: The Prophets: *An Introduction* TB/1421

T. J. MEEK: Hebrew Origins TB/69
JAMES MUILENBURG: The Way of Israel: *Biblical Faith and Ethics* TB/133
H. J. ROSE: Religion in Greece and Rome TB/55
H. H. ROWLEY: The Growth of the Old Testament TB/107
D. WINTON THOMAS, Ed.: Documents from Old Testament Times TB/85

Religion: General Christianity

ROLAND H. BAINTON: Christendom: *A Short History of Christianity and Its Impact on Western Civilization. Illus.* Vol. I TB/131; Vol. II TB/132
JOHN T. MCNEILL: Modern Christian Movements. *Revised Edition* TB/1402
ERNST TROELTSCH: The Social Teaching of the Christian Churches. *Intro. by H. Richard Niebuhr* Vol. TB/71; Vol. II TB/72

Religion: Early Christianity Through
Reformation

ANSELM OF CANTERBURY: Truth, Freedom, and Evil: *Three Philosophical Dialogues. Edited and Translated by Jasper Hopkins and Herbert Richardson* TB/317
MARSHALL W. BALDWIN, Ed.: Christianity through the 13th Century # HR/1468
W. D. DAVIES: Paul and Rabbinic Judaism: *Some Rabbinic Elements in Pauline Theology. Revised Edition* ° TB/146
ADOLF DEISSMANN: Paul: *A Study in Social and Religious History* TB/15
JOHANNES ECKHART: Meister Eckhart: *A Modern Translation by R. Blakney* TB/8
EDGAR J. GOODSPEED: A Life of Jesus TB/1
ROBERT M. GRANT: Gnosticism and Early Christianity TB/136
WILLIAM HALLER: The Rise of Puritanism TB/22
GERHART B. LADNER: The Idea of Reform: *Its Impact on the Christian Thought and Action in the Age of the Fathers* TB/149
ARTHUR DARBY NOCK: Early Gentile Christianity and Its Hellenistic Background TB/111
ARTHUR DARBY NOCK: St. Paul ° TR/104
GORDON RUPP: Luther's Progress to the Diet of Worms ° TB/120

Religion: The Protestant Tradition

KARL BARTH: Church Dogmatics: *A Selection. Intro. by H. Gollwitzer. Ed. by G. W. Bromiley* TB/95
KARL BARTH: Dogmatics in Outline TB/56
KARL BARTH: The Word of God and the Word of Man TB/13
HERBERT BRAUN, et al.: God and Christ: *Existence and Province. Volume 5 of Journal for Theology and the Church, edited by Robert W. Funk and Gerhard Ebeling* TB/255
WHITNEY R. CROSS: The Burned-Over District: *The Social and Intellectual History of Enthusiastic Religion in Western New York, 1800-1850* TB/1242
NELS F. S. FERRE: Swedish Contributions to Modern Theology. *New Chapter by William A. Johnson* TB/147
WILLIAM R. HUTCHISON: Ed.: American Protestant Thought: *The Liberal Era* ‡ TB/1385
ERNST KASEMANN, et al.: Distinctive Protestant and Catholic Themes Reconsidered. *Volume 3 of Journal for Theology and the Church,*

8

edited by Robert W. Funk and Gerhard Ebeling TB/253

SOREN KIERKEGAARD: On Authority and Revelation: *The Book on Adler, or a Cycle of Ethico-Religious Essays. Introduction by F. Sontag* TB/139

SOREN KIERKEGAARD: Crisis in the Life of an Actress, *and Other Essays on Drama. Translated with an Introduction by Stephen Crites* TB/145

SOREN KIERKEGAARD: Edifying Discourses. *Edited with an Intro. by Paul Holmer* TB/32

SOREN KIERKEGAARD: The Journals of Kierkegaard. ° *Edited with an Intro. by Alexander Dru* TB/52

SOREN KIERKEGAARD: The Point of View for My Work as an Author: *A Report to History.* § *Preface by Benjamin Nelson* TB/88

SOREN KIERKEGAARD: The Present Age. § *Translated and edited by Alexander Dru. Introduction by Walter Kaufmann* TB/94

SOREN KIERKEGAARD: Purity of Heart. *Trans. by Douglas Steere* TB/4

SOREN KIERKEGAARD: Repetition: *An Essay in Experimental Psychology* § TB/117

SOREN KIERKEGAARD: Works of Love: *Some Christian Reflections in the Form of Discourses* TB/122

WILLIAM G. MCLOUGHLIN, Ed.: The American Evangelicals: 1800-1900: *An Anthology* TB/1382

WOLFHART PANNENBERG, et al.: History and Hermeneutic. *Volume 4 of Journal for Theology and the Church, edited by Robert W. Funk and Gerhard Ebeling* TB/254

JAMES M. ROBINSON, et al.: The Bultmann School of Biblical Interpretation: New Directions? *Volume 1 of Journal for Theology and the Church, edited by Robert W. Funk and Gerhard Ebeling* TB/251

F. SCHLEIERMACHER: The Christian Faith. *Introduction by Richard R. Niebuhr.*
Vol. I TB/108; Vol. II TB/109

F. SCHLEIERMACHER: On Religion: *Speeches to Its Cultured Despisers. Intro. by Rudolf Otto* TB/36

TIMOTHY L. SMITH: Revivalism and Social Reform: *American Protestantism on the Eve of the Civil War* TB/1229

PAUL TILLICH: Dynamics of Faith TB/42

PAUL TILLICH: Morality and Beyond TB/142

EVELYN UNDERHILL: Worship TB/10

Religion: The Roman & Eastern Christian Traditions

A. ROBERT CAPONIGRI, Ed.: Modern Catholic Thinkers II: *The Church and the Political Order* TB/307

G. P. FEDOTOV: The Russian Religious Mind: *Kievan Christianity, the tenth to the thirteenth Centuries* TB/370

GABRIEL MARCEL: Being and Having: *An Existential Diary. Introduction by James Collins* TB/310

GABRIEL MARCEL: Homo Viator: *Introduction to a Metaphysic of Hope* TB/397

Religion: Oriental Religions

TOR ANDRAE: Mohammed: *The Man and His Faith* § TB/62

EDWARD CONZE: Buddhism: *Its Essence and Development.* ° *Foreword by Arthur Waley* TB/58

EDWARD CONZE: Buddhist Meditation TB/1442

EDWARD CONZE et al, Editors: Buddhist Texts through the Ages TB/113

ANANDA COOMARASWAMY: Buddha and the Gospel of Buddhism TB/119

H. G. CREEL: Confucius and the Chinese Way TB/63

FRANKLIN EDGERTON, Trans. & Ed.: The Bhagavad Gita TB/115

SWAMI NIKHILANANDA, Trans. & Ed.: The Upanishads TB/114

D. T. SUZUKI: On Indian Mahayana Buddhism. ° *Ed. with Intro. by Edward Conze.* TB/1403

Religion: Philosophy, Culture, and Society

NICOLAS BERDYAEV: The Destiny of Man TB/61

RUDOLF BULTMANN: History and Eschatology: *The Presence of Eternity* ° TB/91

RUDOLF BULTMANN AND FIVE CRITICS: Kerygma and Myth: *A Theological Debate* TB/80

RUDOLF BULTMANN and KARL KUNDSIN: Form Criticism: *Two Essays on New Testament Research. Trans. by F. C. Grant* TB/96

WILLIAM A. CLEBSCH & CHARLES R. JAEKLE: Pastoral Care in Historical Perspective: *An Essay with Exhibits* TB/148

FREDERICK FERRE: Language, Logic and God. *New Preface by the Author* TB/1407

LUDWIG FEUERBACH: The Essence of Christianity. § *Introduction by Karl Barth. Foreword by H. Richard Niebuhr* TB/11

ADOLF HARNACK: What Is Christianity? § *Introduction by Rudolf Bultmann* TB/17

KYLE HASELDEN: The Racial Problem in Christian Perspective TB/116

MARTIN HEIDEGGER: Discourse on Thinking. *Translated with a Preface by John M. Anderson and E. Hans Freund. Introduction by John M. Anderson* TB/1459

IMMANUEL KANT: Religion Within the Limits of Reason Alone. § *Introduction by Theodore M. Greene and John Silber* TB/FG

WALTER KAUFMANN, Ed.: Religion from Tolstoy to Camus: *Basic Writings on Religious Truth and Morals. Enlarged Edition* TB/123

H. RICHARD NIERUHR: Christ and Culture TB/3

H. RICHARD NIEBUHR: The Kingdom of God in America TB/49

ANDERS NYGREN: Agape and Eros. *Translated by Philip S. Watson* ° TB/1430

JOHN H. RANDALL, JR.: The Meaning of Religion for Man. *Revised with New Intro. by the Author* TB/1379

WALTER RAUSCHENBUSCHS Christianity and the Social Crisis. ‡ *Edited by Robert D. Cross* TB/3059

Science and Mathematics

JOHN TYLER BONNER: The Ideas of Biology. Σ *Illus.* TB/570

W. E. LE GROS CLARK: The Antecedents of Man: *An Introduction to the Evolution of the Primates.* ° *Illus.* TB/559

ROBERT E. COKER: Streams, Lakes, Ponds. *Illus.* TB/586

ROBERT E. COKER: This Great and Wide Sea: *An Introduction to Oceanography and Marine Biology. Illus.* TB/551

W. H. DOWDESWELL: Animal Ecology. *61 illus.* TB/543

C. V. DURELL: Readable Relativity. *Foreword by Freeman J. Dyson* TB/530
GEORGE GAMOW: Biography of Physics. Σ *Illus.* TB/567
F. K. HARE: The Restless Atmosphere TB/560
J. R. PIERCE: Symbols, Signals and Noise: *The Nature and Process of Communication* Σ TB/574
WILLARD VAN ORMAN QUINE: Mathematical Logic TB/558

Science: History

MARIE BOAS: The Scientific Renaissance, 1450-1630 ° TB/583
STEPHEN TOULMIN & JUNE GOODFIELD: The Architecture of Matter: *The Physics, Chemistry and Physiology of Matter, Both Animate and Inanimate, as it has Evolved since the Beginnings of Science* TB/584
STEPHEN TOULMIN & JUNE GOODFIELD: The Discovery TB/576
STEPHEN TOULMIN & JUNE GOODFIELD: The Fabric of the Heavens: *The Development of Astronomy and Dynamics* TB/579

Science: Philosophy

J. M. BOCHENSKI: The Methods of Contemporary Thought. *Tr. by Peter Caws* TB/1377
J. BRONOWSKI: Science and Human Values. *Revised and Enlarged. Illus.* TB/505
WERNER HEISENBERG: Physics and Philosophy: *The Revolution in Modern Science. Introduction by F. S. C. Northrop* TB/549
KARL R. POPPER: Conjectures and Refutations: *The Growth of Scientific Knowledge* TB/1376
KARL R. POPPER: The Logic of Scientific Discovery TB/1376
STEPHEN TOULMIN: Foresight and Understanding: *An Enquiry into the Aims of Science. Foreword by Jacques Barzun* TB/564
STEPHEN TOULMIN: The Philosophy of Science: *An Introduction* TB/513

Sociology and Anthropology

REINHARD BENDIX: Work and Authority in Industry: *Ideologies of Management in the Course of Industrialization* TB/3035
BERNARD BERELSON, Ed.: The Behavioral Sciences Today TB/1127
JOSEPH B. CASAGRANDE, Ed.: In the Company of Man: *Twenty Portraits of Anthropological Informants. Illus.* TB/3047
KENNETH B. CLARK: Dark Ghetto: *Dilemmas of Social Power. Foreword by Gunnar Myrdal* TB/1317
KENNETH CLARK & JEANNETTE HOPKINS: A Relevant War Against Poverty: *A Study of Community Action Programs and Observable Social Change* TB/1480
LEWIS COSER, Ed.: Political Sociology TB/1293
ROSE L. COSER, Ed.: Life Cycle and Achievement in America ** TB/1434
ALLISON DAVIS & JOHN DOLLARD: Children of Bondage: *The Personality Development of Negro Youth in the Urban South* || TB/3049
PETER F. DRUCKER: The New Society: *The Anatomy of Industrial Order* TB/1082
CORA DU BOIS: The People of Alor. *With a Preface by the Author*
Vol. I *Illus.* TB/1042; Vol. II TB/1043
EMILE DURKHEIM et al.: Essays on Sociology and Philosophy: *with Appraisals of Durkheim's Life and Thought.* || *Edited by Kurt H. Wolff* TB/1151

LEON FESTINGER, HENRY W. RIECKEN, STANLEY SCHACHTER: When Prophecy Fails: *A Social and Psychological Study of a Modern Group that Predicted the Destruction of the World* || TB/1132
CHARLES Y. GLOCK & RODNEY STARK: Christian Beliefs and Anti-Semitism. *Introduction by the Authors* TB/1454
ALVIN W. GOULDNER: The Hellenic World TB/1479
ALVIN W. GOULDNER: Wildcat Strike: *A Study in Worker-Management Relationships* || TB/1176
CESAR GRANA: Modernity and Its Discontents: *French Society and the French Man of Letters in the Nineteenth Century* TB/1318
L. S. B. LEAKEY: Adam's Ancestors: *The Evolution of Man and His Culture. Illus.* TB/1019
KURT LEWIN: Field Theory in Social Science: *Selected Theoretical Papers.* || *Edited by Dorwin Cartwright* TB/1135
RITCHIE P. LOWRY: Who's Running This Town? *Community Leadership and Social Change* TB/1383
R. M. MACIVER: Social Causation TB/1153
GARY T. MARX: Protest and Prejudice: *A Study of Belief in the Black Community* TB/1435
ROBERT K. MERTON, LEONARD BROOM, LEONARD S. COTTRELL, JR., Editors: Sociology Today: *Problems and Prospects* ||
Vol. I TB/1173; Vol. II TB/1174
GILBERT OSOFSKY, Ed.: The Burden of Race: *A Documentary History of Negro-White Relations in America* TB/1405
GILBERT OSOFSKY: Harlem: The Making of a Ghetto: *Negro New York 1890-1930* TB/1381
TALCOTT PARSONS & EDWARD A. SHILS, Editors: Toward a General Theory of Action: *Theoretical Foundations for the Social Sciences* TB/1083
PHILIP RIEFF: The Triumph of the Therapeutic: *Uses of Faith After Freud* TB/1360
JOHN H. ROHRER & MUNRO S. EDMONSON, Eds.: The Eighth Generation Grows Up: *Cultures and Personalities of New Orleans Negroes* || TB/3050
ARNOLD ROSE: The Negro in America: *The Condensed Version of Gunnar Myrdal's* An American Dilemma. *Second Edition* TB/3048
GEORGE ROSEN: Madness in Society: *Chapters in the Historical Sociology of Mental Illness.* || *Preface by Benjamin Nelson* TB/1337
PHILIP SELZNICK: TVA and the Grass Roots: *A Study in the Sociology of Formal Organization* TB/1230
PITIRIM A. SOROKIN: Contemporary Sociological Theories: *Through the First Quarter of the Twentieth Century* TB/3046
MAURICE R. STEIN: The Eclipse of Community: *An Interpretation of American Studies* TB/1128
EDWARD A. TIRYAKIAN, Ed.: Sociological Theory, Values and Sociocultural Change: *Essays in Honor of Pitirim A. Sorokin* ° TB/1316
FERDINAND TONNIES: Community and Society: *Gemeinschaft und Gesellschaft. Translated and Edited by Charles P. Loomis* TB/1116
SAMUEL E. WALLACE: Skid Row as a Way of Life TB/1367
W. LLOYD WARNER: Social Class in America: *The Evaluation of Status* TB/1013
FLORIAN ZNANIECKI: The Social Role of the Man of Knowledge. *Introduction by Lewis A. Coser* TB/1372